ISRAEL–
NATION AND PEOPLE

ISRAEL–
NATION AND PEOPLE

By David Polish

KTAV PUBLISHING HOUSE, INC.

1975

Library of Congress Cataloging in Publication Data

Polish, David.
   Israel—nation and people.

   Includes bibliographical references.
   1. Zionism and Judaism—Addresses, essays, lectures.
2. Israel and the Diaspora—Addresses, essays, lectures.
I. Title.
DS149.P67   956.94'001   75-19301
ISBN 0-87068-290-3

Contents

Preface   IX

1. For Zion's Sake   1

2. The Twofold Task of Zionism   15

3. The State of Israel: Its Moral Implications   24

4. The Uniqueness of Judaism   31

5. The Chosen People   41

6. Israel: the Meeting of Prophecy and Power   56

7. Israel and Christian Conscience   71

8. The Religious Dimensions of Israel   89

9. All Israel's Search for Identity   96

10. The Jewish People and the State of Israel

    (An Interpretation for Non-Jews)   109

11. Pharisaism and Political Sovereignty   114

12. Some Medieval Thinkers on the Jewish King   123

13. Are We in Exile?   131

14. Religious Meanings in Jewish Secularism   139

15. *Mi Yakum Yaakov*—How Can Jacob Endure?   151

16. Israel and Galut: The Unresolved Encounter   157

    Reprise: Warsaw—1943   178

    Notes   186

    Index   190

To the memories of
my Father, Morris Polish
and
my Father-in-law, A. H. Friedland
who taught me the love of Zion

Preface

The Yom Kippur War has brought Israel and the Jewish People to a turning point whose dimensions and consequences we cannot yet assess. In the struggle for survival in which world Jewry is no less involved than the State of Israel, the values which informed the struggle to create and sustain the State have been put to the most rigorous of tests and the most demanding of challenges. These values have been incorporated in the Zionist idea which even before 1973 had begun to lose its hold upon a new generation of Israelis who had not known the Zionist elan of former days or else had come to Israel out of no Zionist motivation. In the Galut, too, vast numbers of Jews who had whole-heartedly committed themselves to the preservation of the Jewish State did not necessarily identify with Zionist thought, nor certainly with Zionism as a movement. While they were in fact engaged in a process which was transforming the Jewish People and their own consciousness, they identified more pragmatically with the building and the security of the State. In the struggle for survival, value-systems were at times obscured, but the Yom Kippur War taught us how indispensable they are to survival itself.

The aftermath of the Yom Kippur War places upon us the task not only of concerning ourselves with Israel's well-being, but concomitantly of restoring, or where necessary, of building a system of Israel-related values to which the State and World Jewry would again aspire. Zionism, as a measure by which the Jewish State and the Galut will test one another's achievements in terms transcending politics or immediacy, needs to be restored as a moral component for the contemporary Jew. In the process, Zionism will have to undergo revaluation and revision. This will be necessary if it is to regain a vigor which it had attained in a time when the unformed Jewish State was fighting for existence, and which is now required when the State enters upon an unpredictable future. Ideologically, the Zionist enterprise may have to resume from the beginning.

The following essays, written over many years, are an attempt at confronting Zionist issues and facing certain Jewish issues from a

Zionist perspective. The first statement was made as the struggle for a Jewish State was reaching its climax. It was made at a debate in the Central Conference of American Rabbis on whether Zionism and Reform were compatible. The decision of the Central Conference was in the affirmative. "Mi Yakum Yaakov" was part of a President's Message to the Central Conference of American Rabbis. Nearly all of the last essay was written shortly before the Yom Kippur War.

I have been prompted to publish the following statements in the wake of the Yom Kippur War, in the hope that Zionist issues, issues of Israel-Galut relations, and the problem of synthesizing Jewish nationalism and Jewish universalism could be faced in joint encounter by Israelis and Jews of the Galut.

Appreciation is offered to the following for permission to publish materials originally printed under their auspices:

The Central Conference of American Rabbis (For Zion's Sake; Israel: The Meeting of Prophecy and Power; Israel and Christian Conscience; Mi Yakum Yaakov).
The Union of American Hebrew Congregations (Are We In Exile? Warsaw—1943; Israel and Galut: The Unresolved Encounter, also published in the "Jewish Frontier").
The Synagogue Council (The Religious Dimensions of Israel).
The Reconstructionist (The Twofold Task of Zionism; the State of Israel: Its Moral Implications; The Uniqueness of Judaism).
Judaism (All Israel's Search for Identity; Pharisaism and Political Sovereignty; Some Medieval Thinkers on the Jewish King).
Christian Century (Religious Meanings in Jewish Secularism).

I wish to thank Dr. Herbert Parzen, Rabbi Samuel Karff, and Robert Milch for reading my essays and offering helpful suggestions. I am especially grateful to my wife, Aviva, for her steadfast encouragement, and to my son, Rabbi Daniel Polish, with whom I have spent many hours discussing the issues raised in these pages. My heartfeld gratitude goes to Earle and Lorraine Iverson for making possible the publication of this book.

May, 1975

David Polish

Acknowledgments

I express thanks to the following for consenting to publish their materials:

To the Central Conference of American Rabbis for the use of Chapters 1, "For Zion's Sake" (June 1943), 6, "Israel: The Meeting of Prophecy and Power" (June 1965), 7, "Israel and Christian Conscience" (June 1968), and 15, "Mi Yakum Yaakov"—How Can Jacob Endure? (June 1972).

To the World Union for Progressive Judaism for the use of Chapter 9, "All Israel's Search for Identity" (July 1968).

To the Union of American Hebrew Congregations and the Jewish Frontier for the use of Chapter 16, "Israel and Galut: The Unresolved Encounter" (November 1973), and to the Union of American Hebrew Congregations for the use of Chapter 13, "Are We in Exile?" (Spring 1971), and "Warsaw, 1943" (1944).

To the Reconstructionist for the use of Chapters 2, "The Twofold Task of Zionism" (February 1945), 3, "The State of Israel: Its Moral Implications" (December 1948), 4, "The Uniqueness of Judaism" (January 1957).

To Judaism for the use of Chapters 11, "Pharisaism and Political Sovereignty" (Fall 1970), and 12, "Some Medieval Thinkers on the Jewish King" (Summer 1971).

To the Synagogue Council of America for the use of Chapter 8, "The Religious Dimensions of Israel" (February 1968).

To the Christian Century for the use of Chapter 14, "Religious Meanings in Jewish Secularism" (May 1971).

1

For Zion's Sake

Jewish nationalism, which is the hope for the restoration of a Jewish homeland in Palestine, was never challenged by any Jewish authority until the French Revolution, and Napoleon's Sanhedrin, by whose fiat Israel ceased to be a nation and became a sect. Throughout our development, the religious impulses and the national nostalgia of the Jew kept pace. Epitomizing this is the aphorism attributed by the rabbis to God: "I shall not enter Jerusalem Above until I enter Jerusalem Below."[1] Not only were the national and religious trends parallel but they were integral, so that no effort was made to establish precise distinctions between the two. There was no rigid borderland separating them, and it occurred to no one that they might be mutually exclusive. They were elements of an organic whole, which no more yielded to artificial dichotomies than a statue acquiesces to a duality between its form and its marble. No one ever suggested that Malkhut Bet David ("the Kingdom of the House of David") and Malkhut Shamayim ("the Kingdom of Heaven") were irreconcilable, and though no sentries patrolled the borders of these kingdoms, none of the Avelei-Zion ("mourners for Zion") dared go marauding in the kingdom of God, nor did the keepers of the sanctuary deem it necessary to stamp out patriotism as a preventive or defensive measure. The osmotic process in which each can come and go in the domain of the other, in which each is simultaneously a citizen in both realms, commands ample evidence in our Bible. The God-enthralled Jeremiah could, without qualms about his membership in the universalist guild, advise his cousin to purchase a tract of Palestinian soil as an act of faith in the restoration of the promised land.[2] The tractate Taanit, with its detailed exposition of the dates of national calamities, posits its discussions about prayers for rain upon the premise of Jewish restoration to Palestine. The identical process persists in times much closer to our own. It persists long after the physical cords between our people and its land had been severed. A galaxy of God-possessed and Palestine-enraptured men attests to an unbroken se-

1

quence down into modern times. In the tenth century, Hasdai ibn Shaprut, vizier to Abd-ur-Rahman III, secure behind the immunities of his office, could write to the king of the Khazars:

> Tell me whether you possess a record foretelling the end of those marvelous events for which we have been waiting these many years during which we have gone from captivity to captivity and from exile to exile. . . . How can I be silent over the destruction of our glorious Temple and over those who passed through flame and water, so that we remain depleted in number, cast down from glory and into exile; we cannot retort when we are told all day long, "Every people has a kingdom, but there is not even a memory of you in the land."[3]

Reverberations of Hasdai's religious nationalism go rolling through the ages. They are speeded on their way by an Ibn Gabirol in the eleventh,[4] a Maimonides in the twelfth,[5] a Nahmanides in the thirteenth,[6] a Crescas in the fourteenth century.[7] They are echoed in the utterances of an Albo in the fifteenth,[8] a Joseph Nasi in the sixteenth,[9] and a Menasseh ben Israel in the seventeenth century.[10] What a narrow crossing from the Spanish Hasdai to the Russian Nahman of Bratzlav. When he said, "The chief of everything is Palestine," his disciples asked him if he was thinking of a spiritual Palestine. He answered, "No, I mean the real Palestine, with its houses and streets, as we see it with the human eye."[11]

It is redundant to heap citation upon citation, for it is up to any anti-Zionist to find a single contradictory expression in all of Jewish literature throughout this period. Even the schismatic Karaites broke with rabbinic Judaism in every respect except Palestine. Throughout Jewish history, every Jewish principle and dogma, including the very nature of God and human resurrection, was scrutinized and debated, but not the principle of the restoration of the Palestinian Jewish state. Not only Israel but his neighbors and contemporaries recognized his national character. "Not only Luther, Israel's violent accuser, considered the Jews a nation who came from Jerusalem to dwell among the peoples, but Reuchlin also . . . regarded the Jews as a distinct nation."[12]

It is clear that Jewish nationalism did not wait for the French Revolution, the Congress of Vienna, or the uprisings of 1830, for its origin and growth. Its unique character is summarized by Judah Ha-Levi, who associates with the longing for Palestine the Jewish God concept, the Jewish festivals, the Torah, Jewish religious values, and messianism.[13]

Just as Jewish religious literature recognizes the national character of Israel, so does secular Jewish literature presuppose the religious nature of Jewish nationalism. Thus, the advent of modern times, and the beginning of modern Hebrew literature in the early eighteenth century, did not interrupt the nationalist tendency in Jewish thought. Moses, Ephraim, and Samuel David Luzzatto, Moses Mendelssohn, Naftali Herz Wessely, Isaac Baer Schlesinger, Solomon Loewisohn, Solomon Judah Rapoport, and many others give voice to the traditional religious nationalism of Israel. Space permits but two out of scores of corroborating passages. The least nationalistic of these is by Moses Mendelssohn. Yet in 1770, in answer to a letter asking his attitude to an autonomous Jewish state, Mendelssohn replied that this could come about only as a result of a great international war. Because of the depressed lot of Israel and its loss of vigor, it must resort to prayer instead of to direct action. "God . . . has had mercy upon our remnant by giving us His Torah . . . as a support, until He shall raise up the booth of David from the earth and say to the fallen daughter of Zion: Rise to your feet."[14] In 1775 he translated into German Ha-Levi's *Zion ha-lo Tishali* ("Zion, dost thou not ask"). Upon reading the translation, Goethe said, "There is a warmth of yearning in this elegy, found in but few poems."[15]

One of Samuel David Luzzato's many Zionistic poems, written from 1815 to 1818, reads: "How long, O Lord, shall our land be the possession of a merciless people, while Thy first-born dwell amidst captivity and murder at the hands of their overpowering foes? Regard Jacob who cries out from his prison. Have mercy and say, 'Rejoice O child of Jerusalem.' In a little while the wrath shall cease, and these things shall not befall you in your own land."[16]

During this period, too, the national character of Israel was generally recognized by non-Jews. Joseph, Prince de Ligne, David Hartley, Lord Shaftesbury, and many others outlined plans for the return of the Jews to Palestine.[17]

We have indicated the unbroken continuity of Jewish nationalism as it developed prior to the burgeoning of European nationalism. We have observed how its character was one with the deepest religious ideals of Judaism. By 1830, nationalism became "a widely contagious and fiercely effective force in European society."[18] At this juncture and in some quarters, the utterances of Jewish nationalists became suspect on the grounds that they are tainted with the European scourge. No one will challenge their contiguity with the thought of European national-ists. Yet to dismiss their contributions to Jewish nationalism as parodies of Europe's jingo professors is an unwarranted conclusion. A careful study of the leading exponents of Jewish nationalism from 1830 will reveal a consistent adherence to the traditional elements in Jewish nationalism. While much of the form is decidedly European, the inner texture is Jewish. In 1836 Nachman Krochmal began his *Moreh Nevukhei Ha-Zeman* ("Modern Guide to the Perplexed"). Its indebtedness to Hegel in its philosophic scaffolding is unmistakable. "We must consider," says Hegel, "the shape which the perfect embodiment of spirit assumes—the State. ... The State is the Divine Idea as it exists on earth."[19] Yet consider Krochmal's approach to the state. The greatest type of society is the nation, he says. In every nation the members devote themselves to attaining the highest degree of spiritual proficiency. This expresses itself in culture, arts, and crafts. Transcending these, however, are the recognition and worship of God. While the spirituality of other nations, which strive for beauty, wisdom, or power, is transitory, Israel's is everlasting because it is absolute and "the source of all spirituality." It is undeniable that Krochmal considered Israel a nation, and was concerned with the rebirth of the Jewish state. "Their power was crushed to earth [deprived of] all those material and spiritual benefits which are necessary for the tranquil existence of a nation in its own territory."[20]

Almost identical sentiments are expressed by Isaac Baer Levinson in his *Zerubavel* and by Shadal in his letters.

The three leading literary exponents of pre-Herzl Zionism, and the most misrepresented as secularists, are Smolenskin, Lilienblum and Ahad Ha-Am. Smolenskin recapitulated his philosophy of Judaism thus: "We are one people, and the rules of faith alone are the cornerstone ... of our national unity. These rules of faith are the belief in One God, the study of Torah in the original ... the hope for future redemption. ... If one adheres to these principles, he is for Israel."[21] These ideas are expressed even more vigorously by Lilienblum.[22] Ahad Ha-Am rejects any possible cleavage between Jewish religion and nationalism. "A Jewish nationalism which does not possess any semblance of those things which have been the soul of our nation ... is such a strange phenomenon that it cannot be imagined."[23] It has been irresponsibly stated that Ahad Ha-Am was concerned with *Geulat ha-Shekhinah* ("the redemption of the Divine Spirit") and not with *Kibbutz Galuyyot* ("the ingathering of exiles"). To the contrary, he indicates that one specific aspect of Israel's dedication to absolute justice is the idea of messianism, the fulfillment of that act of justice by which Israel will be restored to its rightful place. Our national consciousness is identified with faith in the ultimate return to Palestine. Without this, the Torah is doomed.[24]

Hans Kohn, evaluating modern Zionism, writes: "Zionism as a secular movement arose among the secularized Jewish intelligentsia of central Europe as a reaction to economic and political factors, but it quickly became the form into which was cast the mediaeval religious Zionist fervor of the East European and Oriental Jew."[25]

It is abundantly clear that Zionism and European nationalism are not blood brothers. Instead, there is an intimate kinship between Jewish assimilationism, which often passes by the name "universalism," and European nationalism. Modern assimilationism came to life after the emergence of European nationalism, which advanced Jewish escapism to the dignity of a Weltanschauung, and afforded fidgety Jews the opportunity of reduced visibility by total immersion in the state. Assimilationism is a philosophy, barren and slovenly though it be, of Jewish life. It recognizes a social compact with the state to deliver up the identity of the Jew in return for a dose of protective coloration. Jewish nationalism and secularism have been deftly juxtaposed against religion and universalism, thus obscuring Zionism's irreconcilable antagonism to that most vulgarly secularist and hypocritical movement in Jewish life—assimilationism. Nor does the process stop here. The war on Jewish nationalism in defense of the universal truths of Judaism has all too often been nothing but a flanking movement to achieve a junction with Christianity. These tactics also have their origin in the early period of European nationalism. Yehezkel Kaufmann writes:

> Through the weakening of our faith which accompanied the Haskalah, Christianity gained an advantage over Judaism. The Haskalah blazed new paths for apostasy and was the beginning of a conversionist movement which has not yet subsided. The aspirations toward a "national" religion, implicit in Haskalah, minimized the differences between the religions. As a result there was aroused in certain circles of the Diaspora religion an urge to cross over to the dominant Christianity, particularly liberal Protestantism.[26]

He tells us further:

> Even Mommsen, an admirer of the Jews, demanded that they surrender their one remaining "national" characteristic—their religion. For Christianity in his time represented the embodiment of all of human culture, and to stand outside of its borders while remaining inside of the nation, was "possible, but difficult and fraught with danger."[27]

It therefore devolves upon the opponents of Jewish nationalism to bear the burden of proof that Judaism and Jewish nationalism are adversaries. One thing is certain. Jewish nationalism is steeped in ancient and ample precedent. If anti-nationalists insist upon a cleavage where Jewish tradition has detected none, they cannot do so in the name of historical Judaism. They may do so only in the name of their own novel construction of Judaism, and in the name of an altogether unprecedented departure from millennia of Jewish thought. This is their prerogative, but in exercising it let them be mindful that they are launched upon a diversion from the unbroken flow of Jewish history. They may take their stand upon what they consider to be the merits of their position, but certainly not upon the "merits of the fathers."

In our time, the anti-Zionist argument rests upon two spurious antagonisms: nationalism versus universalism, and secularism versus religion. The indictment of Zionism because it is nationalistic is diffuse and irrelevant. The record of Judaism in relation to Palestine indicates that the term *nationalism* neither describes nor defines. Hegel was a nationalist. So was Mazzini. Treitschke was a nationalist. So was Masaryk. During the occupation of Nicaragua, America was nationalist. During this war for the global extension of the four freedoms, America is nationalist. The brutality of Nietzscheanism is not mitigated by dubbing it nationalism any more than the decency and forbearance of Danish democracy are impugned by the epithet. It is a delusion to assume that a word alone must establish a community of meaning. More telling than the word is a cosmos of attitudes, emotions, centuries of living which condition one group to live as though they were little lower than the angels and another group to act as though they were little higher than the beasts. The dragon's teeth of nationalism are not to be drawn by homelessness, nor are the blessings of religion enhanced by denationalization. Denmark is no less democratic for all of its nationalism. India is no less religious for all of its seething patriotism.

Equally vaporous is the term *universalism*. Which of the numerous varieties of universalism are we to accept as legal tender? Shall it be the universalism of Plato? Shall it be the universalism of Spinoza? Shall it, indeed, be the universalism of the prophets? By all criteria, one should be as acceptable as the others. Yet once a distinction is made in favor of Jewish universalism, the choice is no less particularistic than a special preference for Jewish nationalism. Which prophet could pass the rigid requirements of the American Council for Judaism? It is possible by a feat of textual amputation to sever a Jeremiah from *U-vau ve-rinenu vi-mrom tziyon* ("They shall come and rejoice on Zion's height"),[28] but once this is done, there is no Jeremiah, but only a disfigured caricature, stammering a censored and disjointed message to an incredulous world.

The device of stigmatizing Zionism with the secularist taint can be turned upon anti-Zionism by indicating the Christian orientation in its conception of religion. The untenable bisection of personal and social salvation, whereby the former is admitted into the sanctum of religion and the latter is rejected, continues even now to dominate much of Christian thought. Christian religion, we are informed by Niebuhr, is divorced from social morality and has so been construed by many of its proponents from Augustine to Barth. Human society is regarded as corrupt, and these religious spirits have stressed only personal abnegation, the future ideal community, and the love of God as the true requisites for religion. "Pure religious idealism does not concern itself with the social problem."[29] This cleavage has never possessed Jewish thought. Zionism, whose urge for group salvation never deterred saintly seekers for personal salvation from accepting it, confirms this fact. The juxtaposition of religion against Zionism represents, in large measure, the acceptance of Christian terms of differentiation. Judah Ha-Levi was alluding to this specious dichotomy when he said: "Proof of the Divine Influence is not found in well-chosen words, in raising the eyebrows, closing the eyes during prayers, contrition, movement, and talk behind which there are no deeds."[30] Judaism has always laid out its spiritual longitudes and latitudes more universally. The attempt to discredit Zionism because it cannot be wedged into an ecclesiastical bulkhead is a patent example of the unconscious mimicry of Christian dualism. Don Isaac Abravanel had to contend with apostate Jews who insisted that the "deliverance of which the prophets speak does not mean liberation from physical distress and exile, but liberation from sin."[31] The nationalist impetus in our religion and the religious undercurrent in our nationalism, both pressing on uninterruptedly through time, drive home the essentially monistic character of Judaism.

The anti-nationalists would have us explode this monism. To do so would be to alter and disfigure the very essence of Judaism.

Conversely, the religious affirmations of the anti-nationalists are no more convincing than their invectives against secularism. Even in the broadest construction of the term *world religious community*, what do the anti-nationalists have in common with the Jews of Poland, the Hasidim of Jerusalem, the devotees of the Lubavitcher, the Buk-

harians, the Yemenites? They will not be intrigued by champions of a
"world religious community" who will pray *Ve-tehezenah eineinu be-shuvha* ("May our eyes behold Thy return") and will censor *le-tziyon be-rahamim* ("to Zion in mercy").[32] How can the anti-nationalists reconcile their protestations of internationalism with their pronouncement, "Reform has had as its major concern the religious welfare and development of the Jews in America"?[33] This uninhibited confession breathes the blitheness of a Strauss waltz. In a world of butchered Jews and vanishing communities, we are assured that "Reform has had as its major concern the religious welfare . . . of the Jews in America." Are the Jews of Europe therefore *not* a major concern of American anti-Zionists? How can a "world religious community" have as its major concern the "religious welfare" of certain Jews in a specific locality? It would appear that the opposition to Palestine rests less upon spiritual scruples than upon the fact that Europe's Jews do not count as a major concern of American anti-Zionists. But even if they did, the deportees of Warsaw, if they still live, will find such religion a mockery which is long on beatitudes and short on Mitzvot. Moreover, even American Jews, beset by overcast horizons and apprehensions about their future, will find that this credo, by specifying "religious welfare," fails to come to grips with their total needs. Zionism, on the other hand, need indulge in no apologetics for its religious attitude. There is no other Jewish movement to rival the spiritual intensity of the Yishuv and its cohorts. No other Jewish community in the world has so heroically fulfilled the mitzvah of *Pidyon Shevuyim* ("ransom of captives"). No Jewish community has more punctiliously lived the prophetic denunciation, *Hoy magiey vayit be-vayit sadeh ve-sadeh yakrivu ad effes makom* ("Woe to those who add house to house and join field to field until there is no room").[34] No other Jewish community has given not merely of its increment but of its life blood to clothe the naked and feed the hungry. Nowhere else in Jewish life has the principle of man's responsibility to his fellow man been lived with greater integrity than in the kibbutzim and moshave ovdim. Nor need the Yishuv shrink from an inspection of its theological tzitzit. The venerable rabbis of the land, the synagogues in the cities and colonies, the schoolchildren who are taught to memorize *"Pitiysaniy adonal vaepas"* ("Thou hast enthralled me, O Lord, and I am enthralled"),[35] need brook no scolding from without. Should it be said that the Zionism of the Yishuv is not the Zionism of the Diaspora, let this answer be given: Today's Yishuv was yesterday's Diaspora. Before rabbis impeach the religious qualifications of Zionism, let them seek daily atonement for the crassness rampant within their own citadels.

It is more relevant to inquire when anti-Zionists became preoccupied with the welfare of Palestine. They tell us, "We appreciate the position of Palestine, the sentiment that attaches to it, and its capacity to absorb Jewish emigration."[36] Who except an anti-Semite does not? These very sentiments can be found in the report of the Peel Commission, which curtailed immigration and land purchases in Palestine. How sardonic that the alleged concern of anti-Zionists for Palestine has convulsed American Jewish life. Their left-handed blessings have offered only a *pishon peh* ("pretext") to our enemies for tightening the screws on the Yishuv and on European Jewry. It was not their "appreciation" that recently brought a thousand blighted and blasted children to Palestine. It was the grieving compassion of a Yishuv which is too immersed in *Pikuah nefesh* ("Rescue of life") to be trapped in a web of indecision and sophistry. Nor does the anti-Zionist record indicate even a microscopic commitment to Palestine reconstruction. The record will prove that during Zionism's three most dangerous periods—at the end of the First World War, in 1929, and now—anti-Zionists, and in some instances the same anti-Zionists, have selected a time of grief for Israel to lacerate the wound even more. In November 1929, one of them preached, "Some have said: 'The Jews of the world must continue to pour into Palestine thousands and thousands and thousands.' When they are told this policy will lead to more massacres, they answer, 'That's the burden Jews have to bear.' The proposal is stupid and cruel. It is no solution. It is an injustice to the unfortunate Polish and Rumanian Jews who will bear the brunt of it."[37] Since this pronouncement, at least 300,000 Jews have entered Palestine.

Throughout the utterances of anti-Zionism runs an ominous undercurrent. It is the resurrection of the devasting monstrosity once harbored by German Jewry—namely, that we are a religion in the ecclesiastical sense, that Zionism means dual loyalty, and that Zionism accentuates anti-Semitism. The results of these charges, repudiated by events themselves, have taught certain Jewish leaders nothing. They do not seem to have been rendered more temperate even by their professed concern for American Jewry. The recklessness of the following official statements is revealing: "They [the Zionists] are breeding anti-Jewish feeling here in America. . . . Such procedure [the demands for a Jewish commonwealth] is hardly indicative of cooperation in the united war effort, no matter what verbal affirmations or financial contributions Zionists might make."[38] These recriminations say all that need be said about the doctrine of a "world religious community" with particular emphasis upon American Jewry, with special reference to its "religious" needs, and with specific regard for Reform Jews. They offer eloquent testimony that anti-Zionism is no longer content merely to indulge in escape by low visibility. It is bent upon nullifying the Jewish democratic process, which is implicit in Jewish nationalism. In the name of Jewry, it seeks to impose the will of a class whose personal interests are transparent upon Kelal Yisrael. We are conversant with the tactics of minorities who would stifle democracy in the very act of appealing to its sanctions. Within the United Nations themselves, there stretches a second front of those who know that they are doomed if the democracy which they profess should become the possession of the many. In Jewish life, as in every corner of this embattled world, a struggle rages between the many who demand unconditional freedom and the few who would run the risk of defeat itself as a price for keeping the many subdued. The spectacle of a French aristocracy, hating democracy more than Hitler and allowing millions of their compatriots to go down to defeat, is fresh in our minds. The case of privileged classes is that they have denied privilege to the downtrodden in the name of dazzling ideals.

On such an issue, how can a group of rabbis remain neutral? There is no middle course of suspended animation on the destiny of Judaism. There can be no detached objectivity about whether the Jewish body can thrive after an arbitrary expulsion of the red corpuscles by the white. Because Zionists realize that neutrality is a synonym for unconditional surrender of the nationalist ideal, we repudiate silence and reserve. Only those who do not care can be neutral.

The logic of Jewish nationalism in tomorrow's world rests equally upon two alternatives. One is the dream, still misty and elusive, of national pluralism and world federation. The other is the grim fact of the untenability of Europe for the Jews.

Zionism will be valid in the most orderly world, and it will be vital in the most disjointed world. It is hoped that our civilization will emerge from the war with a capacity for multiple allegiance. From union through fear may evolve union through esteem and compassion. Surely, in the minds of the truly free, the loyalties of men must no longer be drained off into the inexhaustible reservoirs of the One Voracious State. The appeal to single devotion is a plea for the totalitarian state and a repudiation of the aptitude of men for many interrelated allegiances. The melting pot is a synonym for *gleichshaltung*. Fidelity to the One State becomes bigotry when it is predicated upon compulsory aloofness from other states. On July 4, 1915, Louis Dembitz Brandeis, champion of multiple loyalties, delivered an address, "True Americanism," in which he said:

The movements of the last century have proved that whole peoples have individualities no less marked than that of a single person; that the individuality of a people is irrepressible, and that the misnamed internationalism which seeks the obliteration of nationalities or peoples is unattainable. The new nationalism adopted by America proclaims that each race or people, like each individual, has the right and duty to develop, and that only through such differentiated development will high civilization be attained. Not until these principles of nationalism, like those of democracy, are generally accepted will liberty be fully attained and minorities be secure in their rights. Not until then can the foundation be laid for a lasting peace among the nations.

The same paragraph appears in Justice Brandeis's essay, "The Jewish Problem, How to Solve It," published in 1915.

The consummation of global union, if it is to be, will not mean the obliteration of national identity. It will level restrictive barriers, and it will restrain savage antagonisms, but it will not outlaw national cohesiveness and internal national autonomy as essential ingredients of worldwide relations. Federation will not mean ethnic dispersal but rather the equalization and the rationalization of ethnic influence. The first act of a new world would be to repatriate the slave laborers of Norway, France, Poland, and Greece. In the perspective of a world aborning, the span between the three-year exile of a Norwegian and the eighteen-hundred-and-seventy-three year exile of a Jew is narrow. Partial surrender of sovereignty in an interdependent world does not require self-effacement any more than American democracy demands the erasure of state identity.

Moreover, in a genuinely united world, the Jew must enjoy not only the role of a beneficiary, but the status of a partner in the global enterprise of rebirth. Peoplehood has been thrust upon him in martyrdom, a martyrdom reserved for Jews only. In the hour of his salvation, he cannot shed the yoke of peoplehood and go slithering back into the disreputable shadows of anonymity. If mankind is to truly undergo a "new birth of freedom," it will not exact national eclipse as the price for emancipation in the very act of resurrecting a whole world of vanished peoples. A callous age is content to let the Jew as Jew symbolize the revulsion engendered by millions of corpses, which even in death haunt the Galut. But it is not ready to let the Jew symbolize the regeneration of the human spirit, to let the Jew raise a hand within his own sphere for the redemption of mankind. In his agony, he is a Jew. In his vindication he may only be a national of this state or that. This paradox offers an ominous demurrer to the faith that through transubstantiation the world's spiritual compounds will be converted from blood to the milk of human kindness. For the world to require, and for the Jewish people to acquiesce to, the role of an *eved nirtzah* ("a slave who refuses to be freed") is a disturbing intrusion upon all the reveries of a transformed society.

To make its contribution to the democratic process, Jewry requires, ultimately, a state and not a laboratory or an asylum. Although we are assured that victory will achieve these objectives without the need for a Jewish state, there is thus far nothing to validate this fond hope. There are more authentic guides than the yet dim mileposts of tomorrow. One is the present, overcast with the suffocating fog of a Christian world's insensibility to Jewish mass martyrdom. The voice is the voice of promised redemption, but the hands are the hands of indecision and moral paralysis. Another criterion is our two-millennia-old past in Europe. A career of unwanted pariahs, relieved in spots by short-lived emancipations during which even Goethes and Schillers recoiled before pathologic visions of a leprous Jewry, will not be annulled at the stroke of victory. Israel has been departing from Europe from the moment he was driven onto the continent. Even now, we are leaving Europe behind as we left Palestine behind, not by choice but by compulsion. This banishment, whose beginnings reach back to Crusades and Lateran Councils and Armleder pogroms, is more convulsive even than the exile from Palestine. We never embraced exile as a blessing, nor do we find anything ennobling or promising in bleak homelessness. We have not invoked expulsion, but understanding its imminent threat, we have attempted to cope with it and prevent it from becoming a chaotic and panicky rout. There can be no comprehension of our problem unless it is understood that Europe has never absorbed us and has never ceased ejecting us.

The currents of history drive eastward. The tides that once surged from the west, bearing with them barbaric invasions, mass migrations, and Jewish expulsion, have been turned. To the east, a whole world has sprung to life. To the east, the enemy swept millions of victims before him. To the east, for generations, Israel has been retracing his steps. To the east, the pilgrimage goes on, a pilgrimage of homeless exiles, a pilgrimage of parentless children. Every land has mourned their fate, and no land has opened wide to them its gates. That bleeding remnant of Israel that yet survives in Europe is on the march—the march of the hunted beggars. No Jew on the occupied continent now lives in the place which four years ago he called home. What shall we have them do? Shall we have them return someday to the place whence they came, where the waters of terror and bitterness have swept away every memory of their presence? They are now in a howling wilderness, a no man's land. If they are to go anywhere when peace comes, where is the wisdom in demanding that they return to a place which shall say "I know you not," while their kin in Palestine wait to receive them? They are doubly in Galut, and the doors through which they have been flung turn outward, not inward. It is blasphemous to demand that a mutilated people return incessantly to the scene of its violation. It is cruel to repeat the callous assurance which only those untouched by disaster can glibly mouth: "This time it will be different." Yes, it shall be different, because Jews will demand rescue through escape, not through the precarious role of hostages. They will demand a home in Palestine as of right, not a *Nachtasyl* in Europe by sufferance. But for the grace of God and Zionism, 600,000 Jews would today be under the sentence of death in Europe. To demand of those who are no longer of Europe in spirit to retrace their steps, is as incongruous as to ask Palestinian Jewry to return to Europe. Who dares accuse Jewry of having little faith when after two thousand years of attempted reconciliation with Europe, it has failed them, and they want to return home? Naked they entered, and naked they shall return. They ask no reparations. They ask only to be released for God's and man's service in a land where the echoes of salvation are heard. They do not renounce Europe. They leave it as a harried victim leaves a place of tortured memories. We are sick, and so is Europe. We cannot live side by side until our wounded souls are restored. Then we may return, but never again as exiled orphans. Zionism is a Jewish People's War against humiliation and torture. In the name of that justice and that prophecy which we affirm, we dare not hold Israel back from his destiny. Others may view the martyrdom of Israel sub specie aeternitatis, but let them not obstruct the path of a lacerated people that implores for salvation *be-haye'khon uve-yomeikhon uve-hayei dekhal bet yisrael* ("During your lives and in your days and during the life of the house of Israel"). A Zionist named Bialik once said:

> Perhaps that which mighty nations have been unable to achieve through their wealth, an indigent people may accomplish in its tiny land through poverty. Perhaps from the walls of the schools shall emerge someday the truth of man's moral responsibility for the destiny of civilization, and perhaps it will spread among all nations. Not in vain has the hand of God led this people

through the straits of Hell, only to restore it to its home for the
third time. The Book of Chronicles, last in the Canon, is not the
final record of Israel's career. To its two sections shall be added a
third. If the beginning of Chronicles is "Adam, Seth, Enosh,"
and its end the Cyrus Proclamation, which after six hundred
years resulted in tidings of salvation for the ancient pagans, so
shall the beginning of its third division be the Balfour Declaration and its end—the new tidings of salvation for all
humanity.[39]

A prophet named Jeremiah once said:

For thus says the Lord, "As I have brought upon this people all
this great trouble, so will I bring upon them all the good that I
promise them. And fields shall be bought in this land of which
you say, 'It is a desolation, abandoned by man and beast, given
into the hands of the Chaldeans.' Yes, men shall buy fields for
money, and shall sign the deeds, seal them, and get witnesses, in
the land of Benjamin, in the neighborhood of Jerusalem, in the
cities of Judah—in the cities of the hill country, the cities of the
Shefelah, and the cities of the Negev—for I will restore their
fortune," is the oracle of the Lord.[40]

2

The Twofold Task of Zionism

Zionism stands on two levels, the immediate and the ultimate. The concern of the immediate level is the elimination of Jewish homelessness through the establishment of a Jewish commonwealth in Palestine. The concern of the ultimate level is the regeneration of Judaism through Palestine. The first is the indispensable condition for the second. The second must be the unconditional consequence of the first. The early debates as to which is preferable have been rendered academic by history. The dispute between Ahad Ha-Am and Herzl on a political versus a cultural center appears unrealistic today. The cleavage was resolved in a classic symposium, which appeared in *He-Atid* under the title *"Al ha-Yahadut v'al Atidoteha"* ("Concerning the future of Judaism").[1] One of the participants, Martin Buber, crystallized the problem as follows:

> In our own time, our youth will go up to their own land. A day will come when a new nation will be born there. But, lest there occur an aggrandizement of life alone instead of an aggrandizement of culture as well, a spark must be struck over that void, the spark of religious revival.

In relation to Palestine, Reconstructionism has contributed significantly, and must increasingly contribute, to the synthesis of both levels of Zionism. This is a task which can most effectively be achieved by a movement whose objective is the cultivation of Jewish life in its totality, and a Jewish national movement in its totality.

On the immediate level, Zionism is based upon two factors— justifiable skepticism and necessary idealism. The skepticism of the Zionist is rooted in history and confirmed by current events.

In our day, a neoemancipation movement has been launched by certain Jewish groups. This movement propounds the following proposition:

15

Implicit in the liberation of Europe will be the liberation of its Jews. Europe will be democratically constituted. In a democracy, special protection and guarantees for ethnic and religious minorities are superfluous because such guarantees imply potential restrictions. In a democracy, the individual, whoever he may be, is assured of inalienable rights, and that is enough. The minority treaties of 1919 failed precisely because they dealt with designated groups rather than with individuals. Therefore, an international bill of human rights within a democratic European society will assure Jews full equality.

This, of course, is the philosophy of the Emancipation all over again. What is the record of the Emancipation? Engendered in an age when concepts of the social contract and natural rights prevailed, the Emancipation sought to cope with the Jewish problem from the point of view of human rights. Christian Wilhelm Dohm, a friend of Mendelssohn, invoked the rights of man in championing Emancipation. The Jews of Paris based their claim on their rights as human beings. So also did the Jews of Alsace-Lorraine and of Holland. In 1796, in the Batavian Assembly, the author of a declaration states that it suffices for the Jew to say, "I am a human being." However, the logic of this position was shattered by the reality of the European world's attitude toward the Jew. He was to learn that formulas do not alter social conditions. Yehezkel Kaufmann tells us:

> True, the Jews were emancipated . . . but their legal condition was based on a fictitious premise, namely, that they had ceased to be a nation. . . . the law might accept the principle that the Jews were no longer a nation but a religious community alone. . . . However, the living people never ceased to feel that the Jew was a stranger to it, that he was not one of its sons. It did not feel inwardly and truly that the Jewish tribe had a share in the national privileges of its land.[2]

Actually, the Emancipation was not a social contract, but a unilateral arrangement whereby surrender of group identity was extracted from the Jew in return for liberties that could always be rescinded. It was to be discovered that liberties could be withdrawn from "human beings" as well as from "Jews." The Christian world was not impressed with this clever distinction. Intuitively, it realized that if Jews organized and propagandized for their own dissolution, this too was a perverted form of group consciousness and group survival. Herder could understand Jewish distinctiveness.

[His] glorification of ancient Hebrew poetry was merely in line with his sincere conviction that diversity of culture, rather than cosmopolitan leveling of differences is the aim of historical evolution. This eloquent proclamation [states] that the older a people, the more distinctive its individuality; that Israel's chosenness is the essence of Jewish history and that the burden of the law is an integral part of Judaism.[3]

The same Herder, confronting "human" Jews, could not understand the elimination of the Jewish ethnic character. He stated that the Jew had been and remained a stranger to Europe. He was bound to a Torah, a way of life, a way of thinking, altogether foreign to Europe. Therefore, the problem is: How can he be assimilated without injury to the assimilating body? The problem is aggravated because it cannot be solved through conversion, since Christianity no longer accepts converts with open arms.

The best refutation of the neo-emancipation doctrine appeared in the January 9, 1945, issue of the *New York Times*. Through a classic irony, the following statement, in extract, was published by the National Committee of Americans of Polish Descent. It was headlined: "The Poles Are Also People with Human Rights."

> We . . . join with you in believing that no force of violence . . . must . . . deter mankind from a full realization of the noble precepts of the International Bill of Human Rights. . . . we appeal to you, not to exclude the Polish people from the International Bill of Human Rights. . . . Let this hard-pressed people, too, share the benefits of the International Bill of Rights.

The European climate has not improved since the Emancipation and post-Emancipation period. It has deteriorated. No one is deceived by euphemistic references to human rights when everyone knows that the fate of the Jew is at stake. Every minority group in Europe will say: "Yes, we endorse an International Bill of Human Rights. Now what are you going to do about *us?*" Thus, the problem is not tackled but merely tabled by a parliamentary trick. Our justifiable skepticism is based on two considerations. The first is the mood of the world today. We ought to be as bitterly realistic as possible. If the American government, with a great show of generosity, admits fewer than a thousand refugees, then this act of political cynicism reflects a very discouraging world situation. Jacob Lestschinsky tells us:

> Just as a sick person cannot be comfortable under any circum-

stances, neither can the ailing and landless Jewish people. The more nationally homogeneous the component units of the future European Federation will be, the more tragic will be the position of the Jewish minority. Remaining virtually alone amid unified national enclaves, the struggle of the Jewish minority for equal rights will become even more difficult than before, while its chances of retaining its own national spirit and mode of living will become even slighter.

The fact that Holland, Denmark, and Sweden have shown Christian charity to the Jew must elicit our everlasting gratitude, but unfortunately, it contributes little to the solving of the problem. These countries do not contain large masses of Jews, nor are they likely to do so.

Our skepticism is aroused further by the very nature of the proposed human rights. They are predicated on nothing more substantial than the aspirations of their authors and underwriters. An orphan ideal—an ideal without a powerful parent to protect it—can prove dangerous because it may lead simple believers to unwarranted expectations. In public affairs, a proposal devoid of the means of giving it life, is regarded as deliberately misleading and deceptive, usually contrived to thwart a rival proposal or to discharge an odious obligation cheaply. Group rights are, at best, arrested and potential realities. They are worthless unless they are conditional upon enforcement and concrete acts demonstrating honorable intent by the givers of the rights. As long as these conditions are not met, no bill of rights can survive. See what the Congress of Vienna did to European Jewry in 1815.

A Jewish homeland, however feeble, holds infinitely greater promise for protecting its Jewish citizens, because its will is enforced by instruments conceived and used by the people for their own benefit. What is more, it represents more than a verbal assent by the nations of the world. It represents a concrete act on their part, niggardly and grudging though it be, intended to give reality to their desire to solve the Jewish problem. To this extent, they have a stake and a responsibility in the matter. They may try to squirm and evade, but they have committed themselves by a deed. A deed, a fait accompli, is harder to undo than a pronouncement. The Greeks betrayed are still Greeks on their own soil. European Jewry betrayed is lost.

The pressure of events has brought many an anti-Zionist to the acceptance of a Jewish homeland in Palestine. But why a government when a refuge will serve the purpose equally well? The essence of Jewish misery has been the inability of the European Jew to regulate, even in the feeblest way, the conditions of his existence. The weaker a people, the more limited its power to manipulate circumstances to its own advantage. But the Jew, far from being able to manipulate, was paralyzed. Galut meant absence of the means of salvation. In this generation, it has meant deterioration from de facto to de jure statelessness, which will not be remedied too easily or too quickly. Self-government means some degree of ability to cope with trouble. It is a form of protection, multiplied as governments draw together for mutual aid. A stateless Jewry in Palestine is threatened with the same disabilities that Jewry suffers in Europe. It means succumbing to the mercies of surrounding powers all over again. It means transfer of the Galut and its evils to Palestine. A people that cannot regulate its own means of defense, its own acquisition of land, its own immigration—a people which depends upon its human status alone, and allows its specific claims as a people to go by default, will suffer encroachment and disaster by enemies who do not recognize human rights.

Just as it is important to scrutinize skeptically events in our time, so is it important to consider the possibility of Zionism in a more liberal world. In that event, the rebirth of the Jewish people in Palestine would be encouraged by the nations of the world. They would not insist upon the obliteration of the Jewish ethnic character. They would be prepared to accept the Jewish people as a co-worker in the building of an interdependent world. If the present blockade of Palestine is a sign of reaction in the world, the sign of liberalism would be free access to Palestine, and self-government in a Jewish commonwealth. A liberal world would not urge Emancipation as an alternative to Zionism, for Emancipation would be recognized for what it is—conditional individual life in return for unconditional group death.

Just as the immediate level of Zionism is devoted to the Jewish people, so must the ultimate level be devoted to Judaism. The long-awaited clarification of Palestine's status—favorable, we hope—will confront Reconstructionism with a unique challenge, the challenge of guarding the spiritual values inherent in Zionism. The Reconstructionist program, by its very nature, embraces these values. Once a Jewish commonwealth is achieved, their preservation will require the sponsorship of a special body, just as the political objectives of Zionism require a special body, just as the men of Safed not only preserved but engendered the sanctities of Israel upon Palestinian soil. The danger of indifference to spiritual values, or of repudiating them, is ever present in a popular movement. Mass movements too often trample upon their own ideals. It should, therefore, be an imperative task of Reconstructionism to serve as the agent that will constantly keep Israel aware of its moral responsibilities to Zionism. It comes to this function legitimately, having consistently stressed the deeper implications of the movement. There are a number of results which can and should accrue from Palestine.

The first is religious. In his *The Jew in Our Day*, Waldo Frank writes:

> This Jewish "remnant"—and only the remnant, through the ages, has preserved the Jew—will be loyal to the classes of social progress; but through its consciousness of God it will be still separate, and must remain so. . . . The God in man will be the still secret treasure it must lovingly nurture against the day when men, free of fear and hunger, learn to look within themselves where God lives. Thus, the Jews will still be a peculiar people. And they will be subject to the dislike and distrust of the zealot for whom the word "God" is anathema; although it was in the name of God that his values of social justice and individual dignity were preserved and prepared, through the barbaric ages.

Certainly, the rebellion against human exploitation has been made manifest in Palestine. The affirmation of human dignity and the worth of the individual have been made manifest in Palestine. Every Jewish settlement, with its own jealously cherished way of life, with its own unique deviations from its sister settlements, represents not only an economic and social experiment, but a serious enterprise in personal and group salvation. (It is surprising that Waldo Frank, whose spiritual program is so challenging, should fail to discern these things in Palestine.) No other self-conscious Jewry has been so uninhibited in casting off the soul-corroding social and economic evils of our time, and in embracing new ways to redemption.

I am aware that this in itself is not religion, even as I recognize the inadequacy of Harold Laski's attempt to classify the social impulses of communism as an expression of a new type of faith. But these elements are nevertheless the raw material from which religion ultimately springs. The attempt to salvage the Jewish religion through minor repairs—such as new prayer books and more felicitously phrased liturgies and lovelier rituals—is inadequate; to limit ourselves to such efforts betrays a failure to understand the basic untenability of religion today. For religion suffers not from aesthetic but from ideological defects—an inability adequately to interpret the problems of the person and of the group. If this interpretation will demand a new type of religious expression, hitherto unheard of and perhaps startling to the traditional mind, it will nevertheless take its place in Jewish life, and it will arise in the Yishuv. What its form will be we cannot tell. But it will be the outgrowth of a way of life, and its symbolism will therefore answer to the people's soul and aspirations as authentically as a bell answers to the push of a button.

The willingness to experiment boldly, not merely to tamper, is the promise of new and significant religious forms and ideas in the Yishuv. We should not be afraid of new and strange departures, raw and crude as they may appear to us. They reveal the gropings of the human spirit, and this is more significant than the hallowed barnacles of ancient formalisms that attach themselves to synagogue, shul, and temple. These groupings are attested to by the expressions of some of the Yishuv's leading spirits. One of them, Bialik, wrote:

> This land has been endowed with a special gift—to convert, in the end of days, small things into great. About four thousand years ago, there gathered in this land bands of wandering shepherds from Ur of the Chaldees, Aram, Egypt, and the Western Arabian desert. From them there grew . . . a small people —Israel. Few and evil were the days of this people upon its soil. . . . Yet it gave rise to simple men—shepherds, farmers, tenders of sycamore trees . . . who bore the storm of God's spirit in their hearts and His thunder and lightning upon their lips. These men, addressing folk and man, prophesying concerning the events of their own generation—these apparently little men dared to face eternity, the heavens and the earth, and they finally gave the world the cornerstone for its religious and moral culture. From beyond hundreds of generations and above the heads of nations rising and falling upon the stage of history, their voice reaches us. Today it is more mighty and exalted and fuller of the power of the Lord than ever before.[4]

Zionism implies certain social possibilities. Palestine has already proved that it alone has been capable of group regeneration. In addition to the rescue of European Jewry's remnants, Palestine has also restored to Judaism withered and decaying communities, which are now taking on new vigor. The Yemenites are one example. Here is a Jewry whose transplanting to Palestine means the preservation of a unique civilization which is already enriching our cultural soil. Palestine will continue to draw settlers from the moribund and deteriorating Jewries of the Near East, Africa, and the Mediterranean areas. These branches of Jewish life, which we had all but written off as remote, obscure, and going to seed, will experience not only a *tehiyat ha-metim* in Palestine but a transformation. They will in turn contribute to its ever-expanding folk life. In addition, these various elements, together with the great bodies of Jews from all over Europe, will go into the making of what may justifiably be called a diversified homogeneity. They will be the many contours of the face of Palestinian Jewry. This homogeneity would be analogous to that of the scores of racial and social elements in America.

Palestine has already contributed, and will continue to contribute, to a revival of Jewish culture. This culture has already proved that it is adaptable for export and can thrive on other soils. Its greatest value has been its folk character. Not since the Ḥasidim gave Judaism folk music, folk dance, folk literature, and folkways, has anything comparable occurred in Jewish life. It is good and well to say that there is nothing magical about Palestinian soil, and that other Jewries can do the same. The fact remains that we in America have strained and groaned with false labor in attempting to create a group cultural pattern. This does not by any means imply that we must be dependent upon Palestine, that we are incapable of creativity. Perhaps Palestine may yet stimulate American Jewry (as it has in some respects already) to produce something comparable. All of which will be for the good. Meanwhile, we have been enriched by the songs, the revitalized festivals fraught with new significance, the educational content, and the contagious fervor generated by the Jews of Palestine. All this is due to the mass character of Zionism. It has touched off enthusiasm and devotion nowhere else approximated in Jewish life. In Zionism, these cultural contributions are the end product of a people in motion, of a people endowed with a sense of direction. This folk character is duplicated in America only in those areas which have themselves been infected with the Zionist impulse.

There is a psychological element in the ultimate level of Zionism. It involves, first, the healing of the schism with respect to the place of Judaism in the world. The long-festering scholastic inquiry into what is Jewish and what is human is the spiritual equivalent of neo-emancipation's damaging distinction between Jew and human in the political realm. The spurious dichotomies that infest the Jewish spirit, as a recent symposium of young Jewish writers indicates, can be shattered in a Jewish homeland, and, by its example, in other Jewries as well. Zionism can also dispel the pathological relationship of many Jews to Judaism by virtue of anti-Semitism. No one has any illusions about the abating of anti-Semitism for a long time, even with a Jewish commonwealth. But it is equally evident that Palestinian Jews do not suffer from the unique mental anguish that accompanies anti-Semitism and plagues many Jews elsewhere.

Finally, the ultimate level of Zionism promises personal satisfactions through the creation of an authentic criterion of the individual's identification with world Jewry. In our time, this identification has depended largely upon suffering, a factor not to be deprecated, but certainly neither beneficial nor of our choosing. The affirmation by some that world Jewry is bound together by religion is hollow. Our religious unity is an objective, not a reality. The convergence of Jews from all over the world upon Palestine, world Jewry's direct assistance to them, world Jewry's concern for the welfare of the Yishuv, its labors in behalf of the Yishuv—all of these factors provide a magnetic center for the unification of our people and for a more personal and positive sense of belonging to one's people on the part of the individual Jew. This prospect, perhaps, underlies the violent anti-Zionism of some Jews, who see in Palestine a force making for their identity with Jewry. More and more, Jews will make trips to Palestine. They will send their children there on scholarships and on visits. The land will increasingly become the personal spiritual possession of widening areas of world Jewry.

In conclusion, it must be stressed that Jewry outside of Palestine need not serve in a passive and receptive capacity. The spiritual gifts that have been mentioned may be our possession too. Perhaps the very intensity of Jewish life in Palestine will awaken us to our own latent potentialities. Perhaps that *hikui shel hitharut* ("emulation through competitive zeal") of which Ahad Ha-Am wrote, will take hold of us. If we can be impelled to achievement which will lift us beyond dependence upon Palestine, that too will be a victory. But implicit in that victory will be the regenerative power whose origins are in Zionism.

3

The State of Israel: Its Moral Implications

When the last defenders were driven behind the barricades of the Second Temple, and the flames were gutting the sanctuary, the priests took the keys of their office and hurled them heavenward. The priests consigned them to the keeping of heaven, for both they and the Temple were doomed, and the doors which once had opened at the turn of the key were already crashing down. Those keys were never lost. They were in good keeping for 1,878 years. On the fifth of Iyar, 5708, the Guardian of Israel returned them, not only to the citizens of Israel, but to Kelal Yisrael, amid world desolation and shattered shrines and amid the never-to-be-dissolved vapors of our people's martyrdom. The keys are now in our hands, either to cast away recklessly by a thousand follies, or else to spring the lock on a new era for all Jewry, yes, for all mankind.

We have not yet measured up, either emotionally or intellectually, to the incredible impact of what has taken place. There are neither tears nor songs, nor declarations nor discourses which can release the flood of Jewry's anguished yearnings, pent up these many generations. Who knows but what the people of Judea, on that calamitous day, Tisha be-Av, in the year 70 C.E., were too stunned and too close to destruction to assess fully the meaning of the destruction. Little did our Judean ancestors know that they were the forerunners of a vast trek in time and space out into the West. And little do we know where the reversal of the journey, now turning backward upon itself, will lead us and our people.

Now that we have witnessed the birth of Israel, we are eager to know what lies in store for it and for Kelal Yisrael. Until now, our goal was the establishment of the state. From now on, we assume a more remote objective, the conversion of the state into an instrument for the attainment of our sublimest ideals. In attempting to discern the future, we are not indulging merely in clairvoyance. Instead, we are taking the first step toward grappling with the future and harnessing it to our will and casting it into our own image. This is the entire meaning and interpre-

24

tation of Jewish history—subjugating the future to our people's obstinacy.

In such a venture, that of determining what lies ahead, we must always predicate our thinking upon another great historical truth— that no historical formula, however accurate when applied to other peoples and other civilizations, applies to the Jewish people. We are a unique people, and no index file has yet been devised which can contain us. Many nations have been exiled, but none has survived. Many nations have been destroyed, but none has been reborn. There is no record of repeated national resurrection, in cyclical recurrence, save our own. No wonder scholars and philosophers resent our defiance of their theories of history. How naive and how malicious their verdicts, steeped in wishful thought, appear in the light of May 15.

Abbott, in summarizing the history of Israel in Europe, ends his work with this plunge into the future:

> It is safe to predict that for many centuries to come the world will continue to witness the unique and mournful spectacle of a great people roaming to and fro on the highways of the earth in search of a home.[1]

And the Jewish Marxist Karl Kautsky concludes *Are the Jews a Race?* in the same spirit:

> We cannot say we have completely emerged from the Middle Ages as long as Judaism still exists among us. The sooner it disappears, the better it will be, not only for society, but also for the Jews themselves. . . . Ahasuerus, the Wandering Jew, will at last have found a haven of rest. He will continue to live in the memory of man as man's greatest sufferer, as he who has been dealt with most severely by mankind, to whom he has given most.[2]

The Spenglers and the Toynbees, having erected symmetrical structures founded upon the rise, decline, and fall of civilizations, have beheld with chagrin the collapse of their edifices for lack of a cornerstone. That cornerstone has been the survival and revival of Jewry, which somehow manages to persist despite its classification by Toynbee as a fossil. Some fossil, which sent the British Empire scurrying out of Palestine in the middle of the night, and which drove the British Empire beneath the robes of Arab tribesmen!

Christian scholars might have sought out Nachman Krochmal, that obscure Galician Jew, who formulated the one authentic interpretation of Jewish history.[3] Reduced to the simplest terms, it propounds the concept that, unlike other civilizations, Israel completes cycle after cycle of rise, decline, and fall, only to swing out into fresh and newer cycles. Why? Because, unlike all other nations, Israel alone is dedicated to the divine principle of *haruhani ha-muhlat*, absolute spirituality, the passionate quest for which will not let us die. Therefore, despite the historians, the course we take and the future we desire are founded upon the truth of our uniqueness and our refusal to be classified. Israel's obstinacy, based upon its will alone, has prevailed. Theories and postulates will have to accommodate themselves to us, not we to them. The birth of the new state is heavy with implications for our future and the future of mankind.

Because we are a unique people, not to be catalogued, the relations between Israel and the Diaspora will also be unique, unlike the relations between any other country and its kinsfolk, citizens of other lands. The fear of the consequences of such a relationship is greater than the wondrous promise of such a relationship. The first illusion that we should dispel is that there must be a political center for Jewish life.

Of late, *shelilat ha-galut* ("deprecation of the Diaspora") has been superseded by *shelilat eretz yisrael* ("deprecation of the homeland"), the assertion that the State of Israel is spent and weary and barren, and that only from America can vitality enough be generated to sustain world Jewry. This cavalier dismissal of the Yishuv reflects an abysmal ignorance of the life-blood, of the moral plasma which the name Eretz Yisrael itself supplied to a hemorrhaging world Jewry in this twentieth century. It ill behooves American Jews to flaunt our spiritual potentials until we have at least drawn abreast of the incredible accomplishments of that tiny Yishuv, whose songs we sing, whose language we learn, whose dramatics we admire, whose culture we emulate.

The conception that there must be a political center is as antiquated as the Ptolemaic theory of our globe as the center of the universe. Democracy cannot tolerate such theories. It is more receptive to the concept of mutuality, of complementation, of interplay and partnership. Israeli and American Jewry must be related, not as the sun is to the stars, but as one eye is to the other. Each depends upon the other, not merely for the combined vision of both, but for its own. When both are healthy, the vision is unimpaired. But when one is blinded, the sympathetic mutuality between the two is affected, and the vision of the other is jeopardized.

While it is true that many in America do not seek citizenship in Israel, we have no intention of abandoning our status as members of a universal Jewish community in which we can identify ourselves freely with our fellow Jews everywhere. Let us not protest too much the obvious truth that as American citizens we owe no exclusive allegiance to Israel. This is a gratuitous statement, for it was just as true before May 1948 as it is now. This kind of disclaimer, if repeated vehemently enough, can lead ultimately to a widening rift, which could separate us from Israel so dangerously that we might become strangers to one another. Jewish history is full of tragic accounts of communities that lost touch with Palestine and withered away, never to be heard from again. The negative approach to our relations with Israel gives deep satisfaction to those American Jews whose philosophy is—Judaism for the people of Israel, dejudaizing for us in America.

The Jewish state will accelerate two processes in America: on the one hand, total assimilation for those who regard the creation of the state as giving them a release from all further Jewish responsibility; and on the other hand, the intensification of Jewish life for those who will want to share in the abundant life that both Israel and America can offer. As members of a universal community, we are bound together by many bonds apart from our particular citizenship, and we need not relinquish any of those bonds, nor reduce our proposed associations with Israel to religion alone, or philanthropy alone. Religion can divide as well as unite. Israel and American Jewry should be like two brothers living in far-off and distant lands. Each is a citizen of his own country, but both are in constant contact with each other, both help one another, both visit one another, both strive to perpetuate their common memories, both have a unique universe of discourse. To be members of a universal community is something more than to be like the Irish or the Swedes in America. God forbid that ours should become an analogous status, for the time is approaching when some ethnic minorities will be swallowed up in the American absorption process.

For the moment, and perhaps for an entire generation, this remains an academic problem. So long as Israel is jeopardized, our task is clear. We did not labor for this day in order to preside over the liquidation of the Jewish state. Let us recall the story of *Tinok Shenishbah* ("the abducted baby"), who was stolen by an evil prince at the very moment that his parents and the pious people in this home ceased from their prayers.[4] In that split second, when they paused from their work of warding off the evil spirits, the child was snatched from their midst. There is much work to be done, and woe to us if we abandon it now, in the deluded belief that the evil prince and all his henchmen can no longer harm us.

The moral implications of Israel are not for ourselves alone. In a tribal world, they are universal. They confront civilization with new truths about itself, truths it has not dared to face, becoming brutal and diseased because of its refusal.

The first superb spiritual value implicit in Zionism is the rediscovery by world Jewry of its own soul. Nations, like individuals, suffer from all the psychological and spiritual afflictions that plague our world. Peace of mind has fled not only from our personal lives but from entire societies, all of which have a unique consciousness of their own. How much more so has this been the fate of our own people. If we could now visualize the inner world of a foundling, shuttled from one orphan home to another, driven by blows from one institution to another, and if we then multiplied this orphan by the myriads of Jews who have lived in Europe these past millennia, we could come to understand the mental snake-pit in which Israel has lived. That he has transcended this pit, refused to go mad, yes, lived gloriously, is a historical miracle. But despite all this, he has felt the brand of rejection, hostility, guilt-accusation, sadism, seared into his inmost being, and the cries of his mutilated soul could be heard down through the centuries.

By the sure instinct with which a hard-pressed victim will often find his own salvation, Israel groped his way unerringly to the redemption of his soul by going back to the earliest sources of his existence, to his earliest memories, to his dimmest childhood recollections. Unaware of the catharsis techniques of psychiatry, Israel, seeking out the inspiration of his prophets and pursuing the course they charted, found for himself the means of spiritual and collective self-redemption which twentieth-century healers of the mind have learned to apply to the individual.

Perhaps this is why Sigmund Freud entertained such a profound admiration for Theodor Herzl. Fifty years ago both of these titans stepped forth in Vienna, each to conquer a different submerged continent, one the continent of the human psyche, the other the continent of a people's soul.

What was Herzl doing? Through his books, his congresses, his impact upon the Jewish masses, he was helping the Jewish people rediscover itself. He was making it reach back into its past, to the origins of its being, to relive its youthful existence, to experience once more the earliest harassing moments of pain and agony and homelessness by which it suffered the initial shocks of hostility. He made Israel grapple with the many contradictions in his own spirit—East and West, the feeling of at-homeness and the feeling of strangeness in the Western world, self-hatred and self-love, the passion to escape and the urge to isolate himself, national hysteria and national melancholy. And these contradictions, he made his people to understand, could be dissipated through seeking and wholeheartedly accepting that of which it had in childhood been robbed—its land, its soil, its roots. This national self-revelation could come about through a great soul-shaking experience, a national crisis in which the people would tear itself loose from its centuries-old moorings and set its face toward home. This was the therapy which Herzl prescribed. The therapy has been applied. The great healing is bound to set in.

What will be the nature of this healing? It will be a source of blessing not only to the Jewish world, but to the non-Jewish world as well. The great yoke of guilt, of self-accusation, which we have borne as a people for ages will fall from our shoulders. This sense of guilt, which some of our sophisticates may not have sensed but which manifested itself in their every move, was a heritage of exile as well as of a conviction that because we were in exile we had been, and continued to be, guilty of a monstrous crime against Providence. "Because of our sins we were exiled from our land" was the perennial explanation of our circumstances. Even in the moment of despising our enemy, we recognized him to be the instrument of our punishment, the rod used by the Almighty to chastise us. Even in martyrdom and in sublimest saintliness, we were atoning for our sins. In recent times, those very Jews who contemptuously rejected this theology, adopted a thoroughly destructive theology in its place, an inverted human worship, rejection of oneself.

Once the Jewish people has been restored to Israel, the greatest incentive for guilt-expression will vanish, for if exile has meant punishment for a national offense, return means not merely that a sin has been expiated, but that we have been a people of supreme merit to regain our heritage. The implications of this new view of our existence are enormous.

Simultaneously, the Christian view of the Jew will undergo a fundamental reversal, like the recession of an evil tide. Much of Christian theology is predicated on the conception of a Jewish crime, the proof of which is exile, the punishment for which is homelessness, the eternal witness of which is the Jewish people itself. The "mark of Cain," "the wandering Jew," are obnoxious epithets which will disappear from the vocabulary and the thinking of the Christian world. If, for two millennia, Christendom believed that Israel was doomed to everlasting wandering, then the very foundations of Christian thought are set upon quicksand; a great crime has been committed, but not by Israel. It is

Christendom that must make expiation. The messianic hope of Israel has attained a degree of fulfillment. A whole people has been resurrected from the dead. If all these things can be, then it is Israel's religious message that has been valid—the message of the end of days, the triumph of good over evil, the power of the human will to shape man's destiny—and what becomes of the crime for which our people has been railroaded to punishment and torture? From now on, the true malefactor, who has been dwelling at ease in Christendom while an innocent victim languished in his place in the dungeon, will take on the thorny crown of an uneasy conscience. That is why some Christians fear and oppose the Jewish state, for they know what far-reaching historical consequences will ensue for their institutions and faiths when Israel becomes secure.

Another moral implication of Zionism, which will be resented by many, is democracy. The real source of irritation to Israel's enemies is not strategic considerations, not oil concessions, not East-West relations. It is that the tiny Jewish community of Israel is throwing the entire Middle East into a ferment of social upheaval, which, if unchecked, will mean the end of medieval and modern fascism in the Arab world. The most infectious element in the world is freedom. It leaps over barriers, and its contagion is irresistible. The reactionaries of the world, who constitute the high command of the war on Israel, judge correctly the meaning of the new state. It brings into a world which has known nothing but slavery guaranteed by ignorance, and exploitation insured by a religion of subservience, a revolutionary way of life. It brings the ballot. It brings the rights of labor. It brings leadership selected by the people. It brings equality for minorities. It brings freedom for women. When this life penetrates deeply enough into the souls of the millions enslaved by emirs and by imperialists, the entire eroded structure will collapse. And with the collapse will go the power of a world conspiracy which began in Europe and continues its operations in Israel. When this occurs, a vast and vital front in the war against the people of the earth will be smashed. And Israel will have helped bring this to pass.

4

The Uniqueness of Judaism

Zionism is a People's revolution against tyranny—the tyranny of exile (both as idea and reality) which Christians perceived as part of the ordained historical order; and tyranny of the belief that redemption must wait for God. Yet, when Zionism emerged, it responded not only to history but to submerged sources in Jewish religious thought which had resisted acquiescence both to the human and the cosmic order. Naysaying to men and to God was the authentic Jewish component out of which Zionism erupted.

One of the most distinctive qualities in the Jewish approach to theology is its rebelliousness. The aggrieved outcry is bound to erupt from some of the most submissive and serene psalms. The Abrahamitic pattern of insistence upon having it out with God is recurrent, and continues to agitate Jewish thought to our own time. In Jewish thought the quest for God and the challenge to His justice are not incompatible with the religious spirit. The search for God is in itself a religious experience. Jeremiah upbraids his people not for their failure to obey God but for their failure to search for Him. "Neither said they, 'Where is the Lord that brought us up out of the land of Egypt?' . . . The priests said not: 'Where is the Lord?'"[1] We know, of course, that the Bible vibrates with impassioned disputations with God, the first of which is ascribed to Abraham. Throughout the spiritual history of our people, this disputatious spirit has not left us, and it continues to vex and agitate us while others have seemed able to lapse into a tranquil and submissive faith.

This persistent effort to break through the veil of mystery, this penchant for the voice of outrage, has played a role in our history as compelling as the Jewish rejection of Jesus. I believe that Israel has brought upon itself the animosity of the world as much for what it has affirmed as for what it has denied, as much for its disturbing religious propensities as for its attitude toward Christianity. There is ample evidence on hand to indicate that before the advent of Jesus and Paul,

31

Israel was condemned for a religious way of life which agitated the pagan world. From the beginning men have been offended by what they regarded as blasphemous treatment of their own cherished beliefs and inner worlds.

It was not only the hidden God but the God with whom one could remonstrate that disturbed and continues to disturb the world. This is a threat to man's yearning for settled answers and closed systems, for the end of searching and the tracking down of the Absolute. A spiritual world of continuous grappling with God, of the endless quest, of searing disappointment, is a dangerous world for those who want to come to easy terms with the universe, and any religious way of life which disturbs this placidity jeopardizes the peace of the world.

When it is said that Judaism has a mission to propagate the concept of monotheism to the world, this touches upon the most superficial aspect of our task. Our task is to carry on the cosmic debate, hoping to discover new insights about man's relationship with God. But in the endless struggles to attain these insights, man will continue to be tormented by his raging need for justifying God's way in the world, and by the inevitable elusiveness of the answers and of God Himself. Israel alone persisted in this quest, and found in its very tragedy and painfulness a depth of experience which has given the Jew a sense of collaboration with God, however fraught with agony that collaboration has been.

Thus to eulogize Abraham as a man of faith alone is to miss the meaning of his faith, which in no way infringed upon his right to his own responses. His faith was analogous to Ben-Gurion's: "We will fight on Britain's side as if there were no White Paper, and we will fight the White Paper as if there were no War." Commitment to God without the abdication of man's moral impulses, this is the essence of the Abrahamitic perception, a perception with which the Bible abounds in the utterances of Jeremiah, the Psalms, Ecclesiastes, and Job.

The great sin of the Jew was that he cherished his view of the universe and thereby plunged the world into misgivings about its own view. The violence with which the world unleashed its wrath upon him attests to the depth of its misgivings. It was not Christianity alone which was outraged by Jewish intransigence. If it were, there might be greater substance to the thesis that the Jews were being punished for alleged deicide. But what of the Mohammedan world? Its pure monotheism did not mitigate its frequent onslaughts against our people. To be sure, the Jewish rejection of Mohammed was a factor, but certainly not equivalent to the rejection of Jesus. It should also be added that, on the whole, Islam was much better disposed to Judaism than was Christendom. But

its onslaughts against Judaism were anything but sporadic. The persecution by the Almohades in Spain, the Maghreb, and Yemen during the
time of Maimonides are examples. They attest tragically enough to a
Moslem anti-Jewish frenzy.

The great offense of Judaism was that it not only propagated a faith of
its own, and propagated it vociferously, but that it propagated a faith
which did violence to the conceptions and preconceptions of the world.
We are so involved in the squaring of Maimonides with Aristotle,
Gabirol with Plato, medieval Judaism's eschatology with that of Christianity, that we are prone to overlook the great irreconcilables which no
philosophical or theological syntheses could overcome. These irreconcilables reside in the Jewish insistence upon the role of man in his
relationship with God. This is the great blasphemy of Judaism: it rejects
the proposition that man is denied an active role in the affairs of the
universe. What Galileo propounded astronomically, Judaism propounded religiously—namely, a radical reorientation of the place of
man in the universe.

The great systematizer of medieval Christian theology is Thomas
Aquinas. His ethics and religion are predicated upon two inflexible
principles—original sin and predestination. Man's original disobedience dooms his descendants to bear the taint of his insubordination
throughout their earthly careers. They are consequently in an unalter-
able posture of hopeless sinfulness before God. Compounding this sorry
conception of man's condition is the even more tragic view of his destiny,
as embodied in the idea of predestination. According to this doctrine,
some men can be redeemed by God from the consequences of their
sinfulness, but this privilege is not necessarily related to one's virtues.
God's grace is vouchsafed to whomever He wills, and this is all pre-
determined.

> Nobody has been so insane as to say that merit is the cause of
> divine predestination. . . . It is fitting that God should predes-
> tine men. For all things are subject to this Providence. . . . As
> men are ordained to eternal life through the Providence of God,
> it is likewise part of that Providence to permit some to fall away
> from that end. . . . As predestination includes the will to confer
> grace and glory, so also reprobation includes the will to permit a
> person to fall into sin, and to impose the punishment of damna-
> tion on account of that sin.[2]

The implications of such a theology, and its heritage of futility, terror,
and despair for man, are self-evident. Man's avenue to God is severed by

God's will, which operates in total divorcement from man's conduct and consequently appears more capricious than inscrutable. Man has been reduced to a passive and cowering instrument, entirely incapable of altering his destiny by deed or prayer.

What was the Jewish conception of man's place in his encounter with God? It was anything but passive. It was anything but capricious. While man is sinful, he does not transmit sin from Adam as men transmit their chromosomes. Each man is guilty of his own sins. His suffering is related to his sinfulness. Sin itself is not so absolute and so heinous as it is in Christianity. "Come, let us ascribe merit to our ancestors, for, if they had not sinned, we should not have come into the world."[3] Moreover, there is a pattern of life whereby man can cope with his moral offenses, mitigate their consequences, stave off punishment, come to terms with God and with man. The quality of doom, the note of inexorability are absent.

This is perhaps best exemplified in Yoma, the Talmudic tractate dealing with the laws pertaining to Yom Kippur, the Day of Atonement. Here one would expect to find the most awesome pronouncements on the dread impact of man's guilt, but instead it may almost be regarded as a guide not only to remission of sin, but to the relaxing of ritual requirements for those to whom they are exceedingly burdensome. Much of the tractate is devoted not to the requirements of the fast but rather to the extenuations permitting the relaxation of the requirements. For example, a pregnant woman, overcome by a ravenous desire for swine meat, may sip its juice through a straw. If this does not satisfy her, she may partake directly of the meat. This is followed by a series of other concessions derived from this, concessions which encourage the violation of the Sabbath in order to preserve life. All this is summarized in the exalted principle that "man was not created for the Sabbath, but the Sabbath for man."

How shall we interpret the principles thus enunciated? In the first place, their very exposition in a text dealing with Yom Kippur reveals a remarkable concern for the well-being of man (even the comfort of a pregnant woman, who is viewed in actual jeopardy of her life out of desire for forbidden food), for whom even the overwhelming awesomeness and judgment of the Day of Atonement can be set aside. The very forces of the spiritual universe are put to his service and for the preservation of his life. The laws of God are canceled so that man might endure. Thus we perceive certain far-reaching implications in these principles. In the first place, the sinfulness of man is not seen as so congenitally imbedded that he need be found unworthy of any intervention in his worldly lot. Second, no discrimination is made as to who may be the beneficiary of such intervention. There is a universal law of compassion for all, and it applies with impartial equality to the virtuous and to the depraved. Third, while salvation in eternity is incorporated in Jewish theology, salvation in this world, within history, through the healing, helping, kinship-giving processes of daily concern, is of paramount importance. It is an irrefragable component of otherworldly salvation. Finally, there is the clear indication that it is possible for man to intervene in, and to contravene, the fixed laws of God.

Man is, therefore, possessed of spiritual maneuverability. He has the power to offer a response to the universal Law. He can say, as indeed the entire body of Talmudic law does in effect, "O God, You have given us the Law, but we declare that we shall so read it that we shall live by it and not perish." This is not a modernized homily on what the contemporary Jew would like to force upon Jewish tradition. In their own genre, the rabbis expressed similar convictions—a famous talmudic story has some scholars, engaged in legalistic controversy, refusing to listen to a heavenly voice which had been invoked to settle the dispute. "The Torah is no longer in heaven," they proclaimed, indicating that once the Torah had been supernaturally revealed, it was for men to interpret and apply it.[4]

The rabbis boldly saw in this incident an illustration of the cosmic tension between God and man, a tension in which, not irreverently, they ascribed to God the proud, paternal comment, "My sons have bested Me."[5] Thus, in Jewish thought, we see man as one who can plot a spiritual strategy instead of being pinned down by angry, wildly flying arrows loosed by God upon a strip of defenseless, untenable human terrain.

Is not the liturgy for Yom Kippur a profound enactment of Judaism's conviction that man is capable of playing a vital part in the redemptive process? Is it not really a grand mystical performance in which man acts out the redemptive role in this world and thereby affirms his belief in its possibility? The entire day enacts a struggle by man to effect a change both in his own life and in his very fate. He relives the experience of the High Priest, who used to intercede for himself, his household, and all the children of Israel. He declares, as he reads the U-Netanneh Tokef, that "penitence, prayer and charity can avert the evil decree." And he brings the day to a close entreating God for mercy before the gates of heaven and justice close once and for all.

Thus we see man in a new context. He is endowed with spiritual maneuverability. He can move in two directions. He can move freely in the direction of his fellow man. He can help shape his society. He can also move in relationship with God. He is a collaborator with God in spiritual processes of cosmic import. Even where doom must come to man, it emanates from his own action, whereby he forces God's judgment upon himself. Thus, God is described mourning over the ruins of Jerusalem, "Woe to Me that I have destroyed My house and exiled My children among the nations of the world."[6] God is pictured as struggling with Himself before His decrees for man issue from Him: "May it be My will that My Mercy will overcome My Judgment."[7] And it is man who helps determine the issue. This theme is reiterated like a litany in tractate Yoma, which tells us, "Great is repentance for it brings healing to the world. . . . It reaches to the Throne of Glory. . . . It brings about redemption. . . . On account of one individual who repents, the sins of all the world are forgiven."[8]

What does this declaration tell us? It tells us that man has some hold upon his own spiritual destiny, and that God, rather than blocking the way, places the opportunity for help into man's own hands.

The role of man as a needed collaborator with God for his own redemption and that of the world does not reduce God, for it is a role assigned to man by God, a role through which God enters into the world of history and acts upon it from within rather than from impenetrable distances. Moreover, this task elevates man to a creature of choice whose moral choices have a decisive bearing upon human destiny. Sodom and Gomorrah are annihilated because men, repudiating their collaboration with God, set their own destruction in motion. It was an act of choice, or, if you will, they gambled that they could successfully evade their collaborative role. Nineveh was spared because it resumed the collaborative role. Judaism is so deeply committed to man's involvement in ultimate cosmic issues that it predicates, rather hyperbolically, the destiny of all mankind upon the single act of a single individual. "He who has saved a single soul is as if he had saved the whole world."[9] "Let each man regard himself as though he could tip the scales of the world for good or for evil." Accordingly, even the presence of a single righteous person in a society could effect its rescue from destruction. Jeremiah tragically cries, "Run to and fro through the streets of Jerusalem and see now, and know, and seek in the broad places thereof, if ye can find a man, if there be any that does justly, that seeks truth; and I will pardon her."[10]

Rabbinic imagery abounds with the concept of God appearing to be bereft by the defection of His children. The necessary expulsion of Israel from its land leaves God, too, grievously affected. The Holy Presence

(Shekhinah) is pictured as exiled, for Israel's calamity has shattered God's design for His creation. This places man in a position of awesome responsibility, for in this conception, he is capable of frustrating God Himself. This is the apparent meaning of Akiba's dictum that "everything is in the hands of Heaven except the fear of Heaven."[11] Also, "Everything is known to God except how to teach men derekh eretz." Inevitably the question of how an infinite God can be limited comes to bedevil us, and no one has successfully resolved the enigma. But Akiba's effort to reconcile the dichotomy by declaring that freedom for man involves even freedom to frustrate God stands as a truthful analysis of man's place in the world.

This is a far cry from a giddy view of the universe in which man's dreams of unmitigated bliss are attainable through his own ingenuity and adaptability. Nowhere does Judaism equate comfort with happiness, freedom from pain with spiritual fulfillment. But it does recognize the redemptive power of history, which classic Christianity and crisis theology seem to despair of. There are great consummations within history, which Judaism considers sufficiently related to man's salvation to be linked with the messianic dream. The ultimate achievement of universal peace, the unification of all mankind, the attainment of the good things of the earth for all, are no less part of man's spiritual hunger than the attempt to cope with his anxious state. In fact, these are profoundly related to his anxiety, and they exacerbate it because they have been removed from the areas of man's spiritual malaise and transposed into economic and political spheres. In Judaism, the transformation of society is placed in the same category with the transformation of nature itself.

The difficulty Christian theologians have about man's inescapable anxiety as emanating from his sinful nature is that they attempt to view him exclusively as an individual alone and not as a social being. In such a context, which aggravates man's preoccupation with himself, which shuts out the world, a radical and unnatural schism of the soul is effected, a schism which alienates man the one from man the many. This forceful cleavage cannot but hurl the divided man into increased anxiety and despair.

Since Judaism has consistently seen man as an indivisible person whose spiritual well-being is dependent upon the spiritual well-being of society, coping with the problem of personal anxiety has not appeared so utterly beyond man's capacity. It is all too apparent that neither man's social plight nor his personal condition can be resolved beyond the context of the other. Surely, not all personal sorrows would fall away in

Utopia, but it is equally certain that a race of redeemed individuals would not necessarily make for a good society, for somehow such people seem to be congenitally incapable of functioning in a group. The saint or the aspiring saint is usually running off into the wilderness, with a contempt for the group altogether unbecoming to sainthood. In Judaism the day-by-day struggle for the attainment of God's kingdom is sufficient fare to stay the hungry soul of man. This struggle, as the Jew knows full well, is not devoid of pain and anxiety and a deep sense of inadequacy.

But—and this is the great difference between rootless anxiety and meaningful anxiety—there is direction and purpose in the tragedy of struggle. As long as he knows his direction and God's directives, to labor for the sake of heaven and to struggle for *tikkun olam be-malkhut shaddai* ("the improvement of the world under God's kingdom"), his anxious state does not come from a knowledge that he is lost. This latter knowledge is foreign to Judaism, and it cannot be grafted on it. It is foreign because Judaism is free of the concept of original sin. Judaism is much closer to the idea of divine restoration. In its deepest context, the idea of the divine restoration attempts to tell us that mankind, together with God, must undergo many cycles of defeat and momentary redemption before the ultimate triumph of man under God. The defeat is never final, and the redemption, momentary as it is, gives man a glimpse of what must yet be.

What is too often overlooked in the early passages of Genesis is the injunction to man: *milu et ha-aretz ve-khivshuha* ("fill the earth and subdue it"). This mission was not canceled by the "fall." Man's task, to become the master, "in God's image," of the earth, still stands. The accounts of one "fall" after another seem to underscore this truth. The fall of Cain, of the generation of the Flood, of the generation of Babel, of Sodom and Gomorrah, of Israel in Egypt, of the nations recorded in the Bible, of the tribes of Israel, of Judah, of the Second Temple—all reveal the tempo of a spiritual impulse in history—the summons to man to go on to that consummation which Judaism holds forth. Even God is involved in the lapses suffered by man. He regrets the creation of man when He brings on the Flood. Moses must plead with Him to preserve Israel.

What purpose, then, is there in the seemingly endless cycles of lapse and restoration, fall and rise? It is this: implicit in the entire structure of Judaism is the promise of *Aharit ha-Yamim* ("the end of days"). This concept stands midway between Christian apocalypticism and utopian temporalism. It is rooted in history, but it does not entertain any illusions about man's capacity to carve out a short-cut to the Kingdom of God. The prophets, who were incessantly holding forth the prospect of national annihilation, invariably relented by presenting the promise of ultimate salvation in this world. There was a goal in men's affairs toward which their tragic collective and individual existences were leading. The vindication of the race would come about "in the end."

The inflexible integrity of this idea, which refused to betray contemporary generations with the lie of instant relief, also required a spiritually disciplined and toughened people to respond to such an idea. If the prophets did not offer palliatives, there were in Israel enough nuclei of religious fortitude to reject palliatives. If the prophets felt the urgency of rousing their people from a smug despair in man's essential mutability, there were enough who responded to warrant the canonizing of the prophets.

Judaism's synthesis of the one and the many has helped obviate the difficulties which any bifurcation of the two presents. The reflection of this awareness is apparent in numerous biblical texts where we repeatedly find admixtures of the singular and the plural in a single context. This free interchange of singular and plural is not accidental. It is an indication of biblical thought's comprehensive understanding of the dual role played by man. One of many examples of this is: "All the commandments which I command *thee* this day, *ye* shall keep that *ye* might live." Thus Judaism does not find itself hopelessly troubled by the plight of the individual, artificially disembodied from the group. Moreover, Judaism has not seen man as essentially different in his inner being from man before the "fall." Judaism, on this account, does not look back to the irretrievable loss in this world of a morally idyllic past, but instead looks ahead to the advent of such an era, when such a human state will represent, not a return to Eden, but an advance into the Kingdom of Heaven.

But still, all men must stand alone and lonely at the grievous junctures of their lives, when they must go forth unaccompanied. How does Judaism cope with man's confrontation of the ultimate reality when the warming campfires of the group have vanished from sight? The response of Judaism to this anguished call for help is that man cannot find help by feeding upon the entrails of his own being, but by relating himself to the everpresent (not impenetrable) God, who can be found in three media of human experience—Torah, worship, and compassionate living. The threefold way to grappling with the human situation —*torah, avodah, gemilut hasadim*—is identified in the Talmud as the very foundations "upon which the world stands." What was meant by this? That life is predicated upon these three elements, without which life could not be sustained, without which life would become amorphous. These three areas embody various levels of human experience—God's revelation to man *(torah)*, man's revelation to God *(avodah)*, man's revelation to his fellow man *(gemilut ḥasadim)*. All these are a synthesis of what in other religions and other disciplines are irreconcilables (or in Christianity, Law versus Love). Here again we observe how Judaism unites disjointed elements into an organic unity, how it reassembles them, not by a grafting process, but by virtue of their essential affinity, into their rightful oneness. This, too, may be an answer to the problem of the sundered human soul.

We see now how Jewish thought could not but come into a head-on collision with medieval Christian thought. We see now that Christian hostility evolved from more than the rejection of Jesus. The very reverse is true. That hostility issued from the violent rejection, through the symbol of Jesus, of the Jewish faith in man and in man's free relationship with God. This Jewish faith put medieval society in spiritual jeopardy, for it confronted it with a challenge to the deterministic approach to man, his static and submissive place in the world, and the moral capriciousness of God. That society betrayed its own misgivings about its cherished spiritual system through the violence of its assaults upon the Jews, and through the violence with which the medieval world eventually brought on its own end.

In a contemporary context, Zionism is a living demonstration of the rebellious impulse in Judaism, leading toward the liberation of the Jewish People and the Jewish spirit. Thus, the Jewish People remains a scandal and an affront to the nations, this time because of Zionism which opposes the inexorability of historic and cosmic fate, reserved especially for this People.

5

The Chosen People

The doctrine about Israel as God's chosen people is a vexation to many Jews, whether they would retain it, modify it, or dismiss it. An examination of the prayer books of the Orthodox, Reform, Conservative, and Reconstructionist movements quickly reveals the vexation and the struggle with the problem. In order to understand it more clearly, we should first examine the basic texts embodying this concept as they appear in the traditional liturgy. On Friday night, many a Jew recites the Kiddush, the prayer of sanctification for the Sabbath, which translated declares:

> Praised art Thou, Lord our God, Ruler of the Universe, Who has sanctified us by Thy commandments and has been gracious to us. His holy Sabbath He has bequeathed to us in love and favor, a reminder of the act of Creation. It is the first of all holy convocations, a reminder of the departure from Egypt. For Thou hast chosen us and sanctified us from among all nations, and Thy holy Sabbath Thou hast bequeathed to us in love and favor. Praised art Thou O Lord, Who sanctifiest the Sabbath.

Each morning, and on Sabbaths before the reading from the Torah, this prayer is pronounced:

> Praised art Thou, Lord our God, Ruler of the Universe, Who has chosen us from among all nations and hast given us Thy Torah. Praised art Thou O Lord, the Giver of the Torah.

Toward the end of the daily, Sabbath, and festival services, the congregation recites:

> It is our duty to praise the Lord of all things, to ascribe greatness to Him who formed the world in the beginning, that He has not made us like the nations of other lands, and has not placed us like other families of the earth, that He has not made our portion like theirs nor our lot like all their multitude.

The Kiddush on major festivals, which is similar to the Sabbath Kiddush, includes this addition:

> Thou has sanctified us from among all nations and hast exalted
> us above all tongues and sanctified us by Thy commandments.

At first glance, these prayers seem to clearly express God's special preference for Israel, Israel's separation and distinctiveness from other peoples, Israel's unique history and destiny, and Israel's elevation above all other nations. That the Jew in the Western world is less than comfortable with these declarations is clearly evident from the manner in which they are translated, paraphrased, or deleted, either in the English or in the Hebrew, or in both. The Reconstructionist prayer book, under the influence of Mordecai Kaplan, who totally rejects the chosen-people idea, has eliminated all reference, both in the Hebrew and in the English, to any suggestion that the Jews are a chosen people. In every passage to which I have alluded, the text has been radically altered. Thus:

> Thou hast brought us nigh to Thy service and in love and grace
> hast given us the heritage of Thy holy Sabbath.

The Reform prayer book, recently displaced by *Gates of Prayer,* is somewhat more ambivalent about the chosen-people concept. In the Kiddush for Sabbath and festivals, and in the prayers for reading from the Torah and the prophetic portion, the original Hebrew is retained, but the English has been revised. However, *Gates of Prayer* now reads, "You have chosen us and set us apart from all the peoples."

The Conservative prayer book states, "Who has not made us like the pagans of the world nor placed us like the heathen tribes of the earth." Most enlightening is one of the Orthodox prayer books, which, although most deeply rooted in traditional theology, nevertheless takes liberties with the translation, thus:

> It is for us to praise the Lord of all,
> To acclaim the greatness of the God of creation,
>> Who has not made us as worldly nations,
>> Nor set us up as earthly peoples,
> Not making our portion as theirs,
> Nor our destiny as that of their multitudes.

It would appear that the Hebrew and English texts are intended for two different audiences, the translations addressed to those who cannot accept the original doctrine and the Hebrew intended to reassure the faithful. But this is rather to be understood as a reflection of an inner conflict which has not been resolved, except in the case of Reconstructionism, which has cut the Gordian knot by rejecting the idea out of hand. The ambivalence between the Hebrew and the English is a dramatic manifestation of a theological dilemma which is yet to be resolved.

The chosen-people concept is not the first which Judaism has subjected to scrutiny, and revised, rejected, or retained as the situation might warrant. The beliefs in revelation, a personal Messiah, resurrection, the authority of the Torah, have all undergone this sort of scrutiny with varying results, depending upon the theological position of the Jewish investigators.

If the idea of chosenness is prevalent in our Tanakh, it nevertheless does not assume the proportions of a dogma but is rather an inference derived from other factors. To the extent that one can speak of biblical dogma involving a faith or a deed commitment, the election of Israel does not enter into that category. Israel is commanded again and again, to love God. Israel is commanded, by the very act of the revelation, to recognize "The Lord your God Who brought you out of the land of Egypt." Again and again, Israel is required "to take to heart." But nowhere is Israel required to believe, as an act of faith or collective acceptance, that it is a chosen people. To be sure, this is unmistakably affirmed by God and by His prophets. There is no escaping the fact. But this doctrine, if indeed it is a doctrine, differs from others in two respects. First, unlike the command to love God, the election principle is challenged in Scripture. Second, it reflects a serious ambiguity, as we shall see, between the popular conception of its meaning and the scriptural and prophetic conception. If the doctrine is an embarrassment in contemporary Jewish liturgy, the embarrassment has biblical roots. Nevertheless, dogma or not, ambiguous or not, the entire Torah represents a unique relationship between the people Israel and its God. It is primarily the saga of Israel's relationship with God, beginning with the call to Abraham and the promise to his progeny, and continuing with the covenant and all the subsequent events in the career of the people. In the main, other nations are virtually ignored, except as their history happens to intersect that of Israel.

Israel's history is the epic of the encounter of one people, and one people alone, with God. Divine history is the reaching down by God to use one people, and one people alone, for His purposes.

Yet this is only a partial explanation. God's selection of Israel is pervasive and implicit, but the specific references to the selection are comparatively few and, if we examine them carefully, qualified and even equivocal. If God chooses Israel, as Scripture plainly states, the reason is obscure. Yes, the element of divine love is clearly stated, but this is an act of grace on God's part, which Israel does not necessarily merit, except for a critical factor with which we shall deal later on. There is no suggestion of any spiritual or tribal qualifications by which the people earns divine favor. If anything, the people is warned against arrogating any special merit to itself by a kind of reverse favoritism, a corollary of which turns up in the prophecy of Amos. In Deuteronomy 7:7–8, the people is specifically admonished that its selection is due not to any inherent grandeur but precisely because of its lowly state. Let us first dispel the altogether unfounded notion that chosen people means superior people. Friends and enemies, Jews and Christians, have fallen victim to this error. Yet if we search carefully in Scripture, where we must begin, there is not a shred of evidence suggesting that Israel was regarded either by God or man as unusually endowed. Quite the contrary: "My father [Jacob] was a wandering Aramean." In this context, the Haggadah for Passover accentuates the less than noble origins of Israel by adding, "At first our ancestors were idol worshippers." Scripture details how God brings a band of dispirited and cantankerous slaves out of Egypt. The essence of this concept is to be found in Deuteronomy 32:5–6: "children unworthy of Him, that crooked and twisted generation. Their baseness has played Him false. Do you thus requite the Lord, O dull and witless people?" Isaiah accentuates Israel's lowliness by referring to it as a worm.

It is important to note the context in which this curious pronouncement from Deuteronomy is made. It is made to a people which but a generation earlier had come out of slavery. It is both a rebellious people and a people still marked by the scars of oppression. But it is also a people which has experienced redemption and revelation. What is there in the smallness of the people, its paucity among the nations of the world, its lowly state, that marks it for divine love and divine selection? We will have to examine Scripture first.

It is well to note that both the concept and the term *selection,* or *behirah,* are not limited to Israel. In the technical sense in which the word is used, it is applied to places, to institutions, to religious practices, and to classes. Jerusalem is chosen as the place God desires. The Temple is chosen as the place where God's spirit is to dwell. But most suggestive is God's selection of the priests. "For the Lord thy God has chosen him out of all thy tribes, to stand to minister in the name of the Lord, him and his sons for ever."[1] Even more instructive is this passage: "And the priests, the sons of Levi, shall come near—for them the Lord thy God has chosen to minister to Him, and to bless in the name of the Lord; and according to their word shall every controversy and every stroke be."[2] Here the function of the selected group is spelled out—to serve God, to bless in the name of God.

Why is this significant? Because Israel, in its covenant relationship with God, is identified as a totally priestly community: "You shall be a kingdom of priests and a holy people."[3] The specialized function of one tribe becomes generalized and is applied to the entire people. The function of the people becomes a universal mission "to be a light to the nations, to open the eyes of the blind, to set the prisoner free."[4] By analogy, then, the chosenness of Israel is related to the fulfillment of certain priestly functions. This is stated specifically in Deuteronomy 7:6.

The classic specific and technical references to selection in the Torah are to be found in Deuteronomy 4:37, 7:7, 10:15, and 14:2.

Scattered throughout the Prophets and the Writings are additional passages referring to the selection of Israel. They are most prominent, although not very extensive, in Deutero-Isaiah. What gradually grips our attention as we study these passages is a common theme which runs through them—almost without exception. Leaving aside the *nature* of the selection, to be a people of priests, we are still puzzled by the *reason* for the selection of Israel. What is there in the text which can give us a clue as to why this lowly people, this "worm Jacob," was singled out for a special place in the divine plan? To gain an insight into this problem, we ask a related question: When the Ten Commandments are proclaimed at Sinai, how does God identify Himself to Israel? "I am the Lord your God who brought you out of the land of Egypt, out of the house of bondage." God reveals Himself to Israel as the redeemer of the enslaved. He does not proclaim Himself as the creator of the universe, an aspect of divinity which is shared with *all* humanity. The self-disclosure to Israel is predicated on the redemption from Egypt. Now, as we study the various citations dealing with Israel's chosenness, we discover that in nearly every instance, the selection is either rooted in the initial redemption or is pointed to a future redemption from suffering, a redemption which is to be a recapitulation of the release from Egyptian enslavement. Why does the text say again and again that Israel has been chosen "from among all the nations"? Because, as the text itself indicates, Isral was taken out of bondage by God. Why does Israel alone merit this particular historical and divine consideration? We don't know, because the Torah does not deal with any history other than that of Israel, and the rest of Scripture is equally silent, with one notable exception with which we will deal. Even the covenant with Abraham, who from the very first is singled out by God from among all other men, is based solidly on a future event—the enslavement of his descendants and their divine rescue. Written as it was *after* the event, it reflects a keen concern with establishing a relationship between selection and redemption. Thus, God's act is not entirely one of inexplicable grace, but has a firm foundation in a historical event into which God enters.

(When Israel fell upon difficult times, it was reminded of its selection by God, who would, the prophet foretold, recapitulate the first redemption. In rabbinic thought, the Exodus becomes the paradigm for all subsequent rescues of Israel.)

When Amos, denouncing the people, wishes to attack it at its most vulnerable point, he reminds his listeners that Israel was not the only people taken out of captivity by God. There is the suggestion here that selection is not limited to Israel alone. But in another passage, Amos clearly links God's special and unique covenant relationship with Israel to the Exodus.[5] He recognizes this relationship between God and Israel, and asserts that Israel must be subject to all of its consequences, however harsh.

As the Torah sees it, even Balaam, a heathen and no friend of Israel, becomes possessed by the awareness of Israel's intimacy with "the God who brought them out of Egypt."[6]

We make our transition from this redemptive aspect of the selection to a second category, which derives directly from it. Significantly, it is apprehended in Balaam's discourse when he says: "For from the top of the rock I see him, and from the hills I behold him. It is a people that shall dwell alone, and shall not be reckoned among the nations."[7] The awareness of Israel's unique place in history, its differentiation from other nations, is clearly discerned. This, too, is a factor which has contemporary relevance.

Third, just as selection is bound up with redemption (and consequently with a deviant role in history), so is it bound up with the derivative of redemption—the Torah. Torah is the third category of the essence of selection. Every Deuteronomic passage referring to the selection also admonishes Israel to be faithful to the commandments. Israel, as Jewish Scripture clearly defines its role, is *the* people of the Torah, the people whose special burden is to bear "the yoke of the Torah." Historically, it is chosen because it is released from captivity. Morally, its consequent obligation is to preserve the Torah. This is stated in almost syllogistic terms in Deuteronomy 7:6–11.

The idea of the selection is necessarily and intimately related to other concepts, such as God's love for Israel, and the covenant. Note Jeremiah 2:1–3 and Hosea 11:1.

The covenant is the culminating act in the divine-historical process. It is the marriage, as it were, of God and Israel, following the engagement.[8] What is significant is that it is indissoluble. Israel may be punished severely. It may be brought to the very gates of annihilation, but the covenant itself is never abrogated, and through it the people is renewed.

In the postbiblical period, the historical aspect, centered in Israel's past deliverance, took on special urgency, particularly during the Jewish people's medieval agony. The concept of selection assumed enlarged characteristics, and in the writings of Judah Ha-Levi, Israel's selection *and* superiority assumed massive proportions. Selection was linked to two factors—the psychological need for justification induced by anti-Jewish oppression, and the futuristic hope, shading off into eschatological expectations, of the messianic advent. But in addition, while Israel yearned for redemption, its sensitivity to the living fact that it alone was the people of the Torah took on special intensity. In the tenth century, the Jewish philosopher-theologian Saadia wrote, "Our people is a people only through its Torah."[9]

Judah Ha-Levi was the great systematic philosopher of Jewish chosenness. Leaving aside a racism which is repugnant to us, and a relegation of converts to second-rate status, which is equally repugnant, Ha-Levi develops a concept of Jewish peoplehood which has special relevance to us today. As Simhah Bunam Orbach tells us, he is "the most original of the Jewish philosophers, the authentic creator of the philosophy of Judaism, of Jewish historicism."[10] Without Ha-Levi's work, we could not understand the special character of Judaism. What is this special character? That through Israel, God is not the remote and inaccessible deity of the philosophers but the One who is engaged in the historical experience of Israel. The distance of the philosophers is shattered, not only by the prophets, who enjoy special access to God, but by every Jew in Israel who draws near through the Torah and the mitzvot.

In the *Kuzari*, Ha-Levi establishes a radical divide between the approaches of philosophy, Christian theology, Moslem theology, and Jewish thought. Through the device of the Khazar king, Ha-Levi discredits the methods of the others, whose primary approach is either speculative or defiant of reason. In the case of the Neoplatonic scholar, stress is placed upon the active intellect and divine emanations. The Christian theologian stresses creation in time and divine providence as

well as immaculate conception, the trinity, and the transposition of the
community of Israel into the "Spiritual Israel." The Moslem, in addition
to acknowledging the Jewish sources of Islamic belief in God's unity and
the creation of the world, stresses the superiority of the Koran and the
culmination of prophecy in Mohammed. Yet none of them convinces the
Khazar, who says: "I see myself compelled to ask the Jews because . . .
they constitute in themselves the evidence for a divine law on earth."[11]
As Orbach comments:

> Ha-Levi's protagonist, contrary to all of his Jewish predeces-
> sors, presents not the universal principles of Judaism, such as
> the Creator-God, the Unity of Man, etc., but rather the manifes-
> tation of God in history, particularly the national history of
> Israel, the marvelous events of which Jewish history is full, the
> most important of which is the giving of the Torah, as well as
> prophecy in general. This particularism arouses the astonish-
> ment of the King who says: "I had at first decided not to ask a
> Jew because I knew that degradation and poverty had left them
> nothing else but to say that you believe in the Creator of the
> world which is the argument of every religious person."[12]

Here Ha-Levi establishes a fundamental difference between speculative philosophy and theology, which at best can apprehend God as the
creator of nature, and this without real certainty—and Judaism, which
offers a different departure defying human understanding—God's historical action, which is beyond nature and gives us a new content based
upon the historical-religious experience of the people.

The king says that the idea of the Creator-God calls for philosophical
speculation, as a result of which there is the possibility of doubt and
disagreement among philosophers. But as for the manifestation of God
in Jewish history—this does not require proof, and all the other speculative arguments become superfluous. The Jewish scholar presses his
point as follows: When Moses addressed Pharaoh, he said: The God of
the Hebrews sent me to you, that is to say, the God of Abraham, Isaac,
and Jacob, because Abraham was known to the nations; and he did not
say, the God of Heaven and Earth sent me. Likewise God introduces his
words to the multitudes of Israel: I am the Lord your God who brought
you out of the land of Egypt, and he did not say: I am the Creator of the
World and your Creator. Says the Khazar: The elements binding the
Jew to the faith of Israel are acknowledgment of God, His eternity, His
providential care for our fathers, the Torah as His, and the proof of all
this is *Yetziat Mitzrayim.*

While God's manifestation in Israel's history is mysterious and beyond explanation, it is nevertheless evident and inherent in the very experience of the people. Ha-Levi stresses the miraculous quality manifesting itself in Jewish history, not merely in isolated events but in the wondrous existence of the people itself. The king is astonished at the Jews' reference to "Israel in whom I take pride." How can God take pride in flesh and blood? The Jewish scholar draws an analogy to the sun: The sun is the pride of Creation, giving life and light to all. In like manner Israel is the spiritual sun of the world, having brought a superior spiritual life and the light of knowledge, especially the special knowledge of Judaism's God. Until the appearance of that people, the world was steeped in idolatry, which represents an enslavement to nature. Even the philosophers were affected by this paganistic bent since they saw God as intimately related to nature. Only the appearance of the people revealed the presence of God within history. This spiritual stress, which Israel impressed upon human culture, is the glory of the people and the miraculous event in the spiritual history of humanity.

Having shown the singular place of God in Jewish history, through Israel, Ha-Levi then establishes the connection between the people and its Torah as well as its coveted land. He states that one can be persuaded of the veracity of the Torah, which alone leads to God, through contemplating the history of the people, when the divine component clung to Abraham, then passed beyond him to the entire people, until the people settled in the Holy Land and ascended ever upward. For Ha-Levi, three elements are required for the special attachment of the *Inyan Elohi* to Israel—the people, the land, and religious conduct. Only in the land of Israel can the highest expression of the Jewish people be articulated. "You see how the law of Shabbat was imposed upon the land, as it is said, 'The land shall rest,' and you may never sell it." It is in the land alone that prophecy arose.

At the end of the dialogue, symbolically enough, the Jew reveals to the Khazar his intention of making aliyah to Israel. The Khazar asks: "What do you seek in Jerusalem and in Canaan, since the Shekhinah is gone from there, and nearness to God can be achieved everywhere with a pure heart and a strong desire." The Jew replies:

> To be sure, the visible shekhinah has disappeared, revealing itself only to a prophet or to a community . . . in the distinguished place. . . . But the invisible and spiritual shekhinah is with every born Israelite of pure life, pure heart and sincere devotion to the Lord of Israel. . . . Pure life can be perfect there only. . . . The yearning is bound to be strengthened . . . espe-

cially in him who travels to the land from a great distance. Jerusalem can only be rebuilt when Israel yearns for it to such an extent that we sympathize even with its stones and its dust.[13]

It was Jewish liturgy more than anything else which spelled out the relationship most explicitly. We can now return to the prayers that were cited at the beginning of this discussion and see them in the light of what we have learned. The Sabbath prayer of sanctification clearly and unmistakably links selection to redemption. So do the festival prayers of sanctification, and all of them proceed to relate essential aspects of the Torah to the selection—the Sabbath and the festivals. The prayer preceding the reading from the Torah more specifically joins the selection to the transmission of the Torah—"Who has chosen us from among all people and has given us [or "by giving us"] the Torah." Even the prayer in the Alenu, jarring and invidious as it may sound, speaks of Israel's distinct history and career, an unequivocal truth. Most compellingly, the prayer preceding the reading from the prophetic portion on the Sabbath links chosenness with specific sacred aspects of the faith rather than with selection in the abstract.

Now, because Jews cannot go about delivering long explanations of a difficult and sensitive topic, we are conflicted about its use in our theology. Those who would return to it do so with trepidation, while others urge the total abandonment of the idea as unworthy of exegesis or reinterpretation. But I suggest that if the measure of an idea is public relations and the danger of misunderstanding, then what important concept could be sustained?

It would be presumptuous for any people or religious community to lay claim to God's exclusive concern. This is what Amos may have had in mind, and that may be why Maimonides chose not to make the selection of Israel a fourteenth article of the faith. But to say this is not to deny that the concept does have relevance, and, particularly, contemporary relevance. Whatever purpose God may have for the nations and the faiths, Israel appears to have been selected to endure *as Israel*. A compelling fact of our time is the very existence of the Jewish people. This is one of the wonders of history and must be confronted at every turn. Biblical insight caught the remarkable link between redemption and selection. This insight applies with special clarity to the condition of Israel, the people, today. With Amos, we assert that Israel is not the only people that has been brought out of the pit, but Israel is in fact the only people whose entire career has been a fluctuation between annihilation and renewal, destruction and resurrection, death and transfiguration. Judaism has seen this ebb and flow in our fortunes as a continuous recapitulation of the original slavery and deliverance. Every exile has been Egypt. Every tyrant has been Pharaoh. Every deliverance has been the first redemption enlarged.

It is told of Pharaoh that he stands at the gates of hell and says to the new tyrants as they enter: "Fools, why couldn't you learn a lesson from me?"

Greater in the dimension of space, greater in time, greater in terror and agony even than Egypt, has been the oppression of Israel in Europe, culminating in the hideousness of the Nazi period. That Israel survived can be explained only in religious terms. To attempt to interpret this sociologically or politico-economically is to make a travesty not only of the survival, but of the efforts at explanation. The sheer fact of survival under conditions of relentless assault, even if Israel were nothing but a nomadic pack for thirty-five hundred years, would in itself be cause for wonder. But it has not been survival alone, but a series of periodic confrontations with evil, confrontations in which Israel has prevailed.

The capacity of Israel to stand at the crossroads of history and by its own witness attest to the indestructibility of Israel in the face of overwhelming evil, is an unassailable fact. This is divine selection.

But there is also demonic selection. During the Second World War, Hitler's agents went all over Nazi-occupied Europe to make what they called "selections" of Jews for transport to the death camps. These selections, then and even before, represented the resistance and defiance of God by the demonic in history. Freud has annotated the specific selection of the Jews for oppression as a rejection by the oppressor of the God whom the Jew represented and, even more, the God who entered into the Christian world from Judaism.

Even as Israel endured, so, as Balaam said, "It is a people that dwells alone and is not reckoned as are other nations." What does this mean in the context of these comments? It means that Israel has a course in history which is altogether different from that of other peoples. Israel defies the deterministic rules of history, which insist that every civilization undergoes a process of rise, decline, and death. It has followed its own solitary course, both living among the nations and preserving its own spiritual impulses intact. What people, once destroyed and exiled for nearly two millennia, has ever been born again? What do the wise men say, who measure the life and death of every civilization, who predict the decline and fall of every living society—what do they say of Israel? For Israel has perished and lived, perished again and lived again, even while the wise men of all the ages have recorded its irrevocable end. Standing over the grave of our most recent oppressor, we see the fruits of Israel's miraculous rebirth. We see the redemption of the land from centuries of desolation and the desert's encroachment.

Moreover, no other people has undergone the unique metamorphosis Israel is experiencing today—to be a people that is both sovereign in a state, the State of Israel, and at the same time living as a world community beyond the confines of the state. It is a metamorphosis, yet a return to a prior condition, before Rome overwhelmed Palestine, when Israel enjoyed both autonomy and a Diaspora existence. This is more than just a unique historical phenomenon. It is a living illustration to the world of the dynamic possibilities of nationhood and universal commitment within our world, where growing disenchantment with nationalism summons the peoples of our globe to a higher goal than chauvinism.

Finally, Israel is the people of Torah. No matter how widely religious parties within Judaism may differ, they all cling to Torah as a central and indispensable aspect of Jewish life. Significantly, and perhaps as a consequence of Israel's martyrdom, Torah is exerting an increasing pull back toward the center. Less and less is it being treated, even in the more radical circles, as an antiquarian, analysis-ridden document, and increasingly as the source of Jewish commitment and direction. Truly, we can say with Saadia, "We are a people because of the Torah." Our distinctiveness is thus rooted in the third factor—that whether a Jew believes in literal revelation or progressive revelation, he can with all conviction declare that Israel's orbit in human and in sacred history is governed by adherence to the authority of the Torah.

Thus, in its repeated redemptive experience, Israel stands alone. In its historical configuration, Israel stands alone. In its spiritual commitment, Israel stands alone.

To many Jews, the task of Israel is to fulfill the terms of the covenant as they are defined in the commandments of the Torah, and as they are enlarged in rabbinical legislation. It is encompassed in the life-style of generations of Jews who adhered faithfully to an existence of sacred study, worship, and acts of loving-kindness. Today, this regimen—especially of faithfulness to the mitzvah, the sacred command, has little validity for some and is undergoing radical mutation for others. The task, defined and systematized by centuries of Jewish living as a way which is readily apparent if only we look into the past, is no longer utterly clear. But clear or obscure, there is no authentic path without mitzvah. More exactly, a path that is not halakhah—the way—is no path.

We cannot refer to Torah in didactic terms alone. Torah as study or edification, or even prophetic ethics, but divorced from discipline, is anomalous to Judaism. The Reform experiment with Torah as the distilled prophetic moralism of our heritage is at an end. We are on the way back to a halakhic approach to Torah, and the signs are not difficult to find. The life of mitzvah, whether as *siyag* in a world where the perimeter of Jewish life is under siege; whether as *ogen* ("anchor") in a world where the foundations of existence are shifting beneath our feet; whether as *brit,* reminding us that our God says, "Kinderlach, while you are trying to find me, here are some mitzvot to keep you from going mad," such a life of mitzvah is Jewish, and only Jewish.

For our own day the task must also be defined in terms of the existential condition of the Jews, rather than in terms of abstract imperatives. This is not the first age in which these conditions have asserted themselves, but it is perhaps the most decisive age. If past history is an index of what may yet be, then out of the existential situation of the Jew may emerge yet another renewal of the spirit which would have its effect upon Israel and upon humanity. It would consist of three components. The first component is that the Jew is and wills to be. His task in the world is to endure. Even when he is uncertain of the purpose of endurance, he feels at times an overwhelming conviction that it has been placed upon him to be, and to wait. This is no small task when, unlike other beleaguered people, who have no choice but to stand up to their ordeal, the Jew today can quietly slip out of his historical role and make his getaway from God and from history. But he chooses not to do this.

The second component, which, like the first, is not a theological abstraction but a reality, is that the meaning of Kiddush ha-Shem, the Sanctification of God's Name, has asserted itself once more within Jewish history, perhaps with greater force than ever before. The martyrdom of Jews and of the Jewish people is a reality in the twentieth century. We need not diminish the agony of all those of other faiths and other nationalities to recognize that the Jewish people was singled out for utter annihilation, for extirpation root and branch. We need not be diverted by the reproaches that Jews were too submissive to recognize that for great numbers submission was an act of faith, and a contemptuous defiance. Both among those who walked into the gas chambers and those who rose up in the Warsaw Ghetto, Kiddush Ha-Shem was manifested by taking death upon oneself as an affirmation of one's humanity.

The third component is the tenacity in saying no. In large measure, the very existence of the Jew represents a negative response to his world. But the Jew has not only been a passive deviant, he has also undertaken this as a task in the world. He has said no to God, from Abraham who challenged, "Shall not the Judge of all the earth do justly?" to Buber, who cried, "How can we say in the presence of Auschwitz, praise God for He is good, for His mercy endures forever?" This is a no of faith. The Jew has said no to man in his insistence on proclaiming, like Elisha, "This is not the way." This, too, is an act of faith, from the slave camps leading out of Egypt to the mountain trails and sea lanes leading out of Europe.

The multiple task is an existential, not a tactical, response to the overwhelming assault upon the very survival of the Jew. Only historical analogy can offer clues as to where this task will yet lead. In the past, however, it has culminated in spiritual regeneration.

In the context of these remarks, the concept of *behirah* takes on awesome meaning following the events of 1945 to June 1967. When, in a time when men were asking whether the end of the Jewish people had come, Israel achieved its astonishing victory, the People Israel may very well have entered upon a new era, whose unfolding will not be for us to see. But we have seen rebirth and collective resurrection, beginning in Auschwitz and proceeding to the Sinai Peninsula. The covenantal character of this event must not be overlooked. Covenant is not only a response to a specific event. It is often the event itself, binding in its compelling nature upon the development of the people, even when it may not be fully aware that it is covenanted. The most extreme form of this is *brit milah,* which makes us Jews without our volition or even, possibly, our consciousness. The *formal* covenant is only one aspect of our relationship to God—whether it be the covenant of Sinai or that of Josiah. But there is also the consequent impact of the covenant, which reaches us with its fullest force only after the event, like the noise reaching us *after* the sound barrier has been broken. When Israel stood at Sinai, it may have been less aware, precisely because of the overwhelming force of the moment, of what was happening to it than it was after the event. We, too, think this day a victory of territory and politics alone. But the inner power of the days of June, restoring Israel to its ancient roots—divine and collective, *this* is yet to be experienced in a way of Jewish existence which will bind us once again to the eternal commitment to be—Israel.

These events also dramatically reveal the chasm between the Jewish and non-Jewish approaches to religious truth. It is the *Kuzari* all over again. The philosophic and theological methods of pure speculation are contrasted once again with the Jewish insistence that it is within history that the issues of life and truth are arrayed, that it is within

history that Israel reflects its encounter with the mystery of existence
and of God. What can Kiddush ha-Shem mean without the number 1096
C.E.? What can the problem of justice mean without the geographical
entity Europe? What can the validation of faith mean without Israel in
June 1967? The return of recent non-Jewish thought to the historical
arena as the place where the issues of eternity are tested is in great
measure the product of Jewish experience and example. Is the renewed
concern with the Old Testament a series of psychological or theological
experiences alone, isolated from the realities of contemporary Jewish
experience? Or has the Christian world been drawn again to our Tanakh
by the reunion of the people with the biblical land? But Israel is not true
to its task merely by conquering nature or by living within history. It is
called upon to transform nature, certainly the nature of man. This is the
meaning of the apocalyptic hope that the leopard and the lamb will lie
down together. It is called upon to overcome history in the end—*Tikkun
Olam*. It is called upon to unite Jerusalem not only horizontally but
vertically, the upper Jerusalem with the lower Jerusalem—and in this
is the *beḥirah*.

6

Israel: The Meeting of Prophecy and Power

First came prophecy, not yet fully aroused, in Israel; then came the kings. Prophecy was inherent in Israel; monarchy was adopted. The issue of power, of ultimate sovereignty, of the nature of Israel, was fought out in the encounters of prophets and kings. In these encounters, the prophet held his ground in his day, and was vindicated in history. It was not only that he denounced tyranny and predicted overthrow, but that there were people who listened and kings who quailed. His was the authentic, though oft despised, voice of God, while the king, though anointed, was God's servant, not His messenger. Yehezkel Kaufmann writes: "Monarchy is rooted in prophesy. . . .The king is only the bearer of God's love through His messenger (the prophet)."[1]

From the first, power and sovereignty were not in Israel what they were among the other ancient states. Mesopotamian laws, prefiguring those of the Torah, established their authority in the "jurisdiction of the king." The monarch was the "son of God" in a mythical, not a figurative sense. His rule was absolute, his power challenged only by the assassin, never by the man of God, for *he* was the man of God. When, at last, monarchy came to Israel, the king was regarded, and often treated, as a limited sovereign whose authority came from God and whose powers were circumscribed by God. Nothing is more illustrative of the king's limitations than his moral surrender to the prophet. The king rules. The prophet often overrules. When the king does assume absolute power, it is because he has usurped it. King Uzziah dares to perform a priestly office in the Temple, and the priests stand in his way, accusing him of "trespass against God."[2] The monarch can be openly diverted from a wayward cause. In a bloody civil conflict, Israel inflicts a heavy defeat upon Judah and takes many captive. A prophet, Oded, meets the victorious forces on their way home and prevails upon them to return the captives.[3]

56

If absoluteness resides anywhere, it is in prophecy. Micaiah ben Imlah is beyond the punitive hand of the kings of Israel and Judah. Jeremiah, even in the pit, is more sovereign than the imperiled king. Many centuries later, a British ruler will demand that Thomas More sanction the king's unlawful marriage. Because More refuses to approve the royal offense and is determined to stand mute, he must die. Prophets denounce unjust wars and often remain unmolested. A prophet cries, "You are the man," and the king cowers. A man of God will not openly ratify a British monarch's sin, and he dies.

In Israel, the kingdom was a development, a necessary development, but subsequent to prophecy. Gideon declines kingship for himself and his descendants: "I will not rule over you, nor will my son rule over you. God will rule over you." At one point, monarchy is held up to scorn. The parable of the prickly bramble, presuming to rule over the trees of the forest, has been called "the most forthright anti-monarchical poem in world literature." The people's fiercely independent, nomadic origin is no doubt a factor. But so is its covenant with the God who brooks no injustice, the God whom a wandering people found in the wilderness.

Yet power did emerge in Israel. The state did assume a life of its own, and temporal sovereignty did clash with divine sovereignty. When monarchy came, it was to graft itself upon the history and the loyalties of the people, never to be displaced except by the foreign aggressor.

However, the encounter of prophecy with power was not for the purpose of displacing power but of taming it. There was no outright rejection of kingship, certainly not of "the dynasty of David." Some prophets may have repudiated the cultic system. But the monarchy, even when individual kings were consigned to destruction—its claim to survival was never challenged.

Thus a polarity unfolded, which was to affect the contours of our ancient development, and once again asserts itself as we struggle to make peace with our identity today. The polarity was formidable because power did not dare to challenge God, while prophecy urged only the transmuting of power, not its annihilation. Yet the impasse was shattered, and by prophecy. If, in the solitary course of Israel's origins, kingship was to be deferred, the subsequent approach of disaster and its aftermath were to effect a lasting mutation upon the body and the spirit of Israel. Kingship is neither rejected while it totters, nor abandoned when it falls. It is appropriated and absorbed into the prophetic expectation of what Israel is yet to be. This is the character of the mutation —that royal power and through it the entire community shall, under sovereign conditions, rise to a higher eminence, and thereby become transformed. A kingdom, but of priests. A people, but holy. This is more implausible even than a dictatorship of the proletariat, yet more true.

The prophets did not seek the withering away of the commonwealth, but its change. The king is to become a wonderful counselor, a righteous judge, a champion of the afflicted. He is "to restore the order of society which the monarchy itself had dissolved."[4] Yet he is not to be an eschatological phantom, but a monarch. The people is not to be disembodied, but a living community. "Israel was still to be regarded as a community bound together by nature and history . . . really a people in the proper sense of the word."[5]

But if the people was to endure, the content of its existence must be altered. Healed of its decimation and replanted in its land, Israel would undergo both a renewal and a radical change. The neglected covenant would be re-established and more deeply imbedded in the people's life. It would be Sinai all over again. "As I pleaded with your fathers in the wilderness of the land of Egypt, so will I plead with you . . . and I will bring you into the bond of the covenant."[6] If ever it was so, the people is no longer absolutely sovereign. A variant in its origins, it developed into a mutant. It is an instrument of a higher purpose, and is not permitted to break away as a vagrant entity. The king becomes messianic. The people becomes utopian. "The tribes of Judah and Benjamin designated Kings by word of the prophets."[7]

In addition, prophecy joined the hope for national redemption to that of the world. One was a precondition of the other. One was antecedent to the other. First came the prophecy, "Out of Jerusalem shall go forth a remnant, and out of Mount Zion they that shall escape."[8] Then followed, "Out of Zion shall go forth the Torah, and the word of the Lord from Jerusalem."[9] Israel stands in an unbroken bond with the world, a bond of conflict and tension, but also of irrevocable concern with the fate and destiny of nations. The interaction between Israel and the world is a reality and a principle of Jewish existence in pre-exilic times. National disaster releases this principle as a living force.

The mutation, to which Israel had been predisposed, takes effect as a consequence of exile. Out of the trauma of the first compulsory exile emerged an ever-widening, voluntary Diaspora wherein Jewish existence and Jewish loyalty were found to be compatible. Palestine was considered the center of Jewish experience to which the Diaspora looked for nourishment, but with which it also interacted creatively. Yes, the constant expectation was ultimate restoration. But in the meantime, Jews chose to remain in the lands of their settlement. It was a voluntary choice, which was possible because the living alternative of resumption of life in Palestine gave them an authentic option. The new factor in Jewish life, and in world history, was the capacity of a people to endure and to create both within and beyond the protection of its own territory. Israel, prone to this from the start, entered into a dual existence of State and Diaspora, nationhood and universalism, space and time. The state was torn out of the orbit of absolute sovereignty. The community was dispatched into a greater trajectory of lasting interaction with the world. So it was until the disaster in the year 70. Now begins a new phase in the meeting of Israel and the world.

With enforced and protracted exile, the course of Israel's voluntary incursion into the world was thwarted. Incursion was replaced by expulsion. Diaspora became exile. The last vestiges of sovereignty were wiped out, and a far-flung community of colonists became captives. The synthesis of time and space was shattered. The mutation, informed with promise, became a hideous distortion. Having begun, at least primordially, to transmute its own being and its own power, Israel now became engaged in an encounter with power not its own.

The central factor in this encounter is that Israel refused to come to terms with it. Of course, it made its accommodations, and it developed a pattern of strategic coexistence to mitigate the despair of exile. But it would not make peace with its own existence or with power. Under duress it endured beyond space and in a timelessness that was more static than eternal. Israel's ability to transcend space, which arouses the admiration of Paul Tillich, was a rope trick in which Israel took little satisfaction. Nor does the poignant nostalgia for the shtetl, indulged in by some Jewish theologians, conform with the Jewish rejection of an exile in which God also languished in captivity. Israel repudiated both the terms under which it was doomed to exile and the world's unilateral conditions by which it could be freed. However we may reinterpret Jewish history, however we may modify the blood-and-tears theory of our European existence, it is clear that to Israel, Galut under any circumstances was unmitigated evil, "the abolition of God's order."

At its very best, Galut was a state of physical and spiritual amnesty, and the amnesty could always be revoked by the captor. Israel was in Europe on sufferance, not as of right, and it yearned to be quit. Under conditions of duress, it was no longer a continuum of the universal vision of prophecy. It was no more a messenger of universalism than a prisoner is a monastic. Coercion makes the difference. If Israel succeeded in preserving its sanity and its sanctity, it was due to its own defenses, not the unsolicited challenge of exile. The passion for restoration, for contraction rather than expansion, became dominant. The process of mutation ground to a halt. The universal impulses of Israel were subordinated, and it is a wonder that they were not wiped out altogether. But the messianic hope, compulsive, pervasive, intrinsic, would not permit this desecration. Israel did not repudiate the content of its prophetic goals. It understood that a precondition for realizing them was redemption. Israel's exile was a sign of the unredeemed nature of the world. Israel was not a *testis fidei,* but a witness, through its own downfall, of the fallen state of the nations. "All later religions . . . served to . . . pave the way for the expected Messiah : He is the fruit; all will be His fruit, if they acknowledge Him and will become one tree. Then will they revere the root they formerly despised."[10]

To be overwhelmed by power, civil and religious, was to confirm Israel in its distrust of power, that of others as well as its own. "With the coming of the Messiah, kingdoms will cease from the earth."[11] Absolutism revealed its demonic proportions. Out of this, Israel learned to pray earnestly for the welfare of the government and passionately for speedy deliverance from bitter exile. Israel was enveloped not only by power itself, but by conceptions of power that did violence to the prophetic view. One of the earliest philosophical contributions to political absolutism appears in Plato's *Laws.* He writes:

> The greatest principle of all is that no one should ever be without a commander. . . . Nor should the mind of any one be accustomed to do anything on his own initiative . . . but in war and in peace he should look to and follow his leader. . . . In a word, he should teach his soul . . . never to act independently. . . . There is no principle, nor will there ever be one, which is superior to this, or better and more effective in ensuring salvation and victory in war. And we ought in time of peace from youth upward to practice this habit of commanding others, and of being commanded by others.[12]

Early Christian views of the state stand midway between prophecy and philosophical absolutism. For our purposes, the critical question is: What kind of judgment does early Christianity make upon the state? It is a judgment always conditioned by the conviction that the state is willed by God. While the Christian must always be critical of the state, his moral resistance is aroused when it infringes upon the realm of God, but, as Cullman puts it, he must "obey every State as far as it remains within its bounds."[13] This division of the sacred and the temporal makes the New Testament judgment equivocal and plants the seeds for a latter-day collapse of Christian morality. True, the early Christian is taught to recognize the "beast out of the abyss," but the state becomes a beast only when it leaves its natural and allotted haunts to prey in forbidden preserves. When the beast prowls, it is still God's instrument serving His vengeance. Also, the nature of Christian resistance, even when the beast invades the sacred precincts of God, is ambiguous. Cullman says: "Of the totalitarian claim of the State which demands for itself what is God's, Paul does not speak directly."[14]

This ambiguity is heightened by two other factors. One is the expectation that the entire historical system of the world would be shattered and that the state, a temporary institution, would then be displaced by God. This eschatological hope reduced, if it did not abrogate, the early Christian's moral resistance. The other factor, stemming from a different set of premises, rested on the naïve assumption of the intrinsic benevolence of the state. Commenting on Romans 12:3–4, Cullman states: "Only he who does evil has to fear the State . . . not he who does good."[15] Thus the judgment to which the early Christian is summoned is a shaatnez of real but circumscribed concern over the possible excesses of the state, and credence in the essential fairness of the civil powers. The judgment to which the early Christian is summoned is not the judgment of which prophecy speaks. It lives in a different realm. "In the world's opinion, [judgment] takes place in that which is visible, either as a cosmic catastrophe (the apocalyptic view) or in catastrophes within history (the expectation of the Old Testament prophets and, in part, of Judaism). In reality the judgment takes place in the decision of men toward Jesus as the Revealer of God."[16]

It is no historical accident that during the Middle Ages, despite some theological efforts to limit the power of the ruler, the weight of opinion shifted to stress on the absolute sovereignty of kings. The source for this was the Pauline doctrine that "the powers that be are ordained of God," and resistance to these powers meant damnation. Gregory the Great even denied the right to judge or criticize a king. This political determinism was part of the broad deterministic system of medieval theology. Herbert Muller writes: "Medieval thinkers, even the saints, seldom took seriously the possibility of basic social reform. They preached charity to the poor the more earnestly because they assumed that poverty and suffering were also ordained by God."[17]

It was during such a period that a Jewish scholar, destined to be jailed and held for ransom, dared to challenge the very suppositions of power. Out of the bleakness of Jewish existence, he dared, and out of the prophetic tradition, he dared. Commenting on a juridical matter involving Jewish and Christian litigants, Meir of Rothenburg demolished the infallibility of the dogma of *dina d'malkhuta* when he decreed: "This is not the law of the kingdom [*dina d'malkhuta*] but thievery of the kingdom, and it is no law."[18] Other medieval rabbis declared: "The law of the king is law, the law of the nation is not law to us."[19]

It remains for Hegel to exalt the state to the ultimate idolatry. "Morality and justice in the State are also divine and commanded by God. . . . There is nothing higher or more sacred."[20] It is enough to say that Hegel acknowledged that he owed everything to Plato.

Paramount in our discussion is the contrast between the prophetic conviction of the mutability of power and an alien conviction not only of its immutability but of its claim to divine origin. The state is absolutized. It is stratified beyond the possibility of mutation. Thus, in our own time, Karl Barth can say: "Every State, even the worst and most perverse, possesses its imperishable destiny in the fact that it will one day contribute to the glory of the *heavenly* Jerusalem, and will inevitably bring its tribute thither."[21]

When the state is absolutized, when in whatever idiom it becomes an embodiment or an agent of the Universal Spirit, Israel cannot abide with it, whether on its own soil or on the soil of Diaspora. The truly absolute state knows, even if many Jews may not, that the people Israel must be totally expunged if the state is to survive.

Historical events now make it possible for Israel to react more freely to power and to alien views of power. The rebirth of Israel the state opens the way for a renewed dialectic of prophecy and power, and offers again an opportunity for a reconciliation of both. Once more, the old mutation, arrested by exile, can be resumed. The discourse between State and Diaspora and the confrontation of Israel and the world can be continued. The identity and destiny of *all* Israel hang largely on this. Will we break apart, nation from people, like a storm-battered ship, or will we break out of the ice-bound fastness of our spiritual condition into open waters?

While there is no going home in history, Israel, once sovereign and dispersed, then homeless and exiled, is now again both a state and a world community, both a political entity and a universal reality with which everyone must reckon and which no one can define. If we are to encompass this separating yet still unsounded being in a category which will not only make sense but will prevent its own break-up, we must achieve a twofold synthesis. The first phase of the synthesis is the coming to terms of Israel the state and Israel the people. The second is the response to external power and sovereignty.

The first condition for our synthesis must be that Diaspora is intrinsic, not merely fortuitous, to Israel. If exile is regarded as a defiance of the natural order, and an injustice which must be abolished, Diaspora is to be accepted not only as tolerable, but organic to Israel. It must be part of the process of mutation. It has been noted by some that the appropriation of the name Israel by the state represents a deliberate rejection of what Israel had come to mean for at least two thousand years. By a historic irony, members of the state are Israel, and those in the Diaspora are Jews. This is a symbol of a dangerous polarity, which, if neglected, could result in a new and more destructive Karaism, with the identity of the new Karaites known only to future history. Only one agent in the polarity responds consciously to the implications of the danger—the State of Israel. It sees the survival, both of the state and of the world Jewish community, as dependent upon the state's own sovereignty. In the Free World Diaspora, however, the awareness of our identity and our relationship to Israel does not move around a comparable magnetic center. What is the difference? A state, whatever its merits in our age, is the matrix out of which society and culture emerge. The State of Israel is conducive to the development of an Israeli, yes, a Jewish society. There is no such entity as an organic Jewish society in the Diaspora of the 1960s. Also, the metabolism of Jewish life in the Diaspora reflects such massive breakdown and disintegration as to tax our survivalist and creative powers. Except for our attachment to Israel, there is little collective awareness of our relationship to history, and the God of history is thereby attenuated. Jewish theology cannot be divorced from this. It cannot be solitary and disembodied in Judaism. It becomes viable only within the dynamics of Jewish history. The kabbalistic adage, "God, Israel, and Torah are one," suggests a warning against abstracting or isolating any component of the triad.

Mainly through Israel's interaction with history, with the nation, in its grappling with power, did the crisis of endurance light up the presence of the living God. Neither synagogue loyalty, nor charity, nor mitzvot, nor social passion, nor vicarious existence in the shadow of Israel the state, can alone long deter the inroads of disintegration. All of these must be imbedded in the processes of Jewish history in which our theology was conditioned. "I am the Lord . . . Who brought you out of Egypt." To the Jew, Galut was both a theological principle and a historical event in which he was swept up. But what does Diaspora mean, except a welcome disengagement from disability, a vague absence? The historical stress emanating from Eastern Europe and the theological stress of latter-day German Jewry must converge once more, and serve as correctives to one another. Neither can exist without the other.

The issue of State and Diaspora, which will become increasingly critical, agitated both Zionists and Jewish nationalists long before the state came into being. When the persistent utopianism of many was voiced in songs promising the imminent return of the Shekhinah to Zion, others no less zealous but more knowing foresaw problems involving the identity of the Jewish people. It is significant that the most constructive concern for this issue arose within East European Jewry. From the birth of the Zionist enterprise, a central controversy was Masada or Yavneh. And another was the equilibrium of Diaspora and State.

For Jewish nationalists to pose these problems, especially that of State and Diaspora, is to acknowledge that an irreversible course had been taken in Jewish history, a course which even the trauma of exile could not push back. Diaspora had become part of the experience of Israel, and it was not to be expunged. Only one sector of Zionism totally rejected the Diaspora. But for most, the very ambiguity about the roles of State and Diaspora is based upon the assumption that both are meant to live with one another. The spirit of Israel vacillates restlessly between these two worlds. In Yizhar's *Yemei Ziklag,* the effort to shatter the tension by falling back upon the state alone as total consummation is despairing. Neither secular Manicheism—the recognition that there are two separate and inherently different domains, *shetei reshuyot,* in Jewish existence—nor secular monotheism—reliance upon power generated from the state—can be helpful. The problem not only of the identity of Israel, but of the existence of Israel, turns around this unresolved issue.

The possibilities of Diaspora both as free choice and as an authentic part of Jewish existence require the fullest exploration. The concept of Diaspora as viable and true was already gestating within the minds of many even before the state came into being.

For example, the spiritual nationalism of Ahad Ha-Am and the Diaspora nationalism of Shimon Dubnow converge upon a most significant point—the recognition of Diaspora as a constant in Jewish history. Ahad Ha-Am saw Diaspora as spiritually bereft and in need of steady replenishment from the Palestinian center. While the relationship was to be inherently unequal, Diaspora was nevertheless to be irreversibly part of the Jewish people. If it was to lack depth, it was to have its breadth.

It remained for Shimon Dubnow to give the Diaspora its own authenticity. Recognizing the merit of the spiritual center, he developed the conception of a Diaspora existence which is organically related to Palestine. For our purposes we need not dwell on his stress on autonomous national life, an untenable notion, but the insight into Diaspora and Palestine as coextensive is paramount.

> Why does the Diaspora, fighting for its life against the "distress of Judaism," fighting as far as it is able with the means at its disposal and not only by emigration to Eretz Yisrael—why does it merit less consideration? To the same degree that the [Diaspora] nationalist is obligated to participate in the revival of Eretz Yisrael, the Zionist who does not negate the Diaspora is obligated to participate in the revival of Israel in all countries of the world. . . .[22]

The understanding by Ahad Ha-Am and Dubnow that Diaspora has become a constant in Jewish existence, but a constant necessarily bound to Eretz Yisrael, is developed still further by Shimon Rawidowicz and Mordecai Kaplan. To Rawidowicz, the organic unity of Diaspora and of the state is embodied in the entirety of the people of Israel.

> *Medinat Yisrael* and *Tefutzot Yisrael* are and must be two which are one.[23]

> *Eretz Yisrael* is not outside the boundaries of the Jewish people. . . . *Eretz Yisrael* cannot take the place of "all Israel." . . . It is not a separate world. . . . Zionist thought errs when it stresses only the "rights" of Jews to *Eretz Yisrael* and posits the existence of the people only on the basis of "sufferance." I refer not only to full and uncompromising equality of Jews in and beyond *Eretz Yisrael,* but fundamental and radical unity.[24]

Mordecai Kaplan develops this concept still further and integrates it with his greater system of the Jewish civilization. For him, this is the direction the "New Zionism" must take.

It is clear that the Western Jew is no longer unwittingly in Galut. He abides in Diaspora by an act of the will which prior to 1947 he could not, however casuistically, have invoked. The transformation of Exile, with all its imperfections, into Diaspora has brought into being a new set of circumstances which enable us to respond voluntarily. We can define our new situation. We can accept or reject it and act upon this choice. We can, with a greater degree of freedom, shape the contours of our collective existence.

Thus, our objective must not be a Diaspora spiritually dependent upon the state, nor a state materially subservient to Diaspora. Nor must it even be one of "first among equals." It must be the organic oneness of the people Israel, in territory and beyond. To talk of *shetei reshuyot,* two distinct peoples, as Klatzkin has indicated, is to sentence the Diaspora to certain disintegration and the state to certain isolation of body and spirit. We are Siamese twins, bound to a common fate, sustained by a common heartbeat. Israel the state must be moved to understand this as well as Israel the people. Let us not be too quick to disown our involvement in Israel's life, or to exclude it from ours. The paramount question is not interference or dual loyalties, but the preservation of the "brotherly covenant." Yes, we must exercise care lest we commit political trespass, but let us not use it as a pretext to build walls between East Israel and West Israel. We are threatened by an enemy within—progressive alienation. It is not aggressive or contentious. It is the alienation of drift and apathy. The brotherly bonds of yesterday can become the cousinly amenities of tomorrow, the pomp and pageantry of philanthropic missions to Israel notwithstanding. We are in danger of becoming separated brethren. We, the first ecumenical movement in history, are forfeiting our claim. If we will be more strident in our stress on our separateness than imaginative in our search for organic unity, the drift will not be arrested. Disintegration, now brooding over us in our benumbed complacency, will accelerate its work.

This is what Julius Wellhausen anticipated when he closed his famous article on the history of Israel in the ninth edition of the *Encyclopaedia Britannica* by citing Spinoza: "the so-called emancipation of the Jews must inevitably lead to the extinction of Judaism wherever the process is extended beyond the political to the social sphere." Whatever may lie ahead for a separated State of Israel, it will not perish through losing its children to intermarriage. Our greatest resources must be devoted to finding the way to organic unity, not to evading the "brotherly covenant" in all its depth.

But even more, separation will compound the mounting spiritual crisis which now holds the State of Israel in its grip. Conscience is being throttled in Israel, and because of the fiction of noninvolvement, we in the Diaspora have been, until recently, silent and overly cautious. A conspiracy of silence enshrouded the spreading scandal of religious repression in Israel, and out of a specious respect for the principle of nonintrusion, we did not protest. It is particularly painful that we, the liberal forces in Jewry, who do not fear to speak and act when civil rights and human freedom are assaulted in America, have failed to oppose bigotry in Israel with sufficient vigor. The time has come to remonstrate not once but persistently, lest we desert and alienate beleaguered free spirits in Israel who have openly wondered why we remain disengaged. In this respect, Reform Judaism is failing its prophetic calling. We can no longer escape the contradiction of an American Jewry fighting for the separation of church and state in this land, while acquiescing to a quasi-theocracy in the State of Israel.

The synthesis of State and Diaspora requires nothing less than a declaration of faith that we are one. This synthesis is both a resumption of our ancient life-style and the assumption of something new. It is yet beyond clear definition, but its conjoining of space and extraterritoriality offers great promise. It will not do to attempt to measure this by conventional categories, such as nonintervention, because it points toward a new condition in mankind. It calls for invoking the ancient but now derelict covenant. The covenant is not a once-and-for-all thing. It is renewable. It has, in fact, been renewed and reinvoked during our history. It is one covenant which is multiple, as our Scripture amply testifies. Its vitality reaches out beyond Israel's biblical history. It is a bond of union between Israel and its God. It is also a bond of union within Israel itself. The political covenant of Basle will not suffice. We cannot say what a renewed covenant might declare, but it must include an affirmation of Israel's commitment to both territory and extraterritoriality. It must compel the recognition that the people of Israel has undergone a resurrection, unknown to any other people, and that the people must respond to this event as to a miracle. The substance of the covenant lies in the task to which Israel is drawn, a task against which death, ravage as it might, could not altogether prevail: a task so compelling that the decimated people has resumed the cycle of renewal for its sake.

If the meeting of Israel with Israel is rooted in the covenant, the meeting of Israel with the world must be rooted in a corollary—prophetic messianism, transposed into a liberal idiom. This is the second phase of our synthesis.

This moment makes it possible for us to resume the prophetic answer to power which history once interrupted. The process of mutation by which Israel was to enter into the world while holding to its territorial base can, if we will it, be undertaken anew, thanks to the creation of the State of Israel. Prior claims to a universalistic mission rang hollow because they tried futilely to convert a tragedy into a spiritual victory. They had made a virtue of necessity. But even more, those prior claims ignored the Jewish conviction that a test of the universal hope is the fate of Israel itself. An unredeemed Israel was a sign that the world had not qualified for redemption. Further, Israel coerced could not pretend to be Israel redemptive. The suffering servant could become a light to the nations only when "the people who walked in darkness" had themselves seen light.

To declare all Israel one is not enough. What is the unifying factor which will offer validity to the union of Israel the people and Israel the state? I believe that it resides in our earliest response to external power, in our arrested but never thwarted mutation when we entered upon a Diaspora of our own choosing, in the fundamental difference between our view of power and that of others. Now it is called upon to respond to the special conditions of our existence as a people and to the special conditions of the world.

One of the special conditions which demands a response is a paradox—the creation of the State of Israel at the very moment in history when nationalism, despite its apparent invigoration by new powers, is declining; the assumption of power when power is becoming either impotent or self-destructive.

Yes, the nation Israel had to be born. The people's way had to be across the path of statehood. The beginning of redemption has to take this form, but we must know that the event intersected yet another—an idea which once conceived cannot be aborted, that the state has passed its zenith. The decline of the tribe, the city-state, the feudal society, monarchies—and now, though it is only a belief, of the state, the sovereign power. Has the weary, blood-soaked march across nineteen centuries of history brought Israel to stand witness to this?

The rise of new nations may obscure the less dramatic disenchantment with nationalism moving about in the world. Perhaps from a less constricted perspective, the young states will be seen less as manifestations of nationalism than of the passion for freedom. In addition, they are the eager children of nationalism's old age, while among more mature powers, skepticism has possessed many minds. Sovereignty and power are undergoing urgent scrutiny. Sovereignty and power are undergoing subtle changes. The state is not yet to be abrogated, but if we are to endure, the state must be tamed. Although it cannot be predicted, the universal community is not a mere hope; it is a fateful necessity. This is no new thing. What is new is that world order, once imposed by conquest, could emerge peacefully as mankind's only option.

Now, both the early conditioning of Israel and the later transformation of the Jewish people demand that we take up the ancient burden of prophecy for the burdened world of our day. We must do this, not out of a pretentious claim to an abstract mission. We must do it because what we must say can be said out of the living situation in which Israel finds itself. To have preached universalism while we were in exile would have rendered us both suspect and fatuous. But out of its own agony and with its own hands and no others, Israel has redirected the course of its existence. It can therefore show a way for such a time as this. Israel is once again, and even more compellingly than ever before, a people of territory and beyond territory, a people of space and of time. "We are a people, one people," said Herzl in *Der Judenstaat,* but the oneness is both centripetal and centrifugal. Israel is a living synthesis of nationhood and universalism, and it will not do to attempt to sever them into separate categories. Our history has amply demonstrated the need for freedom and independence. But sovereignty also requires correctives and controls. For Israel, the correctives are inherent in Diaspora.

And this is what our world must learn. It must learn that while nations cannot and should not lose the love of place, the ardor for native soil, there is a Diaspora of the spirit to which men must be open if madness and chaos are not to engulf us. The nature of this Diaspora must be an open world in which national power is subordinated to international controls. It must preserve local loyalties, that rich earth from which culture and civilization spring. But it must mitigate the virulence of local passion from which conflict arises. For the world, Diaspora must be a sundering of all hope in self-sufficiency, a going forth to the new and even forbidding relationships upon which survival depends. It must be a departure not only from decaying shrines, but an incursion into shifting and bewildering social configurations which are yet to gain coherence. Ideas and institutions have suffered expulsion. Whole populations have drifted across frontiers. And great powers have suffered their subjects and agencies and churches to be exiled from their foreign outposts. What prophecy said to power in Israel, it must now say in the world, and it must teach the world the subjection of power to a higher, more enduring reality.

In his *Study of History,* Arnold Toynbee writes: "I believe that Buddhism and Hinduism have a lesson to teach to Christianity, Islam, and Judaism in the 'one world' into which we are now being carried by the 'annihilation of distance.'" But what people, not by doctrine but by existence, has more effectively shattered distance than Israel? What people, not by contemplation but by encounter, has battered down the barriers, both by the compulsion of others and its own free choice? Israel has a lesson to teach, of home and Diaspora, of power converted, of sovereignty transmuted. Israel has a lesson to teach, of the falseness of historical determinism, refuted once more by Israel's resurrection.

But can we truly say this in the shadow of Auschwitz? If calamity has left us distrustful of the world, if we should now entertain a cyclic and deterministic conception of anti-Semitism, then our strategy is criminally inadequate. Then we are readying future generations for martyrdom, and the only martyrdom we can decently hallow is after, not before, the fact. Then we should either evacuate the Diaspora as soon as expedient or else deliberately abandon the venture of survival.

But there are new factors with which we can reckon with as much hope as we are allowed in this hazardous world. One is that all existence has become a risk, and there is no refuge anywhere from the pervasiveness of danger. The plague which began with the torment of German Jews has now entered the marrow of all humanity. No segment of mankind can any longer escape the chain reaction of hatred, once it is set off. A generation ago, a Jewish homeland was regarded as a sure refuge. Today, we are not so sure. In fact, it is more realistic to see a strong Diaspora as some assurance of Israel's well-being. Thus, Israel's danger has become the danger of all men. And there, also, lies some hope for Israel's safety.

Another new factor lies in the possible reversal of our history. The anti-Semitic myth is a product of two interlinked factors—the crucifixion, and the destruction of the Jewish state. The effects of the first have always been contingent on the second. The restoration of Israel the state already reveals clues to the possible withering away of at least one form of anti-Semitism that has always been identified with Jewish exile. The mark of Cain upon an eternally wandering Israel is no longer tenable. The State of Israel stands as a living refutation of this theological myth. No ecumenical schema, whether approved or deferred, can more eloquently invalidate the myth than a living, sovereign Israel.

Thus, a living Israel and a living Diaspora, together, hold forth the hope that the dogma of deterministic cycles might be broken—the cycle of endless exile, the cycle of inexorable decay and death.

Thus, Israel's renewal is relevant to the world. It is also relevant to Israel in its struggle to rediscover itself. Thus, we can again take up the thwarted task of mutation. From the pit into which we were cast, we have emerged newborn. A time of renewal is again at hand, a time of both death and transfiguration. Even if such a thing has not happened like this before, even if the tradition might shrink from it, its time has come. "That which comes into your mind shall not be, in that you say, 'We will be as the nations'. . . As I live, says the Lord God, with a mighty hand, and with an outstretched arm . . . will I be King over you."[25]

7
Israel and Christian Conscience

Like Scripture, postbiblical Jewish thought is informed with yearning for national restoration, but the essential component of this yearning is rooted in religious and messianic belief. Jewish messianism is both restorative and redemptive.

While Philo reconstructs the Jewish polity into an "ecclesia of the Lord," he does not deviate from the prophetic hope in the dissolution of the Diaspora. "Without mentioning the term Messiah, he deals in great detail with what is known in Jewish tradition as the Messiah and the messianic age."[1] The exiled will be reunited, and a period of national prosperity will ensue. This will be followed by a reign of peace between men, and even between men and beasts.

For Maimonides, the function of the King-Messiah is to restore the dynasty of David, rebuild the Temple in Jerusalem, gather in the exiles, and restore all the laws that have fallen into disuse as a consequence of the destruction. The Messiah is none other than the expected ruler of Israel, and Maimonides goes to great lengths to dispel any other notion.

> Let it not occur to you that the King-Messiah must perform signs and wonders and make innovations in the world or resurrect the dead.... In the days of the Messiah ... the world will go on in the usual way. The reference in Isaiah to the wolf and the lamb dwelling together is only a parable suggesting that Israel will dwell serenely with the wicked rulers of the heathen who govern like wolves.[2]

Judah Ha-Levi regarded exile as penalty for Israel's sins and as God's means of disciplining the people in the way of humility, as well as cultivating a profound "love of that sacred place." He was irked by the complacency with which many Jews accepted a Diaspora existence, and he himself repudiated it by his pilgrimage to Eretz Yisrael. Yet the national existence for which he yearned, both in the *Kuzari* and in his

71

poetry, was predicated on the people's religious rebirth, possible only in the land of Israel. The highest spiritual fulfillment of the Jew could be achieved only in the land to which he must strive to go despite the greatest sacrifice, and where alone he can discharge his most sacred duties.

To Abravanel, who is the most profound student of Jewish sovereignty—and its most unorthodox exponent, because of his rejection of the putative biblical requirement for a king—Israel is an *umah,* and its redemption is contingent upon settlement in the land. God's covenant promise to the *umah ha-yisraelit* is irrevocable. "The inheritance of the land will not be withheld, either through the merit of the Canaanites, or the sinfulness of the people of Israel. . . . Divine Providence can adhere to the seed [of Abraham] only when they are of the Holy Land. . . ."[3] For Abravanel, Israel, unlike other nations, is eternal and has a special relationship to God. But this relationship is conditioned by the inheritance of the land.

Throughout the Middle Ages, Diaspora was the complete rejection of everything Israel affirmed. Nothing redeeming abided in it. It was mitigated by no moral factors making it more endurable. It served only to impress Israel's prior sins upon the people and to intensify to the point of frenzy their yearning for speedy restoration. The yearning was more than an impotent cry for the unattainable. The times were marked by persistent efforts on the part of individuals and groups to break out of their captivity. Frequent episodes of Jews taking to the highways and to the seas in order to reach Palestine are recorded in the chronicles. The despairing courage of Jews, braving the terrors of brigands on the roads and pirates at sea, when capture involved possible slavery or death, attests to the lengths to which Jews ventured to escape exile.

From the period that saw the end of the Nasis (twelfth century), the Palestine community was constantly replenished by immigrants. Even in the face of decrees by various governments, forbidding immigration to Palestine, Jews made their way there. Judah al-Harizi reports an influx of Jews into Jerusalem following its recapture in 1189. He writes: "God's hand was not unavailing to help gather His people and to settle some in their home." Moses ben Nahman (1194–1270) settled in Palestine after his famous disputation with the apostate Pablo Christiani at Barcelona (1263). In the very ruination of the land he saw the promise of its rebuilding, for its desolation convinced him that only the Jews could restore it. One of his students, whose name is unknown to us, writing during the persecutions in England, France, and Germany, stated: "Many people are stirred up to go to Palestine, and many believe that we are near the advent of the Redeemer, for we see that the nations of the world have made heavier their yoke upon Israel in most places."[4]

In 1286 Meir of Rothenburg and all the members of his family set out for Palestine, but they were intercepted in Lombardy, and Meir was held for ransom.[5] Elsewhere we hear of a rabbi, Samuel Shaldstadt from Alsace, who came to Palestine after having been robbed at sea.

In the fourteenth century, the violent attacks upon Jews in Western Europe precipitated further migrations to Palestine, which then was under the benevolent rule of Islam. Ashtori Ha-Parhi, who came to Palestine in the second half of the century, attests to this in his *Kaftor va-Ferah*. He also informs us that the Jews of Syria and Egypt were accustomed to making pilgrimages to Palestine on the festivals.

In the second half of the fifteenth century, Isaac Tsarfati, living in Turkey, wrote a "letter to the Jewish community in Germany to tell them about the benefits of the kingdom of Ishmael." He said:

> Israel, why do you slumber? Come and inherit the land which God gives you. Come, you who are lost in Germany and banished in France, and bow down to God at the holy mountain in Jerusalem. For God has chosen a new way through Turkey, a short overland route by which to flee there [Palestine].

He stressed this route because "there is a decree forbidding Jews to travel to the Holy Land" because of rumors among the Christians in the West "that the Jews have bought Mt. Zion. . . . Therefore they have ordered all ship captains that any Jews found aboard should be cast into the sea. . . . Since then, no one has come."[6] This is confirmed by Obadiah of Bertinoro:

> It is known in Venice that the Jews coming from Edom were responsible for transferring the graves of the kings from the control of the Edomites, and as a result Jews have been denied passage through their land.

In 1428, a decree was issued by the Doge of Venice and endorsed by the Pope requesting all ship captains to refuse passage to Jews seeking to sail for Palestine. Apparently this was abrogated by the end of the century since Obadiah of Bertinoro writes: "Each year Jews arrive with a Venetian galley. . . ."

The Spanish Inquisition spurred movements among Jews and Conversos for settlement in Palestine. Enthusiasts attempted to arouse the people by describing the bliss of dwelling in Palestine. Isaac Abravanel wrote: "They went forth from the West, going in the direction of Palestine, not only Jews but Marranos, and in this manner they are gathering upon the holy soil." This movement was duplicated in about 1500 in northern Italy. In 1538, Jacob Berab and Levi ben Ḥayim attempted to restore ordination and the Sanhedrin to Palestine. Had they succeeded, they would not only have made Palestine the spiritual center of Judaism, but might even have achieved a Jewish government in the land. The plausibility of the first inference derives from a statement by Maimonides that before the advent of the Messiah, the Sanhedrin would be restored in Palestine.[7] This attempt failed because of internal discord in the Palestinian community. In fact, Obadiah of Bertinoro wrote, "if there were in the land a man adept in government, he could be a ruler of both Jews and Ishmaelites."[8]

The intense longing to return to Palestine was not rooted merely in the idea that the dispersion of the Jews was a national calamity. Indeed, the exile was regarded as a disaster of cosmic proportions, a breach in the natural order. With the emergence of latter-day Zionism, some would say, the theological component was eliminated. Furthermore, they maintain, since 1948 the state has assumed the role of power and political expediency characteristic of all nations, and the traditional messianic and covenant pretensions have been discarded by the harshness of historical necessity. Has not the new Maccabean revolution ended, as do all great causes, in another Hasmonean dynasty against which the loyal Pharisees must protest? What bearing can Philo, Ha-Levi, Abravanel, and even Aḥad Ha-Am have upon a state that in its embattled condition appears to be more reminiscent of Mashiaḥ ben Yosef than of Mashiaḥ ben David, more melekh than mashiaḥ? This, apparently, is the problem that vexes Christians who find it difficult to respond to the State of Israel in theological as well as other terms. They seem to be saying: "Jewish tradition—yes; Jewish reality—no." They can be heard saying, "Why try to involve us in the affairs of a political state under the pretext of a religious commitment? Why not be honest and say that you are concerned with the preservation of this political entity, more so than you are concerned with the political entity of the Congo?"

One response would be that we must distinguish between three categories of Jewish existence—the People Israel, the Land of Israel, and the State of Israel. The state is the political instrument by which the land is given renewal and the people is preserved. But in the last analysis this is a specious claim because people, land, and state are conjoined in a unity of faith and purpose, and the only forthright exception is to be found among the Netorei Karta, who, incidentally, do not regard the state as a valid entity but rather as an illegitimate entity. Nor can we plausibly argue that our concern is with the dangers looming over our people, while the state's destiny does not affect us as strongly. This would be a dishonest claim, not only because we know that the people in Israel could not adequately survive without a state, but because the state itself has intrinsic value for us. Taking our stand, then, on statehood, within which the people's destiny is shaped, what can we say about the presumed defection of the state from Judaism's covenant and messianic objectives?

The first thing we can say is that it is the task of the Jews to be vigilant against the corruption of the state. The corruptibility of society, of all social structures, and of man himself is our necessary condition, and a Jewish state is no less susceptible to it than any other human instrument. Our rabbis tell us that among other factors, the land of Israel was given to the Jewish people conditionally. If anything, we have perhaps been more sensitive to this reality than have others, and this is what prophetic Judaism is all about. But corruptibility is the property not only of states but of the stateless, and our Diaspora existence attests to that. Whatever safeguards can be marshaled to mitigate the inherent dangers to any social structure—state, federation, or, for that matter, world-community—should be employed. But allowing for whatever debilitating factors may inhere in a Jewish or any other state, the State of Israel is nevertheless a depository of certain religious impulses within our tradition.

One of these impulses is *kibbutz galuyyot* (ingathering of exiles). We know that this could not have come about without the initiative and freedom which statehood and the expectations of statehood afforded. We know that *kibbutz galuyyot* was obstructed by the mandatory power on the one hand, and by the self-induced impotence or cynicism of the Western powers on the other. If Israel is a political, not a religious, entity in the minds of Christians, then the opportunity for gathering vast numbers of Jewish refugees into the shelter of the United States and other Western nations was a religious imperative and not a political expedient. This imperative was rejected. Israel alone, requiring the instruments of statehood, fulfilled this need and in so doing achieved two things. First, it made the people and the state inseparable. Second, it distinguished Jewish nationhood from all others by building a society exclusively on the immigration of the rejected and the unwanted.

A second religious component of statehood is confrontation with Galut. The Maharal of Prague rightly understood exile as a cosmic imbalance. Certainly it represents a distortion of the universe of the

Jew, which must be redeemed if peace for him and for the world is to be established. It was not only the return to the ancestral homeland but the restoration of peace within it that would abolish Galut. Jews under the Crusaders and the Saracens in Palestine were still in Galut. And as long as the State of Israel is beset by intransigent neighbors, sworn to its destruction; as long as sullen world powers agitate against it and provoke their own people as well as their sought-after allies to hostility against it; as long as it remains a member of the fellowship of nations under a set of moral standards different from those applied to other nations, it remains in Galut. The Galut's dissolution is more than a territorial achievement by Jews. It is a moral, psychological, religious reorientation by the world, and this is yet to be achieved. Even in Israel, the Jew, capable at last of resisting aggression against him, is still the target of an animus which now lies within and yet transcends the purely political equities surrounding the Middle East. This is Galut, but of a kind which only the world can overcome, or perhaps God.

The third religious factor is the rebirth of the people out of the ashes of the Holocaust. This people would not have been resurrected without a state. It would have suffered on, its suppurating wounds poisoning its existence in the lands of its dispersion, but it would have been doomed. True, other Jewries survived their disasters, but there was a critical difference. They lived on primarily because they were convinced of ultimate redemption. "Even if he should tarry." But if a people that had already endured more than any other prior generation of Jews, not only in the astronomical dimensions of its agony but in its demonic depths, were to have had its last hope torn away, it would have been incapable of ultimate survival. Nothing less than a state, or the hope of a state, was required to arouse the despairing spirit of the people.

Fourth, it is within such a state that a mutilated people can undertake the task of unifying its contingent present with its canonized past. If Diaspora Jewry was sustained by its vicarious identification with the land and its historical figures, nothing less than a physical renewal with that land could again evoke the full intensity of the sense of Jewish continuity. With the destruction of the European centers, the existential awareness of relationship to the millennia of Jewish history had become attenuated. And more, the millennial existence of a people in time alone had begun to sap its inner resources, despite the rhapsodic evocations of the beauty of shtetl life. Agnon's description of post–War I Shibush (Blunder) in its moral and Jewish decline should dispel such romantic illusions. With all of his perceptiveness, Tillich misread the meaning of Jewish existence when he deplored the resumption of

Jewish preoccupation with space when Jewry had learned to live so magnificently in time. What he overlooked was that this people could not have lived in time without its dream of space.

What this adds up to is the recognition by Jews that while our European experience was redolent with spiritual achievement, Jewish life was not to be lived in its fullness without the replantation of the land into the withering organism of the Jewish people. It is this fullness of living which Israel the state signifies, and with all the risks that statehood implies, this fullness can be achieved in no other way. This imposes upon the people the obligation to face the issues of Israeli statehood —Arabs, refugees, religion—in their fullness.

But as the Jew faces the Christian world, he finds that within the religious context of a troubled relationship, he is met chiefly and perhaps entirely as a member of a Diaspora community. Not merely that the Jew whom Christianity meets is a Diaspora dweller, but that Jewish existence in its entirety is viewed solely sub-specie Diaspora. This is one of the sources of our ambiguous relationship. It has been assumed on both sides that if only anti-Semitism were banished from the souls of men, the last barriers to dialogue would be swept aside. This, in turn, was based on the assumption that anti-Semitism is due to the single Christian accusation of deicide and the derivative Jewish refusal to accept Jesus. As long as the Jew is seen through the prism of the Diaspora, which by its very historical character circumscribes Jewish existence, his curious stubbornness of heart is understandable. For one thing, the homelessness of the Jewish people represents both a cause of this spiritual peculiarity and a penalty for it. What Judaism always recognized was that hatred of the Jews was related to their homelessness. Hatred could not be extracted by fiat alone, but by an act of restoration. The teaching of contempt was related to its justification —Jewish exile. This is reflected in the conversation between the Kuzari and the Jewish scholar:

> *Scholar:* I see you reproaching us with our degradation and poverty. . . . Yet our relationship to God is closer than if we had *attained* greatness on earth.
> *Kuzari:* This might be so if your humility were voluntary.
> *Scholar:* You have touched our weak spot, O King of the Khazars.

It was even hoped in some circles that restoration to Palestine would prompt the Jewish people to abandon its obstinate hold on Judaism and at last accept Christianity. But the intense concern of Jews with Israel leads in an altogether different direction. By and large the Jewish people want to reconstitute and revive Jewish existence as a consequence of the creation of the state. Whatever the future may hold for us, the possibility of a renewal of Judaism is inherent in the being of the state. The events of May–June 1967 amply attest to that.

I am fully aware that other considerations presently may preempt the attention of Christians. The need to retain friendship with the Arab world, the relationships with Arab Christians, the refugee problem, all seem to be foremost. But I suggest that antecedent to these real considerations are religious factors which have found much of the Christian world unprepared, and perhaps unwilling, to confront the reality of a Jewish state. There is readiness to accept the sinfulness of anti-Semitism. There is not readiness to accept the existence of a Jewish Israel as a people of both place and time. Failure to acknowledge the second factor helps to perpetuate anti-Semitism because the Diaspora and the comprehension of the Jew as a Diaspora figure only are related theologically to the anti-Jewish myth. The Jew must be in exile. But if he is not a deicide, he need not be in exile, and if he is nevertheless seen as a Diaspora being alone, it is a sign that Christendom has not fully cast off the onus with which the historical Jew has been burdened.

Let me attempt to document this by first referring to an essay of mine in the October 1, 1954 issue of the *Reconstructionist*.

> While the World Council of Churches showed itself courageous on social issues and controversial on theology, it proved indecisive on an issue that was not on the agenda but that, nevertheless, proved to be a symbol of the Christian dilemma —the Jewish question. To understand the significance and the magnitude of the question we must go back to the first Conference of the World Council, August 22, to September 4, 1948, in Amsterdam. The vapors of the concentration camp still clung to Europe. The echoes of extermination of Jews still could be heard in Amsterdam, and Israel had become a State but three months earlier.
>
> In one of its committees, the question of the "Christian Approach to the Jews" was discussed. In its report, an introduction on the suffering of Israel leads directly to the need for proselytizing Jews.
>
> "No people in His one world have suffered more bitterly from the disorder of man than the Jewish people. We cannot forget that we meet in a land from which 110,000 Jews were taken to be murdered. Nor can we forget that we meet only five years

after the extermination of 6,000,000 Jews. To the Jews our God has bound us in a special solidarity linking our destinies together in His design. We call upon all our churches to make this concern their own as we share with them the results of our too brief wrestling with it."
Then follows:
"All of our churches stand under the commission of our common Lord, 'Go ye into all the world and preach the Gospel to every creature.' The fulfillment of this commission requires that we include the Jewish people in our evangelistic task."

After the declaration of purpose, there follows another passage which clearly implies Jewish intransigence for failing to accept Jesus.

"For many the continued existence of a Jewish people which does not acknowledge Christ is a divine mystery which finds its only sufficient explanation in the purpose of God's unchanging faithfulness and mercy." (Romans xi, 25–29).

To a Jew, such a declaration, uttered particularly at such a time, reflects insensitivity to the martyrdom of a people which might well have asked the Christian world, Who indeed had failed to "acknowledge Christ"? Clearly, this was the time and place for an unequivocal denunciation of the extermination of Europe's Jewries, and perhaps a call to a great act of compassion for the spiritual forebears of Christianity. Instead, a generalized pronouncement against anti-Semitism as "irreconcilable with the profession and practice of the Christian faith" was issued, but again only as a prelude to the ultimate solution of the Jewish question.

"We must acknowledge in all humility that too often we have failed to manifest Christian love towards our Jewish neighbors, or even a resolute will for common social justice. ... The churches in the past have helped to foster an image of the Jews as the sole enemies of Christ, which has contributed to anti-Semitism in the secular world. ...

"We call upon all the churches we represent to denounce anti-Semitism, no matter what its origin, as absolutely irreconcilable with the profession and practice of the Christian faith. Anti-Semitism is sin against God and man.

"Only as we give convincing evidence to our Jewish neighbors that we seek for them the common rights and dignities which God wills for His children, can we come to such a meeting with them as would make it possible to share with them the best which God has given us in Christ."

As to the emergence of the State of Israel, the Assembly saw no spiritual or religious dimension in the rebirth of Israel, although it did appeal to the nations to treat the problem of Jewish and Arab claims as a "social and spiritual question." It avoided judgments as to the "rights and wrongs" of Jews and Arabs, but appealed to the nations to provide a "refuge for Displaced Persons far more generously than has yet been done."

It is evident that much of the interest manifested in the Jews is evangelistic. It is also quite clear that contrasted with many bold and specific pronouncements by the World Council on a vast range of social issues, the references to the Jews are pallid, highly generalized, and evasive. The first conclusion is borne out by the Committee's first set of recommendations, all of which deal with missions to the Jews. The second conclusion is borne out by the record of the discussion on the Jewish question at a plenary meeting in Amsterdam. The following comments are revealing:

"Dr. Perkins said there were many factors of this great issue which had not been dealt with adequately in the Report: (1) it did not sufficiently emphasize the need for cooperative action between the Christians and Jews; it should be much more emphatic; (2) it was not enough to condemn anti-Semitism; the causes—religious, social and economic—of that attitude must be considered; (3) the emergence of a State of Israel raised cultural and social issues. In accepting this Report, he recognized the need for more detailed study by the World Council of the many complex problems in the field of Jewish-Christian relations."

Rev. A. D. De Vere suggested adding to the recommendations words to this effect:

"That this Assembly send to the Jewish community in Amsterdam a message of sympathy with them over the sufferings of their people in this city during the recent war."

In Amsterdam no less than 100,000 Jews were taken away and murdered only five years previously.

Dr. Golterman thought the Report should state more definitely the right of the Jews to live in their own country, which God gave to Abraham and to his children. Unless this was stated clearly, the Report was unacceptable, in his opinion.

Dr. Herring, [of Holland], said that to himself and to his Church, the Remonstrant Brotherhood, the draft was quite unacceptable. It contained many telling statements, but to all who had at heart the sufferings of the Jews, it must seem impossible to preach to a people which had gone through so much. They must first be given the opportunity of living at all. The statement seemed to him hypocritical, and he moved that it be dropped. This motion was not adopted.

Bishop Oxnam recalled the motion by Rev. A. A. de Vere that a special letter be sent on behalf of the Assembly to the Jews of Amsterdam.

Bishop Dunn, [of U.S.A.], expressed doubts as to the wisdom of such a step, particularly as the trials of the Jews had already been mentioned in the body of the Report. He left the decision, however, to the delegates, who did not adopt the motion.

At Amsterdam, the last decision concerning the Jews was the following resolution:

"That, in receiving the report of this Committee, the Assembly recognized the need for more detailed study by the World Council of Churches of the many complex problems which exist in the field of relations between Christians and Jews, and in particular of the following:

"(a) The historical and present factors which have contributed to the growth and persistence of anti-Semitism, and the most effective means of combating this evil;

"(b) The need and opportunity in this present historical situation for the development of cooperation between Christians and Jews in civic and social affairs;

"(c) The many and varied problems created by establishment of a State of Israel in Palestine."

The linkage of the rejection of anti-Semitism to "the hope for the Jewish people," and the pervasive silence on Israel are of a piece. Theological recognition of Israel as an enduring and viable entity, as the instrument for the renewal of Jewry, is contradictory to the hope for Jewry's redemption in Christ. This is best illustrated in the following.

When the World Council met in Evanston in 1954, the directive of the Amsterdam Council to deal with the "many and varied problems created by establishment of a State of Israel in Palestine" was not placed on the agenda. Instead, a reference to the Jews was made in the proposed statement on the Main Theme. It contained reference to the "ultimate fulfillment of God's promise to the people of ancient Israel and the

consequent special responsibility of the Church of Christ for the proclamation of the hope in Christ to the Jews." A final revised version,
however, stated, "We are not wholly satisfied with the treatment of the
non-Christian religions and are not agreed as to the correct definition of
our hope as it applies to all who, while believers in God, do not know Him
as revealed in Christ." While the new version, deleting any reference to
the Jews, was accepted by a narrow margin, its ambiguity toward the
Jews was clearly reflected. Moreover, the discussion on this statement
was the occasion for a protracted debate on the State of Israel in which
attacks upon it were made in the absence of defenders.

It is also significant that the proceedings of the Evanston conference
carry a strong plea for evangelism to the Jews. It is unofficial and the
product of a large minority, but it is nevertheless prominently embodied
as the view of leading churchmen. It is the one unequivocal statement
on the Jews produced at the conference. "In view of the grievous guilt of
Christian people toward the Jews throughout the history of the Church,
we are certain that: the Church cannot rest until the title of Christ to the
Kingdom is recognized by His own people according to the flesh."

At the New Delhi Assembly of the World Council of Churches in 1961,
the following statement was issued:

> The Third Assembly recalls the following words which were
> addressed to the churches of the First Assembly of the World
> Council of Churches in 1948:
>
> "We call upon all the churches we represent to denounce
> anti-Semitism, no matter what its origin, as absolutely irrecon-
> cilable with the profession and practice of the Christian faith.
> Anti-Semitism is sin against God and man. Only as we give
> convincing evidence to our Jewish neighbours that we seek for
> them the common rights and dignities which God wills for his
> children, can we come to such a meeting with them as would
> make it possible to share with them the best which God has
> given us in Christ."
>
> The Assembly renews this plea in view of the fact that situa-
> tions continue to exist in which Jews are subject to discrimina-
> tion and even persecution. The Assembly urges its member
> churches to do all in their power to resist every form of anti-
> Semitism. In Christian teaching the historic events which led to
> the Crucifixion should not be so presented as to fasten upon the
> Jewish people of today responsibilities which belong to our
> corporate humanity and not to one race or community. Jews

were the first to accept Jesus and Jews are not the only ones who *do not yet* recognize him. (emphasis added)

The statement of the Vatican Council on the Jews contains the same spirit and content as the World Council documents.

The "Consultation on the Church and the Jewish People," held under the auspices of the Lutheran World Federation in Denmark in 1964, stated:

1) In spite of the fact that the outbreak of murderous anti-Semitism on an unprecedented scale has horrified all of humanity, anti-Semitism is still alive in many parts of the world. 2) The Christian church is in a process of reconsidering and reinterpreting its mission, which inevitably also affects missions to the Jews, raising the question anew whether there should be a special mission to the Jews distinct from the mission to other non-Christians and if so what the unique features of missions to the Jews might be.

The section on "The Church and Israel" states:

This division [of Jews and Christians] will be healed when "all Israel" (Romans 11:26) recognizes Jesus of Nazareth as its Messiah. Only then will the mystery of the faithfulness of God toward his people be solved.

But only two short paragraphs later, the statement, which is so confident that it has the key to the mystery—Israel's conversion —disclaims any insight into the meaning of Israel's renewal in "the land of the patriarchs." "We live much too close to this development to make a specific judgment about its religious significance: God's action in history we are unable to discern." The fact is that "this development" represents a sharp rebuttal to "the mystery of the faithfulness of God towards his people." The reconstitution of the people in Israel represents a threat to the missionary program of the church, as the Denmark statement says: "There is no ultimate defeat of anti-Semitism short of a return to the living God in the power of his grace and through the forgiveness of Jesus Christ our Lord."

The cumulative impression we receive is much more disconcerting than any single document might afford. In the aggregate, these five monumental statements, intended to give new direction to Christendom's attitude toward the Jews, say so little as to be irrelevant. In a world where Auschwitz was spawned and Israel renewed, the

statements appear to say as little as possible. While opposing theologically based anti-Semitism, they avoid virtually all reference to its more
virulent and deadly manifestations in their contemporary, secularized
form. The cure they seek to offer for the twentieth-century madness is
more applicable to the fifteenth century. And the relationship of Israel's
suffering to its redemptive aspirations is carefully ignored. Silence on
Israel dominates the statements of World Council and Vatican Council.
By way of illustrating the refusal to face up to the implications of
modern anti-Semitism, the following statement, by Makary el Souriany
of the Coptic Orthodox Church in Egypt, is illustrative: "We agreed in
Evanston and St. Andrews that any theological study concerning ancient Israel in its Biblical meaning must not have any bearing on the
existence of Israel as a political entity. So I reject any mention of Israel
in this statement."

But this is not all. Not one statement issues an unequivocal attack on
anti-Semitism. In every instance, there is a clear call to conversion as
the ultimate escape from anti-Semitism. This effort to enter into a
belated disavowal of anti-Jewish persecution casts a shadow on its
motivation. How can a clear call to "share the best which God has given
to us in Christ" be regarded by Jews who in this generation have just
emerged from hell? How are Jews affected by the knowledge that at
Evanston the study of anti-Semitism was to be "pressed forward in
conjunction with the International Committee on the Christian Approach to the Jews"?

The debates within the councils reflect a clear reluctance on the part
of individual churchmen to say even as much as the statements express.
In New Delhi, one speaker wanted all reference to anti-Semitism eliminated on the grounds that it "was only one form of social injustice and
had no peculiar significance." Another wanted to include the passage
"even their rejection for a time must contribute to the world salvation."
The original statement said, "Jews are not the only ones to reject him,"
but the amended version, "who do not yet recognize him," removes little
of the sting of the original, and suggests that there is a cause-effect
relationship between anti-Semitism and the Jewish refusal to accept
Jesus. How right John C. Bennett was when, during the New Delhi
debate on this subject, he "feared lest the discussion would result in
an uncertain voice on anti-Semitism, and a result which would be
disastrous."

Most significant for our study is the fact that reference to Israel is
scrupulously avoided. What the Jewish people considers indispensable
for its survival and the most effective antidote to anti-Semitism simply

does not exist as far as the formal statements are concerned. The virulence of anti-Israel feeling shows up in Evanston and New Delhi as well as at Vatican II, and the opponents of Israel invariably carry the day. The political factors inherent in the situation are clear. But it is instructive that nowhere does a theologian say: "Can we who come from nations which expelled Jews, which denied them asylum, and destroyed millions because no land would take them in, now remain silent about their devotion to the one land, their ancestral soil, which has given them asylum and reason to exist?"

It has been said that we must not judge Christian attitudes on Israel in the light of pre–June 1967 events, that a new development has been taking place since then. This may be so among various individuals and theological groups, but we must await more definitive positions by official church groups. We would hope that unofficial statements by certain conferences and publications might be a prelude to a radical reorientation within Christendom, but we have no reason to engage in premature expectations. After all, private statements on the Jews have always been far in advance of official church declarations.

To be sure, the General Committee of the World Council of Churches, meeting in Heraklion, Crete, in August 1967, issued a conciliatory statement on Israel. Yet this document suffers from two inadequacies. First, it approaches the issues of the Middle East from a primarily political, not theological, position. That is to say, it fails to recognize Israel in religious terms. Second, even within the context of a political position, the statement is slanted. Why should it say that the Jews of Israel had been threatened only with "expulsion," "at least by word"?

Political and moral foundations will be shaky as long as there is a failure to come to grips with primal religious considerations. No one has seen this more clearly than John Delury, secretary of the Commission on Social Justice, San Francisco Archdiocese, who wrote on June 7, 1967:

> At this moment of grave crisis Christians cannot view the threat to Israel's existence with detachment. We are morally committed because of the centuries of Christian persecution of Jews. . . . We are morally committed because Nazi anti-Semitism, though racist and not religious in immediate origin, capitalized on the Jew-as-scapegoat. . . .
>
> We are morally committed because of the passivity of so many Christians in response to the anti-Semitism of very recent times. . . .

There are complexities in the Middle East situation. There must be an answer to the Arab refugee problem. . . . But one factor stands out clearly: The survival of Israel is not only a Jewish concern: It is a Christian concern.

This leads to another fundamental issue in Christian-Jewish relations—that the concern of Christendom with a new relationship to Judaism stems from Auschwitz. This implies that the Holocaust induced Christian compassion and contrition, which in turn prompted Christian declarations on the Jews that were the product of Christian initiative. Yet the circumspect declarations of Amsterdam, Evanston, and the Vatican Council could raise some questions on this score. But we must raise the additional question whether Christian initiative could have been effective without the accompaniment of Jewish initiative. I do not refer to the deplorable efforts by Jewish agencies to influence Catholic deliberations at the Vatican. I refer to something infinitely more significant—the initiative of the Jewish people in bringing the State of Israel into being out of the people's own martyrdom. If Jewish existence would have been jeopardized without the state, how would Christian opinion have been affected without the state? In the alchemy of new attitudes and pronouncements, would the utter hopelessness of a decimated and depleted and homeless people have led to contrition and "absolution," or might this condition not have led, conversely, to intensified calls to Jewry to see its suffering as an appeal to turn from its spiritual blindness? This is what Amsterdam does say, and what Evanston barely hints, and what Vatican II implies.

Thus, we must not only consider the radical change in our history, but we must insist that this came about as a result of Jewish initiative. From a political aspect, the Jewish people fulfilled the mandate set forth by Pinsker to undertake the task of "auto-emancipation." From a theological view, the Jewish people at last released the pent-up messianic forces imprisoned in the walls of Jewish suffering. Thus, it was not the world that liberated Israel, it is not the world that can "absolve" Israel. Israel brought about these circumstances, which made "absolution" absolutely essential, because that people, no longer exiled, reduced any accusation of sinfulness, of which exile was a seemingly compelling proof, to a fatuity.

Jewish-Christian dialogue, as a theological experience, is consequently subject to misgivings by some and repudiation by others. There are Jews, however, who reaffirm dialogue despite the events and recriminations on both sides. Some Jewish spokesmen denounce opponents of dialogue and insist that organized Christianity did indeed rally to the support of Israel. I consider such statements mischievous, not because they want to rescue dialogue but because they tamper with historical reality. Some Jewish organizations continue their programs for interfaith activity without uttering a word of regret about the silence of great Christian institutions, thus giving the unhappy impression that nothing really happened and that business can go on as usual. If dialogue is to be resumed, and there are those who ardently wish this to be, it will be doomed to failure if it does not honestly face the disappointment Jews experienced, and the shallowness of a relationship that could not elicit the kind of concern the occasion warranted. I am not even sure that the instances of signing of declarations of conscience were worth eliciting, because too often they were not spontaneous and were elicited rather than offered. There is little depth in such gestures, and I do not believe that arm-twisting, even under such grave circumstances, is beneficial either to a cause or to the integrity of a cause.

All this points to the need for helping Christians to become more sensitive to the realities of Jewish existence. It is clear that Jews, despite defense agencies, missions to Christian students at college campuses, fellowships to Christian theologians, and interfaith colloquies, have dismally failed to convey the existential situation of the Jew to the world. We, too, have presented ourselves not only as a Diaspora community but worse, as a disembodied theology adapted to Christian misconceptions about what Judaism properly ought to be. The best of us have kept the Jewish people's redemptive aspirations as a legitimate religious expression out of sight, and have mustered our theological speculations as the only fit subject for discourse with Christians. And in this respect we have shown less courage and understanding of Jewish history than some of our ancestors, who stood up to their opponents in Tortosa, Barcelona, Paris, and rejected the messianic claims of Christianity. Misgivings about dialogue must not preclude a more effective program of making authentic knowledge of Judaism and the Jewish people available to the non-Jewish world. And suspension of dialogue is an eloquent form of instruction.

Nor must misgivings preclude continued cooperation with all men in the areas of social concern. The issues of conscience—race, peace, poverty—must continue to unite all men of conscience in a common endeavor, even if the memory of Jewish aloneness will agitate some of us who wondered where our comrades were.

But theological dialogue has been impaired, if indeed it ever really functioned. For one thing, the sort of dialogue that is "motivated" by defense agencies is not dialogue but apologetics, and we should be quit of that. For another, the sort of dialogue prompted even by the most subliminal desire for winning the other over is futile as well as anachronistic. A proper respect for the inevitability and desirability of religious diversity precludes such motivation. But if by dialogue we mean the intimacy of insight and relationship embodied in the I–Thou relationship, we should be wise enough to know that the time is not yet. By its very nature I–Thou is a sometime thing, uncontrived, momentary, suddenly emergent and retractive like revelation itself, an act of grace and not of committee structuring. Sometimes silence is to be preferred to premature discourse for which the soul of a man or a community is not ready. Even within a family, the exchange of intimacy is not an everyday occurrence, and it is hallowed precisely because it is rare. And even in a family, there are depths of feeling that had best be confided to God alone. There are times in the history of man when some issues of existence had best be tabled for better days, lest forcing them might exacerbate our lives and our relationships. In such a time of history do we live.

8

The Religious Dimensions of Israel

Eretz Yisrael is an indispensable theological component of Jewish existence. This is validated by our literature, which has linked the land with Israel's covenant and with its messianic aspirations. This is a central tenet in our Tenakh, and it is a continuous principle in our subsequent literature. With all of its reservations about political sovereignty, Pharisaic Judaism conceived of the land as indispensable for the fulfillment of Israel's covenant with God. Upon that sacred stage were to be enacted the sacred obligations of the community. In the course of time, a synthesis of political and redemptive messianism was achieved by the emergence in Rabbinic thought of Mashiah ben Yosef and Mashiah ben David. One is the Messiah militant. He is to conquer for Israel, then die in battle. However, rabbinic opinion about him is restrained. He is to be a great military figure, but is not to excel in spiritual qualities. He is a necessary factor in overthrowing Israel's captors. But he is subordinate to Mashiah ben David, who is destined to exercise truly extraordinary powers. Early in the postdestruction period, Mashiah ben Yosef fades into the shadows and Mashiah ben David looms larger and more imposing. The political factors are not obliterated. They never will be as Jewish history advances. But they are augmented by expanding, universal expectations. The fusion of "king" and "Messiah" in the term *melekh ha-mashiah* is a reconciliation of the political and eschatological in the Jewish hopes for the future.

Exile was more than a national disaster for the Jewish people. It represented a breach in the very order of nature. To the Maharal of Prague,

> The exile of Israel is a change in the order of the world. . . . God created every nation for its own existence. . . . Every nation must be free. . . . Exile is non-existence for Israel, who cannot be considered a nation as long as they are dispersed. . . . Even when Israel is in another land (even when not oppressed) and they do

89

not (wish to) return to their place, this is insupportable because even in exile the (holy) place has not been removed from their midst, and the Israelite nation must be in its place, because there can be no connection between it and the nations.[1]

With the emergence of latter-day Zionism, it would appear that the theological component had been eliminated. Some authorities go so far as to reject any relationship between traditional messianism and political Zionism, spawned, they contend, by nothing else than raw nineteenth-century nationalism. If this were indeed so, then how can we explain the remarkable episode in Zionist history when the East European delegates to the Zionist Congress refused to consider Uganda even as a temporary asylum for the Jewish people? If this were so, then Jewish territorialism, fostered by Zangwill, would not have perished so prematurely. There can be no doubt that under the direction of Smolenskin, Lilienblum, and Ahad Ha-Am, Zionism underwent radical secularization, but this is not the same as saying that it underwent apostasy to European nationalism. The role of Eretz Yisrael as a retentive factor in the preservation of Jewish values (Smolenskin, Lilienblum), as the instrument for reviving Israel's passion for *ha-tzedek ha-muḥlat* (Ahad Ha-Am), and as a means of cosmic awareness and the fulfillment of the personal *Ani* (A. D. Gordon), is a legitimate, if inadequate, heir of traditional Jewish identification with the land as a spiritual stimulus.

What is the meaning of May–June 1967? In the retrospection of history, it will not stand isolated but will represent a towering peak of a great mountain range dating back to 1948. It is the rebirth of the state that will be known as the humanly redemptive event. The Six-Day War will be a supreme occasion in that event. Like the recorded encampments of our people on the way out of Egypt, which are all linked to the most monumental occasion—the Exodus, so will the trials, the vindication, the heroic and saving episodes, be linked to the most amazing event of all, the rebirth of the people in its land.

And this leads us to another point. In the hierarchy of our sacred historical occasions, the restoration of sovereignty to Israel stands second only to the Exodus, is in fact a contemporary expression of the Exodus, and is yet to be enshrined not only in our calendar but in the rhythm of our lives, personal and collective, as a hallowed time, capable of interpretation only in theological terms. Political and social explanations cannot alone raise us or the events to the level, not merely of understanding, but of experience, and only as they are appropriated by the power of the spirit which moved our people can they become both sacred and human.

Moreover, these events must be understood as the release of the redemptive forces latent within the Jewish people. If the People Israel acted in history, it was in response to the imprisoned redemptive impulses which for a hundred years clamored with rising intensity to be set free. This is important for two reasons. First, even the most secular Jew will have to recognize that the messianic idea played as much of a part in the redemptive process as did the rise of European nationalism. And however each of us interprets the Messiah idea, it is clear that when the Jewish people returned to Eretz Yisrael, it was in response to a call that issued, not from the Congress of Vienna or the uprisings of 1848, but from the depths of the Jewish spirit. The second inference to be drawn is that it was Israel the people, not the world, which made the redemption possible. We are confronted with United Nations declarations on Israel. We are confronted with church pronouncements on a new approach to the Jewish people, prompted, we are told, by compassion for the martyrdom of Israel. But we must not permit the world to appropriate our achievement. The messianic passion came from within Israel, not from the world. The United Nations responded to the reality of a Jewish community in Eretz Yisrael, which it had to recognize. And the religious community of the world was moved to a spiritual reassessment by the reality of Israel and not of Auschwitz. If all that postwar Jewry had been left with had been the soil of the death camps and not the soil of Israel, then it is questionable whether the pronouncements would have been forthcoming. Instead, there is ample evidence to indicate that a massive effort would have been launched to persuade the People Israel that the lesson of its ordeal was the acceptance of the truth of Christianity. I say this not for polemical reasons but simply to illustrate the more positive truth that just as the Exodus was not from the side of Egypt, the twentieth-century redemption was not from the side of the world. "Not by might and not by power, but by My spirit, says God."

The emergence of the state makes it possible to bear the horror of Auschwitz. No man can explain Auschwitz. But Israel in some measure adequate to our needs vindicates Auschwitz, especially in the days of June 1967. That Israel could be born at all is a wonder. That it came into being out of the pit of our people's martyrdom is the miracle—that is to say, our capacity to wish to endure is *the* miracle. It would be cruel to say that Israel could not have come about except through martyrdom. This was not our wish. But this is how the world would have it, and in these two events, conjoined in tragic union, the Jewish people showed its capacity to undergo resurrection within the historical process. This is not the first time this has happened, but it has never happened with such intensity and over such a massive historical stage.

A Western world, fighting for its survival, and mesmerized by the deterministic dogmas of the rise and fall of civilizations, may ponder this mystery.

What is Israel for us today? What is the Diaspora? What is the nature of their relationship?

As Israel was the center of Jewish hope in the past, it is the existential center of Jewish life today. I say this with fullest awareness of the inner imperfection, flaws, and contradictions of the State of Israel. But the prophecy "Out of Zion shall go forth the Torah" is also a reality. Much as we may believe in the viability of the Diaspora, history has compelled us to realize how risky these convictions are. What would Diaspora existence be like without the emergence of Israel? Would our renewal as a people have come about in the absence of a state? Would we not instead have become spiritually traumatized, even more than the generation which stood on the edge of despair in the time following the Chmielnitzki massacres and the Shabbetai-Tzvi debacle? We would have only the memories of Auschwitz, and difficult as it is to live in a post-Auschwitz world, we are redeemed from madness by the redemptive reality of Israel.

Even in the area where Jews and Israelis try to flagellate themselves, the realm of the spirit, Israel manifests a vitality whose effects inform our lives. Where, on the most primitive of all levels, would our Hebrew teachers be coming from? But there is much more. The projection of the kibbutz movement, small as it is, as a great option in the social and spiritual world, the expansion of Hebrew culture, the proliferation of Hebrew letters, are all Torah out of Zion. They reflect not only literary but great spiritual creativity. The Diaspora has given rise to its Bellows, Malamuds, Fiedlers, and Roths, but first, they are clinical, occasionally prophetic diagnosticians of a people in disarray and in defection from itself. They are one generation beyond Ludwig Lewisohn and Maurice Samuel, whose work was redolent with the love of Israel. Second, they do not proliferate like Israel's creative spirits—the Lamdans, the Yizhars, the Sh. Shaloms. Third, they are more bent on demonstrating that the American Jew can "make it" on the American scene than on the continuity of Jewish existence. But, we will be told, Israel is deficient in the Diaspora's one great gift—religion. Even this is wishful thinking. In the first place, the level of our religious achievement, setting aside the institutional grandeur of American Jewry, is questionable. Our desire to quicken Israel's religious sensibilities is admirable and should not be thwarted, but ultimately, religious awakening, once it responds to the initial proddings of the American Diaspora, will be deeper and more impassioned because the historical sense of peoplehood and covenant is nowhere more intense than in direct association with Israel. It would suit our egos to rejoice in an equalitarian relationship of Diaspora and Israel, but we will have to learn to accept our moral and spiritual dependence on Israel. Modern man is no different from medieval man. We want to be central to our world. But just as we have learned that we are not at the center of our solar system, so will it contribute to the Diaspora Jew's humility if he realizes that he is not at the heart of Judaism. This is not to say that the Diaspora is not indispensable to the Jewish existence. It is. There could be no Israel without a strong Diaspora, just as the reverse is also true. But the inner substance of Judaism will flow from Zion, enriching us, quickening us, challenging us.

Which leads us to the Diaspora. First, we should reject the notion that it is expendable. Eliezar Livneh once tried to persuade me that if in the year 66 the Diaspora had been transferred to Israel, Rome could not have overcome us. I cannot indulge in historical speculation, but the analogy is totally invalid for our time. The political dynamics of our day require an influential Jewish community in the Western world, and a Jewry concentrated in Israel would court disaster. The American Jewish community is a demonstrably effective instrument for the strength and the stability of Israel. Perhaps it is not as powerful as it claims to be, and our efficacy in May and June of 1967 may be debated. But a radically weakened American Jewry would, at the very least, stifle the one certain pro-Israel voice, the one medium capable of interpreting Israel in the Western world.

At the same time, as a consequence of May 1967, I am driven to the persuasion that wherever we live, we live in Galut. There are varying gradations of Galut, and the American Galut is not the same as the Soviet Galut. But neither was Moslem Spain the same as Christian Germany in the twelfth century. And yet it was out of Moslem Spain that aspirations for redemption came.

American Jews who lived through May 1967, the time of mortal indecision and abysmal silence before Israel's action unsealed the lips of statesmen and decision-makers, realized once and for all how equivocal our status is even here. This is not to suggest that we must adopt the traditional attitude of despair and hopelessness toward Galut, but to refuse to recognize the existential truth of our age-old condition is to be psychosomatically blind. Jews are not absolved, and would be criminally negligent, if we did not fulfill our proper role as citizens and Jews in resisting the malign incursions of which Galut is capable, but we must never deceive ourselves about the very condition of Galut—insecurity. Therefore, the land of Israel is necessarily precedent to Galut in our scale of values. True, each needs the other, but historically as well as existentially, life is not worth living without Israel. The same cannot be said for Galut at its most golden period. There is no Galut *shel zahav.*

Recognizing this fact, we must predicate our relationship upon it. First, if we are in Galut, then our affinity to Israel is more than one of patronizing benefactor to the object of his generosity. Then we become, in fact, at least as much a recipient of aid and strength as does the State of Israel. But in a deeper sense, we enter into an affinity of the spirit with Israel which makes us, in a spiritual sense, contiguous to Israel. I would go even beyond contiguousness and state that modern man, living as he does in many realms of loyalty, is capable of dwelling in multiple relationships. In this context, Jerusalem is of a piece and the term *Israel* applies with equal force to us all, not only as a religious fellowship but as a community in which the people, wherever it is, is one, as a very principle of its faith. On this level of existence, it would be possible for the Jew, echoing John F. Kennedy's declaration—*Ich bin ein Berliner*—to declare *Ani Yisraeli.* On this highest level, there is no break between Galut and Eretz Yisrael. They are inextricably one in terms of their spiritual union, just as to some of our mystics this world is an extension of eternity. The dichotomy exists only for those who are already detached from Jewish existence. We are all bound together not only by an interdependence of fate and destiny (the events of May–June 1967 made this clear enough), but there is a part of us that transcends our immediate world and lives within the experience of Israel.

Second, while we are one we must recognize that even unity has its nuances and variations. The atom consists of neutrons and protons. Israel the state and Israel of the Galut embody different qualities, which modify and balance one another. Israel the state represents the people's need to live in space. Israel of the Galut represents our people's capacity and even requirement to live in eternity. Like it or not, this is the unique nature of the Jewish people, and it is not likely to be changed. Tillich was mistaken when he stated that we had attained our highest level when we ceased to occupy space and became a people of time. This people of time could not have survived if it had ever abandoned its dream of the restoration to space. We are both of place and of eternity, of the land of Israel and the sea of Galut.

Third, the relationship of Galut and state must be one of tension, in which each acts as a corrective and deterrent to the other. What corrective does Israel exert upon Galut? It is the refusal of Israel to allow Galut to die. The irony is that while Zionism in its classic sense wills the end of the Galut, its dynamic influence upon the Galut has always exerted a compulsion to survive. Galut without Israel is the enshrinement of a collective death-wish. While some in the Galut see Israel as the sanction for unwilling Jews to cut themselves off from Judaism, the events of 1967 indicated the reverse.

But the Galut also plays a vital part in the tension. It can serve as a deterrent to nationalism run riot. In a world where the state is deified, the danger of such a possibility must not be ignored. The holy can become demonic, and this applies to Israel as well as to any sacred entity. The American Galut, outside the currents of Israel's internal political embroilments, can, because of its commitment to Israel, serve as a moderating influence whenever the tendency asserts itself to equate the nation, the state, with Judaism. The constant insistence that we are a people, one people, which lives only partially in Israel, which is not entirely a people of space, can act as a monitor upon the impulse to transform the people into a nation alone. Our task is to unite the sundered elements in the Jewish spirit—God, Torah, Israel; we cannot survive without the restoration of all of these to a single organism. They must counterbalance one another, if any of them is to exist.

9
All Israel's Search for Identity

For the Diaspora Jew, crisis came with the power of a black revelation during May and June 1967. He was no longer the easy dual dweller in the Zion of the Diaspora and the vicarious homeland in Israel. Suddenly he found himself confronted with a challenge he had never envisioned—to be passionately fearful for Israel in places where his generation-old roots suddenly seemed to shrivel. We must not berate ourselves for having expected too much of the new Diaspora. And we must not be diverted by a debate as to whether the lands of Diaspora let us down in the moment of Israel's peril. What is significant is that suddenly we felt alone and abandoned, and whether the psychological experience of bereftness in a silent world was justified or not, the pain and the fear were there, and these were true enough to compel many of us to ask whether our prior assumptions about our Jewish being in a benevolent non-Jewish world were valid. Suddenly we found ourselves emotionally and spiritually uprooted, and our entire beings, which until then we were capable of sharing generously both with Israel and with our own Western society, were violently torn from their moorings. During those days a Midrash kept recurring, of the Babylonian Diaspora going forth to meet the victims of the Judean conquest. Like their fellow Babylonians, the Jews celebrated the triumph over the Judean state. But beneath their festive garments they wore black, and Jews furtively addressed passing captives: "How is father, how is brother?"

To understand the depth of the paroxysm that seized many of us, it must be realized that American Jews were not merely integrated into their society or even wholly engaged in its economic and political life, but many were also fully committed in the critical issues that have been besetting our nation. We had entered unreservedly into the struggle over America's Vietnamese war. We had taken unequivocal positions on the issue of race. I refer to Jews who had entered into these causes as Jews, convinced that there was a Jewish mandate to speak and to act, who at the same time felt bound by covenantal ties to the survival of the Jewish people. Even after the first shock waves of our desolation in the face of the threat to Israel in its solitude had subsided, we continued to be beset by the pull of loyalties that had never before challenged us. They were of a piece. Being Jewish meant waging a battle for Jewish existence and justifying that existence by concern for the world in which we lived. But after June 1967, we were not so sure. Could we in fact sustain the multiple burdens of defending not only Israel but the Jewish people and at the same time spend ourselves on the issues of peace and race and poverty? What for the better part of our lives appeared to be a multiple yet homogeneous agenda for religious existence suddenly turned into divisive and irreconcilable demands upon our time and our loyalties. Then, as the months passed, it was America's turn to become convulsed and to see the abyss opening at its feet. The terrors of Vietnam proliferated; and the apocalypse of the racial struggle grew wilder. Once again many of us were driven to the other end of the spectrum by the gyrating events which took possession of us. Not as citizens but as Jews. Jews of the Diaspora, we found ourselves driven by the events themselves to make our commitment. It was impossible to stand aside, and our response to the death of Martin Luther King symbolized our impassioned immersion in the moral struggle which could determine America's fate.

Israelis may not fully understand our schizoid state. We are fiercely bound up with Israel. We are deeply committed to the social struggle in America. This alone does not make for the schizoid state. It is that we swing so wildly from one to the other, swept up by the violence of events that tear us from one orbit to the next. And to an Israeli, whose existence appears to be of a piece, this is incomprehensible. At the inception of the civil rights struggle in the United States, a prominent and highly informed Israeli friend asked me: "Why must Jews be involved? Why can't the Negroes practice auto-emancipation like the Zionists did?"

We must not dismiss those Jews, not only in Israel but in growing numbers in the United States, who argue that it is not the function of Jews as Jews to enter so deeply into the issues that beset Galut Jewry. They maintain that Jews may take whatever positions they wish as private citizens, but to enter into the fullness of Jewish commitment is not only inexpedient and tactically unsound, but Jewishly inauthentic. They say, let us walk our Jewish path alone. And the weight of Jewish precedent is on their side. This has always been the way of the Galut. When, at any time of our history until the Emancipation, did Jews expend themselves in universal causes? Our history both in the land of

Israel and in Galut has been concerned with the preservation of the people and its Torah. Our conception of our history was that it was deviant and contemptuous of the history of the nations. We had learned from disastrous experience that our entrance into history in the form of intimate relationships with empire and world affairs proved costly again and again to our vulnerable people. When the Hasmonean dynasty courted imperial Rome, Pharisaic Judaism rejected this course because it felt we had no business being diverted from our isolate and sacred way in the world back into the gravitational pull of temporal history. What did we, the people of the covenant, have to do with powers which could never right the wrongs of existence as long as they stood outside the sovereignty of the God of Israel? The prophets spoke for God and within the context of God's time, not for Immanuel Kant, or for Karl Marx within the schedule of revolutionary time. While our tradition was fully committed to the rights of the stranger, it must be understood that it referred to the stranger who was under our jurisdiction and not to the oppressed of other nations. Our expectations were universal. Our existence was particular, and especially when we entered upon the long night of the Galut. Our unfulfilled hopes for the world were concentrated inwardly upon our own morality, our own sense of justice, our own piety. This, too, is prophetic. With this construction, Jews who follow a single track of exclusive concern with Jewish existence and survival can certainly appeal to an authentic tradition. In this context, those who found themselves standing alone in 1967 can validate their separation from the world and can find precedent for their withdrawal into the struggle for Jewish preservation. After all, who demonstrates for Soviet Jewry? Who is appalled by the recrudescence of Polish anti-Semitism? Who is contrite for the Western world's moral if not physical complicity in the murder of our martyrs? When nations were silent in May 1967, when Negro leaders proclaimed an anti-Jewish, pro-Arab line, why should Jews feel summoned to risk so much? Jews hear the bitter disappointment of a poem in the Psalms:

> For it was not an enemy that taunted me,
> Then I could have borne it;
> Neither was it mine adversary that did magnify himself against me,
> Then I would have hid myself from him.
>
> But it was thou, a man mine equal,
> My companion, and my familiar friend;
>
> We took sweet counsel together,
> In the house of God we walked with the throng.[1]

We must confess that whatever the merits or inadequacies of this position, it has the value of two strong conditions. One is that there is no lack of a sense of Jewish identity. The Jewish ego is strong. The crisis of existence is intensely severe, but there is no identity crisis here. At its best, it is the crisis of the Warsaw Ghetto fighters, who were illusionless not only about their fate, not only about the stony indifference of the world, but also about the cause for which they were dying. They were dying not to quicken world conscience, not to redeem humanity, not to be suffering servants, but to perform a despairing act for the Jewish people. The second authentic quality of this point of view is that it is a product of Galut. Even within the beleaguered borders of the Jewish commonwealth, we experienced a foretaste of Galut in the omnipresence of threat. And certainly, until the Emancipation, Galut was pervasive.

But as a consequence of May–June 1967, we must abandon an illusion about Jewish existence which we have embraced like a mother clinging to a dead infant. Galut is still with us. When we confront the Jewry of the Soviet Union we automatically reject the possibility that we, too, might be living in Galut. I think that we would see our situation in a more correct perspective if we realized that Soviet Jewry lives in captivity, but that our status of Galut remains unchanged. The term *golah,* Diaspora, is an evasion of our true condition, which is now as it has always been, contingent. The uncertainty of existence is what characterizes Galut, and no polls, no scientific studies, which after all objectify only what they can presently sample, can project the unexpected shift of winds and currents to which Jewish life is subject. This is precisely what the Jew alone, not the social scientist, felt in May 1967, when our world turned cold overnight. This is why I consider Podhoretz's *Making It* so fraudulent, because it is predicated on the naïve assumption that the American Jew, in attaining success, has at last entered upon his inheritance. Peretz Smolenskin, writing toward the end of the nineteenth century, had a different interpretation of Jewish success.

It is true that Israel has a strong hand in Germany and finds shelter in the shadow of the law. . . . But who knows what may happen? Hatred will increase and will send forth its shoots in secret and pass from land to land. . . . Our shortsighted brethren refuse to see, and they imagine that all will be well with them . . . but it is a vain dream. . . . Whereas at one time those who hated them despised the faith of Israel or else paid usury to a single Jew and blamed all Israel, now the enemies increase who (hate us) both because of the faith and because of the usury, and

even because of a prominent seat in the theater which the Jew
can afford to buy. . . . When the government will have need for
such a rabble . . . then will come a time of trouble for Jacob.[2]

In addition Galut has psychological and existential dimensions, as
well as historical. To *feel* contingency, or to apprehend it when it is not
yet a reality, is itself Galut. And this the Jew of the West possesses in
great abundance. This is perhaps one of his greatest contributions to the
culture and spirit of the West, the ability to transmit the intuition that
the atmosphere of the world is charged with ominous storms, the sensitivity which led a Zalman Shneour to write in 1913:

Again the Dark Ages draw nigh! Do you harken,
    O man, do you sense it,
The whirling and swirling of dust and the
    sulphurous scent in the distance?
The air is with omens impregnate, with omens
    grim evil foreboding:[3]

Friedmann caught this existential Galut of the Western Jew when he
wrote of his "consciousness of the precariousness of life" as his "essential
dignity."[4] It has been suggested by him and by Hazaz that the Galut
Jew does not really want to abandon the anxiety of his insecurity.[5]

Having granted all this, I must nevertheless depart from the conclu-
sions toward which this analysis would seem to drive us. The assumptions implicit in the argument I have developed are theologically based
on two interrelated principles: God alone governs history, and He alone
will change history by destroying the Galut. These assumptions made
life possible for the Jew, but if we read some of the reconsiderations of
Jewish history, we will discover that even this was not good enough for
great numbers of Jews, who preferred instant apostasy to deferred
redemption. What has happened to us is not that our history has undergone a real transformation. The twentieth century reduced the Emancipation to a fleeting interlude just as Hitler demolished the interlude of
the Weimar Republic. What has changed is our attitude toward history,
and in this respect Zionism has played a mighty role in changing our
theology from one of waiting for God to one of acting for God. At the same
time the realities of Zionist history have revealed to the Jewish people
that for good or ill, Galut has become an inescapable and ineradicable
part of Jewish existence, and no Jewish state will alter that reality. We
can take Jews out of the Galut but we cannot take Galut out of Jewish
life. Out of the historical process has emerged a people which is altogether different from any other people and perhaps may be a forerun-

ner of other communities of man. By the re-creation of Israel the state, we are again a people of both space and eternity. We are again an amphibian people, capable of existence on the land, without which our existence is imperiled, and on the many seas of contingency where the currents of history bear us. The Zionist contribution to Jewish theology—the mandate to the Jew to assume his responsibility for redemption—has further implications—that the Jew must also now unlock the prophetic hopes once deferred to messianic time, which are part of the moral treasure of the Jewish people. If Galut is to have redemptive meaning for the Jew, if it is to transcend "making it," or anxiety about our fate or our destiny, then as Jews, not merely as citizens, we are called upon to bring prophetic visions down from heaven into earthly endeavor. For those to whom this is an impudent tampering with the will of God or of Jewish history, it should be pointed out that Zionism, predicated on similar assumptions, was also a tampering with the will of God. Only the loyalty of Netorei Karta to the eschatological hope could permit the Jews of the Galut now to withdraw from the human struggle. But entering the struggle requires of us an unprecedented expansion of spiritual and moral capacities. Being inhabitants of land and sea, we will have to learn to encompass both our commitment to Israel and our concern for the world.

To us is given, for perhaps the first time in history, to yoke the national and the universal, not only theoretically but dynamically. To us is given to repudiate the course of self-rejection by some Jews in the interests of a spurious liberalism and to avoid the counsel of isolation by others in defense against the assimilating influences of a more honest liberalism. To us is given what Moses Hess taught—that Judaism requires a union of our intensest social concerns with our love for the Jewish people. But we must try to apply this lesson to Rome as well as to Jerusalem.

The Galut Jew can rediscover identity not by swinging erratically from loyalty to loyalty, from Israel to the social crisis and back, but by integrating them both into his being and making them an organic aspect of his Jewish existence. Even here, however, there is a scale of priorities, and I will deal with them later. Only when Galut becomes more than a historical accident or a deliberate choice for the entrenchment of success and power, only when it becomes a value, however painful and deceptive, a value by which the Jewish ethic can be released into the world, can we justify Jewish existence outside of Israel. I do not suggest that the intrinsic values of Judaism are not cardinal, such as learning, mitzvot, the community, and the synagogue. But unless the urge "to perfect the world" is taken seriously, these very ingredients of Jewish life can become subverted as symbols of Jewish banality and exhibitionism. A Jewry existing only for the sake of glorifying its own success will quickly become corrupt and decrepit.

If we see Israel as an expression of the messianic impulse in Judaism (and all of us are aware of the need for self-preservation and viability, which cannot help but obscure the messianic impulse in these difficult days), then there is another front on which this Jewish task must be carried out—and that is the Galut. It is precisely because it is Galut and not a more assuring Diaspora that this task devolves upon us.

There are those who will say that this is too great a risk, that in Jewish involvement in the sociopolitical issues of our society are imbedded the seeds of anti-Semitism. Our response should be that the risks lie not in what we say but in who we are, not in our action but in our identity. The centuries should have taught us that there is no tactical escape from the nature of our confrontation with the world, and the hard events that beset the State of Israel indicate that this is as true of a sovereign Jewish state as it is of the Jewish people wherever it may be dispersed. Our risk is in being Jews, not in pursuing the paths of justice and freedom. Yet we must always be aware that there is the gravest difference between the Galut of the West and the captivity of the East. It is only in Galut that the Jew may take risks. In the captivity no one would be fool enough to call upon him to assume his prophetic role. It is risk enough if he stands and waits. And this should be a lesson to us that only if the Galut remains Galut may we summon the courage required for these days. Therefore realism demands that a further qualification be made. Our universal commitment cannot be unconditional. If the world closes in upon us too much, we will be too embattled for any concern except our own survival. The Jews of every generation who would march to Utopia on the trampled bodies of the Jewish people expose the lie of their cause, since in the name of a new life they would deny life to this people; in the name of freedom they would enslave this people; in the name of redemption of every group they would thwart the redemption of this group. Even now, we stand on the narrow ledge of Western society. This has been our historical posture. Nevertheless, despite the sorry record of the twentieth century, we must cling from that ledge to our identification with the ethical impulses of Judaism. If we abandon them, where can we turn? But this is conditional upon the stability of the Galut. If it falters, we have no choice but to turn inward. We will be prophetic if we can, defensive if we must. Those of us who are engaged in the issues of the world have cherished eternal hopes. Those of us who are detached have ancient memories. From a coldly scientific view, their memories have more substance than our hopes. If it comes to that, the Jewish people's courage to be in a hostile world is also a prophetic act. In the revolution in which the United States is now convulsed, on what shores can we yet be swept up? If our hopes are dashed, it could be for always. If we are driven in upon ourselves, it will not be for primitive self-preservation alone. It will be because we believe that locked within this people are possibilities for itself and the world which, in God's time, are yet to be released, as similar possibilities were released again and again for three thousand years. Ultimately, and I hope we will not be driven to this ultimacy, the endurance of the Jewish people is paramount. Why? Because the faith of the Jewish people is the most authentic test yet devised of the world's integrity. The truth of every cause is validated or found fraudulent in the way it confronts the Jewish people. Thus if the Galut should fail us, as it did in fact in May 1967, then not only are we in jeopardy but so is Israel, and in this lies the ultimate truth of our identity. In *this* world, the State and the Galut are one, and if the domino theory applies anywhere, it applies with grimmest realism here.

But Israel is not without its own crisis of identity. Agnon understands it well, and his work reflects a special kind of schizoid gyration to which sensitive spirits in Israel are victim. His *Oreah Natah Lalun* evokes the tragedy of the Jew who is torn by the conflicting pulls of Jewish existence in Galut and in Eretz Yisrael, and *Tmol Shilshom* reveals the even more radical tension between the secular Zionist world and the sacred religious world struggling for the soul of the Jewish pioneer in Eretz Yisrael. The identity crisis in the state is the crisis of Jewishness as against Israeliness. The Six-Day War did not resolve it, touching episodes reflecting sudden Jewish awareness notwithstanding. The Jewish consciousness that emerged among many was a sudden conversion experience with all the defects of this kind of phenomenon. Like fox-hole religion, it rarely survives the moment of intensest crisis. The breach in the soul of the Galut Jew is matched by a schism in the Israeli spirit. There is the fateful danger that we and they may become separated brethren because they, like us, are separated and disjointed personalities. The sense of kinship is becoming more and more jaded as older-brother generations yield to younger-cousin generations. If Israeliness ultimately supercedes Jewishness, then a new identity will emerge in the Jewish state, and while it would be foolish to make predictions, we have reason to fear that the Galut would become exceedingly lonely, because Israel has brightened our lives, and whatever

Israel may become, it could (except for a stubborn enclave here and there) become lost to the Jewish people. Having lost most of European Jewry by annihilation, Soviet Jewry (possibly) by spiritual strangulation, how could we endure if an entity called Israel, on which we had staked our greatest hopes, were to cease to be Israel?

The search for identity must ultimately drive us to ultimate questions: Who am I? What is the meaning of my existence? What is my task in the world? How can I bridge the abyss between myself and the universe? How shall I submit to death? Our times are mistakenly regarded as irreligious or antireligious because the sounds of the destruction of the old forms and the old institutions possess our consciousness. But beyond the clamor one can hear less strident voices, not only of theologians and scholars, but of simple people, asking these questions with mounting urgency in a world where the foundations are crumbling and apocalypse hangs like a deadly missile in orbit. It is no accident that among the thinkers, the writers, the cultural leaders, Jews are frontiersmen in the desperate search for meaning. This is not a time for answers. It is a time of questing, which is in itself a great religious experience. It is no accident that in circles outside Jewish life, people are again turning to the teachings of Judaism, from the Tanakh to Hasidism to this very day, for insights and direction in finding a way for man. So what we seek in Medinat Yisrael is not a cheap device for linking Israel to the Galut. What we seek is the restoration for us all—Galut and Israel alike—of the spiritual and moral impulses that make us one people, pursuing our solitary way in a world that has learned again and again to follow in our wake. This should not be novel or revolutionary for Israelis. In particular, it should not be novel for Israelis who still find satisfaction in the formative influence of the labor movement and its gifted spiritual leaders upon the land. Aaron David Gordon was such a religious spirit. He spoke to his generation of man in the universe. He spoke to his generation of the problem of the *Ani,* the I.

> When you perform your work . . . you will feel that you absorb something hidden . . . something you do not understand . . . but which will add light and life to your spirit. Moments will come to you when you will melt into the Infinite.[6]

He spoke to his generation of the cosmic significance of human existence.

> On an evil day when suffering comes upon you, your suffering shall be sacred. You will know trouble which will shed upon you a spirit of transcendent holiness and transcendent love for all

who live and suffer. You will know neither ordinary life nor
pettiness nor empty existence. ... Then all of nature will be
close to your heart. ... Then you will see eternity in a moment
... for man will be a brother to man and to the stars of the
heavens, for there will be enough heaven in the soul of every
man ... and no man will fall upon his neighbor. ... On that day
your wisdom in science will not be a cold and terrible light, but a
living light, pouring out from all the worlds.[7]

When the absorption in antireligion or nonreligion becomes a weari-
ness, when men are no longer content to live by national slogans alone,
they will turn again to the sources of our being for assurance that their
life is not a deception. This eagerness is to be found here. We seek to help
to awaken it, not for the sake of this brand of Judaism or that, but for the
sake of Am Olam. In the Ben Zvi Library of the Hebrew University, I
came upon this extract of a letter from a young soldier from En Harod,
writing from a North African battlefield during World War II to his
father.

Yesterday we celebrated the first of May. ... If Marx said that
the workers will ultimately triumph and establish absolute
equality, our prophets said this thousands of years before he did.
... They proclaimed fifty-two "first of Mays," the Shabbat. ...
The prophetic aspiration for justice serves as spiritual food. ... I
have hardly spoken of this holiday and to my sorrow neither I
nor the youth in general know enough about it. If we are to be
reproached for this, then our shame must be turned against you,
our parents.

Nevertheless, I believe that the secret of Jewish survival is imbedded
chiefly in the State of Israel. This has been true historically. The expectation of redemption, wrapped up with the faith in the redeeming God of
Israel, alone made existence possible for the otherwise hopelessly en-
trapped people. This is also true currently. How else can we account for
the primal upsurge of Jewish energies and creativity as well as instinc-
tive identity if not through the redemptive forces released by the State
of Israel? We like to think that the creation of the state and everything
consequent to it are the products of certain forces generated within the
Jewish people and within the world. Quite the contrary. It is Zionism
and Israel that have set loose mighty moral and spiritual currents in the
modern world. It was not humanity's contrition for the Shoah, but the
Jewish people's determination to redeem the Shoah, that triggered a

measure of expiation on the part of the nations. After the Holocaust the World Council of Churches could say nothing about either the martyrdom or the newly created state except to issue a call to conversion. How much more urgent would have been the call, not to atonement by the world but to apostasy by Jewry, if we had been left without a state, with only the torn limbs of a beaten and demoralized people. As for us, we need only look about to see how the dynamics of the state and the community within the state have sent waves of moral power and influence coursing throughout our lives. We who properly wish to bring the message of religion to Israel must be mindful of the enormous motivation for our work, for the new lease on life Israel has given to our movement. We might add that Jewish religion will immeasurably benefit from once again joining itself, as it always has, to the historic experiences of our people as the ground of Jewish thought about man, God, and eternity. The ingredients for Jewish survival are here—from the reminders of our origins at Hazor and Qumran, to the kibbutz movement, which has already moved beyond Israel's borders, to the doctrines of a Buber, to the proliferating universities, to the rebirth of the Hebrew language, to the mysticism which may yet again enrapture the world, to the literary, scholarly explosion of creativity as nowhere else.

Most of all, Israel contains the secret of survival for us all because through it the Jewish people has demonstrated the historically unprecedented capacity to undergo resurrection. Ezekiel's vision of the valley of the dry bones has been fulfilled before our eyes.

To have crawled out of the sewers of Warsaw, the barracks of Auschwitz, the forests of Poland, and to give birth to a people again is a marvel that no deterministic interpretation of history, no economic dialectics, can possibly cope with. *This* is the moment from which Jewish theology and a theology of consolation for men everywhere arises. And this is the saving event which rescues the Jewish people from ultimate terror and despair. No one should dare to speculate about the meaning of Auschwitz, least of all those who reject all meaning and deny its victims the title of martyr. But this can be said—the State of Israel and the people within it represent a measure of vindication of Auschwitz. The capacity of a people to face the demonic in man and to overwhelm its own fate is a vindication not only of this people, Israel, but of the spirit of man, flickering desperately in the dark night of human anguish. If there is no meaning in Auschwitz, there is transcendent meaning in remembering Auschwitz from the midst of a people reborn to be a witness to the world.

Wherever I go I hear footsteps
—My brothers on the road, in the swamps, in the forests
Swept along in darkness, trembling from cold,
Fugitives from flames, plagues, and terrors.

Wherever I stand I hear rattling
—My brothers in chains, in chambers of the stricken—
They pierce the walls and burst the silence.
Through the generations their echoes cry out
In torture camps, in pits of the dead.

Wherever I lie I hear voices
—My brothers herded to slaughter—
Out of the burning embers, out of the ruins,
Out of cities and villages, altars for burnt offerings;
The groaning in their destruction haunts my nights.

My eyes will never stop seeing them
And my heart will never stop crying "outrage";
Every man will be called to account for their death
The heavens will descend to mourn for them.
The world and all that is therein will be a monument on their
grave.[8]

If there is no meaning in Auschwitz, there is meaning in the surge of
hope released by the reality of Israel.

Seal me into the Wall with Jerusalem stones.
Set me in mortar, and from
The midst of the stones my bones shall call,
Proclaiming the Messiah.[9]

This is the miracle—not military victory, not the defeat of the many
by the few, but Jewish existence itself, the return, the rebirth, the
renewal. God wants Israel to endure. This wish is a paradigm for God's
wish that man should endure. This is why the state is called to higher
statehood. This is why the wisdom of the Pharisees was greater than the
statecraft of the Hasmoneans. Even in the midst of a world caught up in
nationalist frenzy, the possibilities of community beyond national
idolatry are beginning to emerge. Can it be that this people, rooted in
soil and drifting in the world at the same time, can show a new way—a
love of land and a kinship with mankind, an attachment to home
modified by an openness to the world? The Galut says to the state:
"Remember, you were born for prophecy and for messianism." The state

says to the Galut: "Remember, you have gone forth into the world to live and not to die." But the world, which is also in Galut, must learn this lesson of the twofold existence. Because of all this, we want Israel to be exemplary of our people's moral and spiritual, yes, and pietistic, genius.

And in learning this lesson, we may begin to find the path back to our true identity.

10

The Jewish People and the State of Israel
(An Interpretation for Non-Jews)

To many Christians it must be puzzling that the Jews in the Western World should manifest such a deep attachment to the State of Israel. Why should a religious group be so concerned about a political entity? Are the American Lutherans heavily committed to the preservation of Sweden? Are American Catholics preoccupied with the fate of Poland? On an elemental level, it can be said that among all religious bodies there is something more than a casual interest in lands with which their faith has a historical relationship. The Catholics of Polish descent do in fact manifest a deep involvement not only in the faith of Catholicism in Poland but in political developments there. In this we note a significant aspect of the relationship between the theological and the ethnic components, which, as the study of world religion reveals with increasing clarity, cannot be segregated without destroying the religious factor in life.

But the analogies I have cited are adequate to only a limited degree. It is demonstrably true that Jews in the Diaspora have a deeper attachment to the State of Israel than do other American ethnic or religious groups to the lands of their origin. And here the paradox is further complicated because in a strictly historical sense, the land of Israel is not the place of origin of Jews, except in the broadest collective sense, and only in the context of ancient history. For most American Jews today, the United States is the land of their birth, and for their grandparent generations, it is not Palestine, but Russia, Poland, Lithuania, Germany, Hungary, or some other European country which is their native home. Yet as the events of May–June 1967 revealed, Jews throughout the Diaspora responded to the danger confronting Israel with an intensity that would have been out of character for most other third- and fourth-generation citizens. It has been demonstrated frequently enough that while there are far more Americans of Polish,

Italian, or German extraction, a threat to their ancestral land by a foreign power has never evoked anything like the passion manifested by American Jews. Even more, no religious persecution anywhere has ever aroused American Protestants or Catholics to such levels, not only of anxiety, but of commitment. So we return to our question: Why should a religious group be so concerned about a political entity? By posing the question, we answer it in part. The Jews are not, in the generally accepted sense, a "religious group" alone, and for vast numbers of Jews, the State of Israel is more than a political entity.

First, the nature of the Jewish people is beyond definition, although the people is endowed with high visibility. The people can be observed, but not categorized. It is aware of its being, it is existentially authentic, but it cannot conform to any of the accepted categories of identification. It is a unicum in history, even as it is in contemporary events. We can only indicate what it is not, and then proceed to suggest how it functions. It is not a theological community. It is not an ecclesiastical institution. It is not the third wing of religious America. If it is equated with Protestantism and Catholicism, this is only by way of indicating that at certain points, as in the areas of worship and belief, they converge and intersect, reflecting a kind of unity even in their credal diversity. But the Jewish people and Judaism cannot be contained within this limited configuration. Some segments of American Jewry, more concerned with acculturation than with authenticity, attempted to force themselves into this Procrustean bed, with disastrous results. As some Christians are becoming increasingly aware, Judaism is a way of life that includes theology (of the most disparate varieties) and at the same time transcends it. I hesitate to use the term *secular* because it does not adequately capture the essence of Judaism. Biblical Judaism did not recognize the existence of secularity as we understand it or even as it has been reconstructed by radical theology. Life was unitary to the Jew, and radical dichotomies did not exist. There was, of course, the realm of the holy, but the nonholy (except for the out-and-out unclean) was not viewed as clearly distinguished from the unrelated to the holy, but rather as embryonic holiness. All existence was under the jurisdiction of the holy, and as such was not arrayed against it or unsusceptible to being appropriated by it. Later Jewish mysticism carries this much further and speaks of the "lifting up of the sparks" of divinity that have fallen into the world and given the false impression of evil. Evil is only unredeemed holiness.

Within this kind of spiritual situation, Judaism found it incompatible with its own life-view to restrict itself to false antinomies. The divine spirit held sway everywhere, and therefore nothing was beyond the scope of the sacred in its most unstructured form. This is why the Jewish Prayer Book, without embarrassment or anxiety about what is "religious" and what is "secular," can provide a beautiful prayer for a person going to the bathroom and thanking God for his bodily functions. Out of this undefined state, Judaism underwent developments in which the underlying principle that all of life is the legitimate concern of Judaism was asserted again and again. Out of this principle emerged, not an ecclesia but a community, which established responses, disciplines, a literature, and institutions that attempted to grapple with the whole human situation. Thus, not the synagogue, not the school, not philanthropy is central to Judaism, but the people itself, ranging broadly like a free-flowing river with many tributaries, is central and encompassing of the life and history of the community. The sacred is not an isolate. It is an unfettered reality touching every aspect of Jewish existence. Two of the elements Judaism invested with religious content are the people of Israel and the land of Israel. The people and the faith are born together. Abraham is the man who both discovers God and fathers the people. If we go behind the biblical accounts, we find a primordial community out of whose experiences the faith and civilization of Israel emerged. But the biblical sources do more than fuse faith and people in their common origin. They identify the essence of the people, which is dual—a covenant with the Eternal, and continuity in history.

The land of Israel has also been endowed with a special character by the Jewish people. To live in the land was always considered a supreme objective of life. Throughout the Middle Ages, Jews made pilgrimages to Palestine, risking the terrors of highway brigands and of pirates at sea. At no time since the expulsion of the Jewish people following the destruction of the Second Commonwealth was the land empty of a Jewish community. At no time did the Jewish people relinquish its claim to the land, and every day pious Jews the world over would face toward Jerusalem and pray: "May our eyes behold Thy return to Zion in mercy." The attachment to the land represented more than a physical or a political impulse, and it was informed with overwhelming religious and spiritual content. Even with the emergence of the Zionist movement, which is generally regarded as a response to the eruption of European nationalism, Jews were willing to settle for nothing less than Palestine as the Jewish homeland.

Thus one cannot cope with the question of Israel unless he understands that there are spiritual and psychological factors which may be hidden from view by the exigencies of Israel's struggle for existence.

One must understand that the ideas of the people and the land of Israel are so deeply embedded in Jewish existence that even the secularized Jew still responds to them, sometimes in a manner he himself may not have considered possible. This was, in fact, true of large numbers of presumably alienated Jews in May and June of 1967.

But there are other factors as well, and they must be dealt with as the historical ground of reality out of which Jewish life flows. If the yearning for the land of Israel animated the Jew as a theological principle, it was given special impetus by the realities of the exile that had been imposed upon him. For some years, the land of Israel was a cherished goal even in times and places of security, few though they may have been. It should come as no surprise that large numbers of Jews would (and indeed did) abandon any hope for national restoration in return for freedom and endurance in the Diaspora. Early American Reform Judaism was predicated upon the idea that the Jewish exile had come to an end and the hope for Palestine was a vestige of the medieval past. The plunging of the world back into the age of barbarism soon dispelled this short-lived illusion. Not all Jews are Zionists, but the rise of Hitler convinced most that the state of the world as inhospitable to Jews had not really changed. A Hebrew poet, Zalman Shneour, apprehended this prophetically when in 1903 he wrote: "The Middle Ages are approaching."[1]

Two events, one violent, the other silent, imposed an awareness upon twentieth-century Jews of their true situation in the world. One was the annihilation of six million Jews. The other was the failure of the world to respond to the Holocaust. It would be false to say that the second proved to be as shocking as the first. But while the Holocaust was an event of the past, the silence was a foreboding about the future. *The Deputy* by Hochhuth and *While Six Million Died* by Arthur Morse detail both the apathy and the complicity of spiritual and temporal powers while Jewish lives could yet be saved. The knowledge of the world powers that Jews, doomed to annihilation, could be saved if places of refuge were opened to them, and the refusal by those powers to help, could not fail to convey their message to Jews living in an "enlightened" age. In 1903, the Jews were not ready for Uganda. During the dread period 1933–45, Jews would have seized upon a Uganda with passionate gratitude, but no such place was available. World conferences were held to consider the plight of the refugees, and they invariably concluded that there was not a single place on earth susceptible to Jewish immigration. The pious justifications were monumental. The escalation of the assault against the Jews of Europe was prosecuted with a mounting and massive evidence of world apathy. Consequently, the Jewish people was left with nothing but Palestine, and even Palestine had to be acquired by Jewish travail and not by world intervention. The Jewish state came into being through the intercession of the Jewish people with the acquiescence of world opinion. The Jewish case for Israel is thus predicated upon the proposition that the Jewish people was denied any other authentic options. Had Ugandas, in the symbolic sense, been open (in the United States, Canada, Australia, far-flung colonies), and had the Jewish people declared, "We will accept Palestine alone," world opinion could more justifiably have felt a "narrow Jewish nationalism." But such an option was not forthcoming, and Jewish nationalism, however narrowly one might choose to construe it, was driven toward Palestine as the solitary recourse.

This is not to suggest that all is well with Jewish nationalism. An impressive array of Jews—Ahad Ha-Am, Martin Buber, Judah Leon Magnes, Ernst Simon, and many others—all of whom were deeply rooted in Jewish national aspirations, had been critical of trends within the Zionist movement, and later within Israel. The problem of the Arabs has vexed Jewish thinkers almost from the inception of the Zionist movement. The possibilities of Arab-Jewish federation long antedate the Six-Day War. In my book *The Higher Freedom,* I have put forth the hope that the State of Israel might be the first sovereign body to endorse world government, which would mean nothing less than the renunciation of full sovereignty by all states that assent to such a concept. But with full awareness of the magnitude of these issues, it must be pointed out that similar concern for reconciliation and ultimate peaceful solutions has not been manifested in Arab intellectual circles. Yet even this does not absolve responsible Jews from seeking to break out of the circle of hostility and intransigence against Israel.

Jews will seek far afield for a peaceful resolution of the Middle Eastern crisis, but they will stop short at the renunciation of their claim to independence and freedom within the State of Israel. Borders, free of encroachment and subversion, may be negotiable. But the continuation of the state, and through it of the people, is not negotiable, since both the physical endurance and the spiritual renewal of the Jewish people are at issue.

11
Pharisaism and Political Sovereignty

The antimonarchical strain in Pharisaic Judaism was rooted in great measure in the impulse toward separation from the nations. Its antithesis, the urge for monarchy, was predicated on "let us be like all the nations." Schalit, in *Hordos ha-Melekh*,[1] suggests that Jewish Hellenism was a derivative (albeit corrupt) of prophetic universalism, which reached out into the world, while the anti-Hellenistic spirit in Judaism was rooted in prophetic particularism, which sought to preserve the people's spiritual integrity by withdrawal from the morally polluted world. The initial motive of the Maccabees was to achieve separation by overthrowing the external enemy and destroying the Jewish Hellenizers, and their goal was the defeat of anyone, Jew or gentile, who sought to join Israel to the corrupting gentile world. This is why the Hasidim were, at first, among the most zealous supporters of the Maccabees, but withdrew following the victory, out of concern that political power would lead to immersion in, and defilement by, the pagan world.

The Hasmoneans, who had fought to free their people from foreign domination and influence, were, nevertheless, increasingly driven to political entanglements as the only way of preserving their hard-won independence. They had gained sovereignty in order to be free, but through sovereignty they exposed themselves to the very dangers against which they had rebelled. The Hasmoneans hoped to escape the fearful dilemma of power by counting on national strength as a deterrent against aggression, and even as a means of imposing the will and doctrines of Israel upon all non-Jews under their jurisdiction. The Hasidim, however, rejected this course with all its obvious pitfalls, and separated themselves from the center of power when the national crisis had passed. They reasoned that in a hard decision between religious and political considerations, between religious integrity and international

114

involvement, the latter would prevail, and they feared it as an ever-present danger.

Schalit finds corroboration for this attitude in the Book of Daniel, a product of Hasidic thought, where the significant distinction is made between the preordained role of the nations and that of Israel. Political power had been granted by God to the nations of the earth from the earliest times. "The history of this world is the history of the nations," and here Israel had been assigned no role. It was part of the divine plan that Israel be subjugated as long as the domination of the nations persisted. This condition would prevail only for a time, but with the fall of the last tyranny, the rule of nations would cease, the kingdom of God would ensue, bringing redemption to Israel, and then all the nations would serve God. Thus, Israel was reserved by God and kept separate for a special purpose. This is the mystery of creation, and for this purpose was the world created. This mystery is not to be made clear to all until the end of days, but in the interim it is known to the chosen ones, the Hasidim. Therefore, "Israel is not like all the nations. The place of Israel is outside the normal course of life which obtains among the nations of the world. This course, that of the state, does not apply to Israel. The effort to force the Jewish people into the cast of a political state is a perversion of its spiritual image and a constriction of its task in creation as conceived by God."[2] To apply political criteria to the people is to render its position untenable in the midst of greater and overpowering nations. The Hasmoneans' intent was, therefore, a violation of the divine will, which intended for Israel to be apart from the nations. As it turned out, the apprehensions of the Hasidim were justified. The Hasmonean dynasty took on more and more the aspect of power in its external and internal affairs; it imposed taxes, shed blood in the conquest of territory, and hired mercenary warriors. The Hasidim considered all this to be contempt of God. The rule of Israel was God's alone, not men's. Thus began the alienation and, ultimately, the opposition of the Hasidim to the Hasmonean dynasty.

But the very immersion of the Hasmoneans in power politics attracted even as it repelled. Ultimately, the forces in the community that saw Israel's destiny as bound up with its national aspirations, who increasingly stressed the possibilities of this world, were drawn into what came to be known as the Sadducee party. In contrast to them, the Hasidim eventually evolved into the Pharisaic party, dedicated to overcoming the influence of the Hasmonean dynasty.

What was the fundamental premise on which the Pharisees mounted their opposition to the Hasmonean dynasty? The Pharisees clung steadfastly to the belief in the King-Messiah, who would be a descendant of David, and whose kingdom would be everlasting and accompanied by an era of peace, while the Hasmonean kingdom, supported by bloodshed, was a usurper because it was both non-Davidic and transitory, like all human kingdoms. It was a defilement, a usurpation of a divine prerogative, which was primordially ordained, and a repudiation of Israel's authentic task: "to live in holiness and to prepare for the true kingdom which is yet to come."[3]

This persistent adherence to the ultimate disclosure of God's kingdom made it possible for the Pharisees, and earlier for the Hasidim, to tolerate foreign rule as long as it was not oppressive. During the Seleucid reign (which began in 312 B.C.E.), Israel managed to achieve an accommodation, living under Syrian hegemony, yet in a state of spiritual withdrawal from it. When rebellion came under the leadership of the Maccabees, it was not against foreign rule but against the special tyranny of Antiochus.

With the growing entrenchment of Hasmonean power, the Pharisees came to look upon their Jewish rulers as the heirs of the pre-Antiochus period, the Seleucids. The comparison was, however, invidious, because while the Seleucids had been concerned chiefly with administration and taxation, the Hasmoneans sought to convert the people to an acceptance of their regime as the authentic Jewish kingdom "as it had been sanctified over the generations."[4] The dynasty's fall, in 63 B.C.E., was seen by the Pharisees as a retributive act of God, against whom the Hasmonean house had rebelled, and, according to many of the faithful, the ensuing subjugation of the Jewish people to Roman rule restored the divine order of the world. Worldly power, ordained from the beginning, had been imposed over Israel, and Israel would endure under its domination until the advent of the Messiah and the Kingdom of God. Thereafter, it would live a holy existence in absolute separation from the outside world, as befits the chosen people. The divine plan required Israel's subjugation so that it might be purified for the events of the End of Days. Aside from rulership, the Imperium of Rome had no special function assigned to it by God, Israel had nothing in common with it, and Rome, as such, played no part in advancing the coming of the Messiah. The Pharisees hoped only that Rome would be no different from the other kingdoms that had ruled Israel (except for the tyranny of Antiochus) so that the people might not be driven to rebel. Thus, the people should avoid arousing the wrath of Rome while separating itself from the power of Rome, from "the defilement of the nations," and preparing itself for the authentic Kingdom of God.

But the role of the Pharisees must not be misunderstood. In the ensuing struggle with Rome, though they were overruled by the more militant elements within the nation, the Pharisees counseled restraint. Yet their policy of moderation, and, in some instances, of submission, never attenuated their bonds with the people and with the land of Israel. Whatever the internal conflicts, all factors shared the fate and destiny of the people and struggled to secure survival upon the soil of Palestine. In this respect, they differed irreconcilably from the Jewish Christians of Palestine, who not only opposed active resistance to Rome, but saw themselves as completely removed from the struggle. These early Christians departed from Jerusalem during the insurrection against Vespasian and removed to Transjordan, justifying their action by quoting Jesus: "There shall not be left one stone upon another that shall not be thrown down."[5] From that time forward, the action of the Christian Jews went far beyond taking issue on matters of internal policy, and became a total severance from the Jewish people. The strategy of non-resistance propounded within the Jewish community, however, was conceived out of a passionate determination to preserve the people as well as its divine destiny.

It would be proper to say that Pharisaism, rather than being antinationalistic, subordinated political nationalism and sovereignty to the sacred, covenanted community for whom a fundamental, life-giving requirement was its land, where, alone, the highest obligations could be fulfilled. "Whoever lives outside the land is as though he had no God" may be an extreme example of the people's attachment to their country, but it reflects the profound emotional and religious attachment of the Jew. Yet this attachment was not to a homeland in the way in which it is understood today, but to God's land on which He had chosen to settle His people. "That your days may be long on the land which your God gives you." Thus, neither the land nor the nation was the ultimate object of loyalty, but the God of Israel who conferred the land and could also expel the people from it. The land was to be the scene of Israel's deliverance, which could come about only through the return of the exiles. "Gather together the despised of Israel. . . . Gird [the son of David] to purge Jerusalem from the nations that trample her down to destruction."[6]

If the Pharisaic leaders could have rid Palestine of their Roman masters without violence, they would gladly have done so. They saw no inherent benefit in being subject to a foreign power, but if the cost of keeping the sacred community inviolate on its own soil was submission to Rome as a political power, they were ready to pay the price. One may question the wisdom or even the morality of such a course, but it can be understood only in terms of the ultimate allegiance the Pharisees paid, an allegiance that transcended both the political pretensions of the Maccabean dynasty and the claims of imperial Rome.

The Pharisaic position was anchored in the ultimate sovereignty of God—*malkhut shamayim.* The radicalism of this allegiance to God as king is best comprehended against the background of a world where kings were regarded as gods, and the Jewish breaching of this concept is significant because it rejected the divinity not only of foreign kings but of the kings of Israel as well. The rabbinic declaration "Praised be His name whose glorious kingdom is forever and ever" was an affirmation that the only kingdom worthy of absolute fealty was God's. Rabbi Akiba's insistence upon reciting this statement before his execution by the Romans caused them to change his sentence from swift decapitation to torture by fire, for they well understood the implications and the dangers of loyalty to a heavenly kingdom. Even in the messianic age, the wonders to be performed would be done by God through the Messiah, but not by the Messiah alone. Not even the King-Messiah was to be anything but a divine instrument.

Thus, it would be grossly misleading to identify the Pharisees with opposition to national Jewish existence in Palestine. They were not rejecters of the sacred land and the sacred community, which were not only bound to one another but were inescapably joined to God's promise and God's covenant with Israel. In addition, unlike their opponents, they manifested a great concern for the Diaspora, which they sought to incorporate into the universal hierarchy of Judaism. Even before the destruction of the Temple, Pharisaic Judaism was already developing a system of observances and institutions that could encompass Jewish life everywhere, unlike the Palestine-based Temple and priestly cult. The ubiquitous synagogue, the mobile Torah, these were the products of Pharisaic reaching out into the Diaspora.

But were not the wars against Rome, culminating in the destruction of the Temple in 70 and the annihilation of national existence in 135, a manifestation of intense nationalism? A close look at the historical facts reveals sharp conflicts over the policy of resistance. Great segments of the people, including the Sadducees, who had abandoned their nationalistic fervor after a century of submission to Rome, were reluctant to be drawn into a war for statehood. Josephus tells us that the most influential men in the land attempted to dissuade the rebellious elements from insurrection and even engaged in a futile deterrent attack upon them.[7] Baron writes: "It was a tragedy of the Jewish people that, in a most decisive moment, it had to stop its ethno-religious expansion to take up arms in defense of a political principle from which it had become estranged, and in opposition to the very embodiment of that principle, the Roman empire."[8]

The uprising of 135, sanctioned by Rabbi Akiba, who regarded Bar Kokhba as the Messiah, was, to a significant extent, a response to Roman religious repression. When Rome had conclusively imposed its political will on the Jewish community of Palestine, resistance came to a halt, but renewed opposition came with the Roman efforts to eradicate the spiritual life of the people as well.

A revolt in behalf of religious freedom may sound implausible to a secular, modern society, but even in our own day conflicts that have their origin in religious animosities are not unknown. The India-Pakistan struggle over Kashmir is one such example. For over half a century, within the materialistically oriented society of the Soviet Union, many Jews have made sacrifices and risked official displeasure in order to adhere to their faith. In all cases of this type there are interlocking political overtones, to be sure, but the depth and integrity of the religious components must not be dismissed.

Joseph Klausner suggests that the insurrection, under the leadership of Bar Kokhba and the inspiration of Akiba, was politically inspired and that, as a result, religious repression followed.[9] It is true that the cruel decrees of Hadrian were a consequence of the aborted rebellion, but we must not overlook the initial causes. It must be remembered that Hadrian had announced his intention of transforming Jerusalem into a heathen city, and he had invoked an old Roman decree which would have proscribed circumcision. This dual threat, against the sanctity of Jerusalem and against the perpetuation of Israel's covenant, may have been politically motivated, but it was, nevertheless, correctly seen as a blow against Jewish religious existence. Hence, here too the desparate response of rebellion was undertaken, certainly by Akiba, if not by Bar Kokhba, out of primary concern for the religious integrity, and not only for the political sovereignty, of the people.

It would be futile to speculate whether a united front on the part of the Jews of Palestine might have brought about different results. Klausner believes that this failure of national unity was the cause of the people's disastrous defeats and even changed the course of human history. It may well be argued that such a conclusion is not only speculative but dubious. We might regard the admonition of Agrippa, appealing to the people against taking up arms, as more persuasive: "If great advantages might provoke any people to revolt, the Gauls might do best of all, as being so thoroughly walled round by nature. . . . Yet these Gauls . . . are kept in servitude by twelve hundred soldiers. . . ."[10] Retrospective speculation could lead to the conclusion that a less militant policy by a united people might have spared it disaster and exile. There is no way of knowing, and even contemporary analogies are not helpful. Would there be a State of Israel if the Yishuv had not resisted? But what kind of resistance are we discussing—the disciplined and restrained resistance of the Haganah or the more violent tactics of the latter-day Zealots, the Irgunists?

One matter, however, does seem certain. Even during the most critical period of national subjugation, the community was not monolithic in its confrontation with the adversary. It was deeply divided. Yohanan ben Zakkai, making his peace with Vespasian, was not a deviant, but a consistent champion of a widely held but embattled position. What is more, the Pharisaic conception of Judaism, which included not solely a territorial-cultic position, but an ethnic and universal one, ultimately gained the ascendancy and molded Jewish thought and existence. Thus, prophecy found its continuity in a popular movement and fixed the direction of Jewish aspirations, at least for the long exilic period.

It must be reiterated that Pharisaism did not represent a renunciation of the land, which it regarded as indispensable for the fulfillment of Israel's covenant relationship with God. Upon that sacred stage were to be enacted the sacral rites and obligations of the community. In addition, however, the Diaspora was to become an authentic part of Jewish experience and concern. We must, thus, be careful to distinguish between the Pharisaic strategy of submission and a totally un-Jewish concept of renunciation.

Let us not, therefore, equate the position of the Pharisees, as does Moore, with that of Paul: "Let everyone be in subjection to the authorities that are set over him, for no authority exists except by God's will."[11] We must remember the difference in motivation between the Pharisees and the early Christians, who had abrogated their claim upon worldly existence and submitted to temporal power because the true kingdom was not of this world. Pharisaic Judaism, believing as it did in the kingdom of heaven, also cherished Jewish existence in the Holy Land which God had allotted to Israel. If survival in the Holy Land was conditioned upon submission to Rome, the price would have to be paid. But submission had its limits, as it did with the early Christians, yet with a significant difference. Both early Christianity and Pharisaic Judaism agreed that there must be no obedience to the encroachment of tyranny upon the religious life of the community, but while in Christianity this took the form of disobedience without resistance, in Judaism it became open rebellion, as Akiba's part in the Bar Kokhba uprising attests.

It is in this light that we can understand the occasional benign references to the rule of a foreign power. Prayer for the welfare of the government "without the fear of which men would swallow each other up alive" represented a realistic awareness of the restraining power of government, but it was neither an endorsement of tyranny nor Judaism's exclusive judgment on political power. One of the most damning indictments of ruthless power was made by Rabbi Simeon bar Yohai, who overheard a conversation in which imperial Rome was praised for its fine forums, baths, and bridges. He commented: "They build forums in order to house harlots there, baths to refresh themselves in, bridges to collect tolls from them."

It is important that this attitude be understood lest we assume that rabbinic Judaism, like one aspect of New Testament Christianity, believed in the divine rule of kings. George Foote Moore cites references to prove that, according to the Talmud, "the kings of this earth rule by the appointment of Heaven." "Blessed is the All-merciful who has made the earthly royalty on the model of the heavenly and has invested you [Rome] with dominion."[12]

The most striking refutation of Moore comes from a passage that he himself cites:

> When Rabbi Jose ben Kisma was ill, Rabbi Hanina ben Tera-dyon went to visit him. He said to him: "Brother Hanina, do you not know that it is heaven that has ordained this [Roman] nation to reign? For though she has laid waste His House, burnt His Temple, slain His pious ones, and caused His best ones to perish, still she is firmly established! Yet, I have heard about you that you sit and occupy yourself with Torah, publicly gather assemblies, and keep a scroll of the law in your bosom." Hanina replied, "Heaven will show mercy."[13]

The significant point here is the pronouncement by Hanina ben Tera-dyon, who says, in effect, "The rule of Rome is transitory. It is not the wave of the future. God will employ it for whatever purposes He requires and will then discard it."

The isolated citations by Moore will not suffice to establish a normative Jewish view on the matter, and can be more than outweighed by extensive rabbinic references to the cruelty and injustice of Rome. "Why is Edom called a villain? Because it has filled the world with villainy."[14] The crucial difference in the Jewish view is that foreign domination over Israel is not part of the order of the universe but is, rather, a provisional means by which God manifests His providential care, or His displeasure with Israel. Temporal rule is not a divinely preconceived institution, like the Temple or the King-Messiah. It is, rather, one of God's many provisional devices for chastening or protecting His people. Earthly rule, either as God's surrogate or as the necessarily permanent condition because of man's innate depravity, is not authentic in rabbinic Judaism. On the contrary, invidious references to earthly sovereignty abound to the effect that the rule of kings is an intrusion upon the moral system of the universe, rather than indigenous to it. God is conceived as saying: "You asked for kings and when they felled you by the sword you cried out: 'We don't want the king to replace our original King. We want God, our King.'"[15] "Three things were given conditionally—Palestine, the Temple, and the dynasty of David."[16] "In days to come an arrogant king will rise upon a poor people, and he will 'obtain his rule by blandishments.'"[17] "They said to Nebuchadnezzar: 'If you impose a poll tax or a tax for crops on us, we will call you a king, but if you impose idolatry on us, you and a dog are the same.'"[18] "Fools despise knowledge; this is the evil kingdom which has not accepted the yoke of the kingdom of heaven."[19] "The kings of the heathens are like wild beasts trampling about in the woods in the middle of the night."[20]

We see, then, that out of the Pharisaic response to sovereignty—Jewish and foreign alike—two new elements entered into Jewish existence: a special kind of messianism, and a theology of Diaspora. They represented a response both to the power to which Israel was subjected, and to Israel's powerlessness to resist with the conventional weapons of national sovereignty. Neither of these could run its course without leaving some lasting impression upon Jewish history and thought.

12

Some Medieval Thinkers
on the Jewish King

Speculation about Jewish kingship is subordinate to messianic considerations in medieval Jewish thought. The Messiah embodied the dominant redemptive hopes while the king represented the ensuing Jewish sovereignty. Yet it is significant that kingship was considered as a political option at a time when Jewish aspirations gravitated chiefly toward the initiative of God in history. The viability of political concern as incorporated in theorizing about Jewish monarchy attests, thus, to a deep-seated temporal strain in Jewish thought despite centuries of depoliticization. Three approaches to the issue can be isolated—the acceptance of monarchy as divinely ordained and required; monarchy as implicit but subordinate to a higher value; and monarchy as optional and not a mitzvah. In this essay, these approaches are represented by Moses Maimonides, Judah Ha-Levi, and Isaac Abravanel respectively.

Transposed into a modern secular idiom, the speculations of these writers bear upon a wide range of political issues in contemporary Jewish life. Maimonides represents the most conservative, traditional approach, which regards monarchy (nationalism) as indispensable to Judaism. Judah Ha-Levi stresses prophecy (ethical Zionism) over monarchy, while the most radical is Abravanel, who challenges the claims of monarchy as the only legitimate expression of nationhood.

Maimonides considers kingship mandatory for Israel. "Israel was given the commandment, when they entered the land of Israel, to select for themselves a king, to destroy the memory of Amalek, and to build the Temple."[1] The initial refusal by Samuel to grant Israel a king did not reflect a rejection of monarchy, but was due to Israel's sinful motivation—its rejection of Samuel rather than its wish to fulfill a divine command.[2] The position of the king was so exalted, according to

Maimonides, that even a prophet had to prostrate himself before the king.[3] (But Maimonides also writes: "Whoever disregards the decree of the king because he is performing mitzvot, even a slight mitzvah, is exempt. And it goes without saying that if the king decrees that a mitzvah be nullified, he is not to be heeded.")[4]

Though Maimonides stresses the functions of the king rather than his limitations, yet it is apparent that he is not an absolute sovereign. For example, a king may not be elevated to office except by a court of seventy and by a prophet. A high priest is not required to come into the king's presence, and if he chooses to do so, he is not required to stand in the king's presence, although the king is required to stand in the presence of the high priest.[5]

What, then, are the king's functions? They are both generalized and specific. Generally, he is expected to advance the "true faith," to advance the cause of justice in the world, to overcome tyranny, and to wage the wars of the Lord.[6] Specifically, his task is to restore Israel's pristine national and spiritual condition. When he discusses kingship abstractly, Maimonides uses the term *melekh*. Yet in presenting the specific prospect of Israel's renewal, he writes of *ha-melekh ha-mashiah* (the King-Messiah). He insists upon the human and nonmiraculous as well as the historical character of this future sovereign. The Messiah is none other than the expected ruler of Israel, and Maimonides goes to great lengths to dispel any other notion.

> Let it not occur to you that the King-Messiah must perform signs and wonders or make innovations in the world, or resurrect the dead. . . . In the days of the Messiah . . . the world will go on in the usual way.[7]

Within the limits of the historical world, the King-Messiah will restore the dynasty of David, rebuild the Temple in Jerusalem, gather in the exiles, and restore all the laws that have fallen into disuse as a consequence of the destruction of the Temple. The test of authenticity is in the performance of the claimant. When Bar Kokhba failed in his mission, it was recognized that he was not the Messiah. The true Messiah will be a king from the House of David who will study the Torah, fulfill the written and oral law and succeed in restoring the Temple and in gathering in the dispersed, thereby fulfilling the requirements of leadership.[8]

This messianic rule will have moral consequences for both Israel and mankind, for the advent of the King-Messiah will be preceded by universal peace. Israel will have renounced any aggressive designs against other nations, and it will be free of the tyranny of oppressors. Famine, wars, envy, conflict, scarcity will cease from the earth, and the chief preoccupation of man will be to know God.[9]

It is important to note that in the fusion of king and Messiah into one personality, monarchy on the one hand is removed from the various categories of kingship that obtained in Maimonides' world, and messiahship, on the other, is secured to a worldly, historical base. Both elements in this combination represent a unique departure from conventional conceptions. The king segment of *melekh mashiah* does not fit the Aristotelian conception of the ruler as either a tyrant, an absolute monarch, a representative of the aristocracy, or a democratically constituted limited monarch; neither does the messianic segment conform with the eschatological and divine character of the Christian savior. The distinctive factor making for this differentiation lies in the distinctiveness of Jewish history—exile. This special condition requires a special response—historical redemption—which is antecedent to, and in a sense an earnest of, universal redemption. Before the king can rule, he must restore. Before he can reign, he must redeem. But his government must also usher in a new and different era in the history of the people and of humanity. This an ordinary king cannot do; only the Messiah can achieve it. In this fusion the king achieves a deeper dimension by performing messianic feats, while the Messiah plays a redemptive role within the confines of human affairs. Thus, the king is not a mere precursor to the Messiah, and the Messiah does not come to abrogate kingship; they are one and the same. The transition from early biblical monarchy transformed by prophecy is complete and irrevocable.

Judah Ha-Levi, in the twelfth century, and Abravanel in the fifteenth, were vigorous exponents of Jewish nationalism and detractors of Diaspora. While both saw Palestine as the means of rescuing the people from its degraded lot, they viewed restoration primarily in terms of the moral and spiritual, and not the political, consequences. The political implications of Palestine are muted.

Ha-Levi has been properly termed "the most national and the most patriotic of all Jewish poets." He regarded exile as a penalty for Israel's sins and as God's way of disciplining the people in the way of humility, as well as a way of cultivating the profound "love of this sacred place." He was irked by the complacency with which many Jews accepted a Diaspora existence, and he himself repudiated it by his pilgrimage to Palestine. Yet the national existence for which he yearned, both in his philosophical work, the *Kuzari*, and in his poetry, was predicated upon the people's religious rebirth, possible only in Palestine.

Both in the dispersion and in the expected restoration, Ha-Levi sees the unprecedented nature of Israel and its distinctiveness among the nations. The survival of Israel in the midst of exile distinguishes it from other conquered and obliterated nations, while its apparently moribund nature is sustained by the promise of ultimate redemption.[10]

To Ha-Levi, medieval Judaism's outstanding philosopher of Jewish history, both the land of Palestine and the ultimate restoration to it are part of a sacred relationship between the people and its God. The political note, the monarchical quest, are absent. While the yearning for restoration attains its most passionate articulation both in the poetry and in the philosophy, it is the covenantal character of the land which envelops Ha-Levi's thought. The land is endowed by God with a sacred character; the supreme events in the people's past transpired there, and the supreme fulfillment of the people's duties to God can be consummated only there.[11] The messianic goal is, of course, implicit, although it is subordinated to the acts of God in history, rather than to the manifestation of the Messiah. But the role of monarchy is not alluded to, and appears to have become subdued and indistinct. In its place, the land itself assumes a unique and hallowed character. Prophecy, not monarchy, is identified with Palestine.[12] The divine presence has a special affinity for the land. Prophets proclaimed their messages either in it or concerning it. The gift of prophecy was transmitted among Abraham's descendants and was retained by them as long as they remained in the land and fulfilled the requirements binding them to God. All this is predicated on the covenant God made with Abraham once he settled in Palestine. The highest spiritual fulfillment of the Jew can be achieved, therefore, only in Palestine, to which he must strive to go, even at the greatest sacrifice, and where alone he can discharge his most sacred duties.

Ha-Levi has been regarded as the Zionist par excellence of the Middle Ages, yet his Zionism, land-oriented as it is, concerns itself with renewing the covenant with God rather than with ancient power. "My longing for the living God has impelled me to seek the place of the throne of my anointed. . . . I have set my paths in the heart of the seas, so that I might find the footstool of my God."

We can best appreciate the radicalism of Abravanel in relationship to royal power when we understand that he is altogether opposed to the Maimonidean and the more generally accepted views of kingship as obligatory in Israel.

A refugee from Spain, where, as both courtier and exile, he tasted the extremes of royal favor and tyranny, Abravanel was concerned, as no other medieval Jewish scholar was, with the evils of monarchy and of human government. His work represents a response to two conceptions about the king: the prevailing Jewish one that Israel was required to have a king, and the Aristotelian view that concerned itself with the art of government in the ancient world. Abravanel was mindful of both conceptions and possibly, of the position of Aquinas on the role of kings. In a daring manner, he rejected the conventional Jewish view, and disposed of the Aristotelian position by declaring it to be relevant only for the non-Jewish world. In this way, he attempted to differentiate between a Jewish philosophy of government and that of other states and scholars.

In Abravanel we find a more extensive investigation of the concept of sovereignty than in any other medieval Jewish writer. This is initially due to his own political experience as a courtier under Ferdinand and Isabella of Spain, but his exile from Spain compelled an evaluation of the kind of sovereignty to which the Jewish people should aspire. To Abravanel, Israel is a nation, an *umah*, and there is no question about its redemption being contingent upon settlement in its land. God's covenantal promise of the land to the *umah ha-yisraelit* is irrevocable. "The inheritance of the land will not be withheld, either through the merit of the Canaanites or the sinfulness of the people of Israel."[13] "God has given the land to Israel as a bequest and as a full-fledged government."[14] "Divine Providence can adhere to the seed [of Abraham] only when they are in the holy land."[15] Israel, unlike other nations, is eternal and has a special relationship with God, but this relationship is conditioned by the inheritance of the land. "Your seed shall inherit the land of your sojourning; then will I be their God, not before."

Given this premise grounded in Jewish tradition, Abravanel develops a thesis which flows from the belief in Israel's differentiation from the nations and is predicated on the covenant relationship in which God fulfills the role of king over Israel. Therefore, monarchy is not even necessary to the Jewish nation! But is it not required, according to Scripture? Abravanel denies that it is, maintaining that it is only a concession to the people's insistence upon being like the other nations. Scripture does not *require* a king, but *permits* a king. It is remarkable that Abravanel ascribes this fatal predilection to the yetzer ha-ra, the evil inclination, which is usually identified with the aberrant sexual impulse. But to Abravanel, one of the most mischievous aspects of the yetzer ha-ra is that it seduces a whole people to place itself under the yoke of human domination. He refers to monarchy as a "cursed leprosy." "He who entrusts man with [power] gives it to a wild beast, for this is what his appetites sometimes make of him; for passion influences those who are in power, even the very best of men."[16]

It is also important to note that not the king, but the prophet, most authentically speaks for God. Moreover, *if* a king is to be selected, he must be God's choice, not the people's. Unlike Aristotle, who sees the ideal society as remote, Abravanel believes that it is attainable through the Torah. Aristotle's ideal of vesting supreme power in God and in the laws is, according to Abravanel, possible of fulfillment through God's moral legislation to Israel. While Abravanel acknowledges that he differs with the tradition on the mandatory nature of monarchy in Israel, his deviant position holds out many implications for us. That position may be summarized as follows: Kings may be selected in one of two ways—either, as in Israel, they submit to the laws of the Torah, or else, as among the nations of the world, they arbitrarily make their own laws and rule by decree. The first category, ordained by the Torah, is desirable, while the second is harmful, since the king, because of his absolute power, will not administer justice. When Israel demanded a king, it was in accordance with the second way, "so that we too might be like all the nations."[17]

Abravanel inquires into three problems: Is the rule of a king mandatory in a nation? Is it required for Israel as well as for other nations? Will Israel be required to have a king in the future? He cites Aristotle, who believes that kingship "is mandatory, and that the relationship of a king to the body politic is like the relationship of the heart to the body." Yet, disputing Aristotle, Abravanel feels that this must not be regarded as an immutable political law. The abominations of tyrants require that states should be governed by elected leaders, not kings, for fixed periods of time. In fact, such governments do exist, and, therefore, "the king is not mandatory, neither for the well-being, unity, or stability of the community." Abravanel concedes, however, that absolutism was the first form of government. "This cursed leprosy spread so that a man could arise to repress his people." Whether monarchy is absolute or limited, it is undesirable.

Yet even if it were to be admitted that kingship is mandatory among other nations, it is not for Israel.

> The reason for this is that the need for a king [among other nations] involves three functions: to save the people from their enemies, to arrange the customs and laws necessary for the well-being of the body politic, and, under special circumstances, to punish not in accordance to the law, which is compatible with absolute authority. These three functions are necessary for the

nations because they have no Torah or divine commandments, nor are they protected by divine providence in time of trouble. But the Israelite nation does not require any of these royal functions because . . . God fights for them. . . . "Moses commanded the Torah to us" . . . and God Himself [not the king] will make [legal] innovations in the time of need.[18]

Abravanel's third position follows. Israel was not commanded to have a king and need not have one when it is to be restored.

The commandment [to select a king] is dependent upon free choice. If you want to do this, *then* the king must be selected by God and from the midst of their brethren. . . . Israel was not commanded by the Torah concerning a king . . . since God fought for them, since they conducted themselves in accord with the Torah, and *since God's prophets were with them.* . . . Their sin was in rejecting divine kingship and in choosing human rule. [emphasis added][19]

It is all the more surprising that Abravanel is, nevertheless, opposed to deposing kings, even when they are tyrannical. The problem arises in his discussion of the passage *Zeh yihyeh mishpat ha-melekh* ("This should be the practice concerning the king").[20] He construes it to mean that the mishpat of the king will be evil. Yet while Aristotle, who conceives kingship to be as connected to government as the heart is to the body, endorses the overthrow of tyrants, Abravanel, who despises all forms of monarchy, rejects the deposing of kings. By what reasoning does he arrive at this conclusion? First, a people enters into an absolute covenant with a king when it enthrones him, and there can be no breach of that covenant. Second, "a king in a land is in place of God in the world." He is given absolute power, even to annul the general law, just as God can annul nature's law. These two arguments apply specifically to kingship among the nations, and what Abravanel seems to say is that if nations are foolish enough to accept kings over them, they must learn to endure them under all circumstances. Covenants cannot be abrogated, says Abravanel, who sees Israel under covenant with its own divine king.

It would appear also that Abravanel, adhering to Aristotle's distinction between kings and tyrants, wishes to preserve the lesser of two evils rather than run the risk of tyranny, which could follow in the wake of revolution. Aristotle writes: "A kingdom is formed to protect the better sort of people against the multitude, and kings are chosen . . . either for their superior virtue . . . or from their noble descent."[21] The tyrant, however, "is chosen out of the meanest populace." Kingly government should be preserved against overthrow, which brings tyranny and disorder in its wake. The king is the guardian of the community against anarchy; therefore, tyrants may be overthrown in order to reinstate benevolent kingship. Abravanel seems to say that for nations under moderately disposed kings, it is better to endure "the cursed leprosy" than to suffer a worse fate under their evil successors. As for Israel, this reasoning does not apply.

Abravanel's third argument against deposing kings applies specifically to Israel. Since the people does not have the authority to select a king, it has no authority to remove him. The selection of a king is God's alone ("You shall take for you a king whom the Lord your God chooses"). The people, therefore, do not have authority to rebel, even if the king is a tyrant, but "they should cry out to God who rules above the kingship of man."[22]

The disparity of views concerning monarchy reflects an openness to the subject which belies all monolithic views normally attributed it. Amidst debates raging on Jewish nationalism today, all concerned must be impressed both by the diversity of views and the radicalism of Abravanel, whose Jewish authenticity cannot be challenged by the equally authentic nationalists among us.

13

Are We in Exile?

When Diaspora becomes malignant it is Galut. Consider French Jewry directly before and after June 1967. Through the retrospective eyes of an American Jew, Golden Age Spanish Jewry lived in Diaspora, but we know it to have been Galut.

Not until the Emancipation were fine distinctions made between Diaspora and Galut. Existence, however benign, outside the land of Israel was exile, not merely historical and physical but a breach in the cosmic scheme of things, which had to be, and would be, rectified. The distinction was made with increasing finality in the Western world where, too hastily, Jews felt themselves released from exile by their native lands, where they believed they had at last found permanence. Many were ready to surrender the identity of the Jewish people (except for certain religious differentiations, which were stripped of all ethnic contexts) in return for personal liberation from the Galut stigma. This was an overeager, but understandable, response to the variously proclaimed slogan originating in Emancipation France: "For the Jews as individuals, everything; for the Jews, as a people, nothing." The formula did not work because the collective identity of the people could not be shed.

Theodor Herzl came to his Zionist solution only after he had abandoned as hopeless his scheme to persuade the Pope to accept all nonadult Jews into the Church. (For Jews who reject the principle of Jewish survival, the thesis underlying Herzl's scheme is valid and still applicable on the American scene. This essay is not concerned with them but only with those to whom the survival of the people is significant.) The glaring error in the rejection of peoplehood lay in the failure of emancipated Jewry to recognize that as long as there was a Jewish people by the millions in Eastern Europe, and as long as that people languished in Galut, Diaspora was not a permanent, triumphant reality but a tentative, vulnerable possibility. This was to be cataclysmically demonstrated by the Dreyfus prologue and by the apocalypse of Auschwitz.

Thus far, only the experience of Jews in the English-speaking world has validated the use of the term *Diaspora*. For other Jewries, it has proved to be a fatal illusion. Even in the post–World War II world, emancipated Russian Jewry finds itself plunged back into Galut, and French Jewry once again is confronted with attacks upon its loyalty to the state. To be sure, segments of those Jewries do not feel that their status is endangered, and at least subjectively they are not in Galut. But by the same standard, those who do feel a radical deterioration of their status experience Galut.

If the American Jew looks to our history for precedent, he will find little that is reassuring. He can rely only on his belief in the radical uniqueness of the American experience, which for less than a century has been an unparalleled success story. But we must stress—for less than a century. For the American Jew for whom this nation has finally resolved the contingent Jewish condition, the United States is beyond Diaspora. It is the ultimate leveler of all extraneous distinctions, the ultimate guarantor of inalienable rights. This claim is based on America's drastic severance from the deep-rooted bigotries of Europe and its record of constitutional protections. But neither history nor law offers adequate protection against human irrationality. Both the irrationality of bigotry, fostered by national adversity, and the irrationality of revolution, prompted by justifiable or unjustifiable despair, are familiar foes of the Jewish people. The ground for both is being assiduously seeded. Should either prevail, and the Jewish community must take a stand along both fronts, Galut will have come to America. In a sense, revolution is the more insidious enemy of the Jewish people, because it invariably comes with the pretense of resolving the Jewish problem and ends up with the expulsion of even the most faithful Jews from its ranks. This is basic Marx. For the unconvinced, even the most recent example in Poland will not be illustrative. Gilboa, one of the editors of *Maariv*, wrote, "The Trotskys make revolutions and the Bronsteins pay for them."

If Jewish history is so contingent even in America, this alone is Galut. If Jews begin to ask, "Can it happen here?" that is Galut. Should our apprehensions prove to be unfounded, the possibilities which reasonable Jews envisage place them in Galut. This is not to say that Galut is "merely" a psychological condition. The very realities of historical possibility, which are intrinsic to the land and its people, reduce us to Galut status. Members of the black community ask the same questions, and presently offer more somber answers. The questions are not minimized when we say that even the three-centuries-old black issue in America will be resolved before the two-millennia-old issue of the Jewish people in the world will be put to rest.

There is a qualitative difference between both tragic issues, in that hostility to blacks, irrational as it is, springs from social, economic, and historical roots, while anti-Semitism is still the product of a diseased world consciousness which sees the Jews as allied with demonic conspiratorial forces in history. The medieval theology of the Jew as the devil's agent, poisoning wells and sacrificing Christian children, thus leading to the Crusades, has been transferred to the secular doctrine of the Elders of Zion conspiring against Christendom at the Prague cemetery and leading to Auschwitz. This dybbuk, lurking for ages in the psyche of the Western world, has not been exorcised, and to mistake remission for cure is to do a frightful disservice to the Jewish people. The last lines of Camus's *Plague* could have been written about our condition.

> As he listened to the cries of joy rising from the town, Rieux remembered that such joy is always imperiled. He knew what those jubilant crowds did not know but could have learned from books: that the plague bacillus never dies or disappears for good; that it can lie dormant for years and years in furniture and linen-chests; that it bides its time in bedrooms, cellars, trunks, and bookshelves; and that perhaps the day would come when, for the bane and the enlightening of men, it would rouse up its rats again and send them forth to die in a happy city.[1]

Certainly such a condition is not confined to the Jews alone. It might be said with some justification that all mankind, unfulfilled and facing possible apocalypse, is also in Galut. If the purpose of such an assertion is to stress that Israel is not alone on the precipice of history, the assertion is true. The Western world enters upon an exile of its own as it confronts the possibility of its own twilight—the end of its physical and spiritual hegemony in the world. But if this is meant to equate the Jewish with the human experience (and the Jew also shares in the human experience), then the Jewish condition is robbed of all meaning. It is to make Auschwitz and its moral issues another strategic (and avowedly hideous) operation like Hiroshima; Warsaw and its moral issues another stupid police action like Watts. Galut means a condition which is Israel's alone even when the Messiah has come for all the world. In *Canticle for Leibowitz*, the eternal Jew scrutinizes a savior in an age to come and says, "He's not the one."[2] Galut means permanence, continuing beyond world improvement, beyond the restoration of Jews to Israel, racing with God to the end of days.

At the very best, Diaspora waits with a metaphorical suitcase. Nevertheless, Diaspora-Galut is now intrinsic to the Jewish condition, and we will have to confront it. More of this later.

Galut is more than political and historical precariousness. It is also a condition of the inner and collective life of the Jewish people. While we must exert every effort to create a satisfying Jewish culture in America, we will fail if we look to our own resources alone. No amount of indignation will alter the fact that without Israel, with all its imperfections, American Jewry, especially after Auschwitz, would be morally and culturally lost. Intermarriage is making steady inroads into the Jewish community. It has been defended by some as a process by which non-Jews are won for Judaism. But how can we defend a new phenomenon, the co-officiating by rabbis with Christian clergymen in churches at weddings of Jews and Christians? The fact that there has been no outcry against a practice clearly contrived to dissolve Jewish individuality is indicative of dangerous lethargy within Jewish life. This lethargy is the product of various factors—a Jewish education which by its very nature cannot by itself resist the erosion of Jewish commitment; Jewish homes which are bereft of Jewish identity; Jewish youths who in their multitudes reject the Jewish community for both valid and invalid reasons; the leveling of the distinctions between Judaism, Christianity, and secularism, which would lead to the rejection of Judaism even if the Jewish establishment were above reproach. This is Galut, and our greatest exertions will not overcome it with American Jewish resources alone. Islands of Jews will persist as committed Jews. Vast numbers of Jews will prosper as Jews who possess identity and nothing else. But Judaism as an American product will fight a losing battle. I cite from two essays by confirmands concerning their self-image as Jews:

> Other people have labelled me as a Jew because I have a big nose and my mother wears a full length mink coat. People see us go mysteriously out all dressed up on Friday night. We may have a *mezuzah* on our front door, we always have hundred dollar bills falling out of our pockets. . . .

> I'll tell you that if I had my druthers, I'd not be a Jew. It's too hard, and the risks outweigh the rewards.

The condition illustrated by these adolescent comments is more than qualitatively, though not quantitatively, offset by the proliferation of Jewish day schools and university departments of Jewish studies. But if they should contribute to a recrudescence of Jewish depth and consciousness, it would be closely related to the reawakening of Jewish concern accompanying the restoration of Israel. Had the Second World War brought the Jewish people nothing but Auschwitz, the Jewish world would have fallen into a moral and spiritual decline which would have allowed for neither Jewish studies nor massive response to Jewish misfortune abroad. When the collapse of the Shabbetai Tzevi messianic movement occurred, it took over a century for the Jewish people to emerge from despair and deterioration. Auschwitz only, without the redeeming quality of Israel, would have plunged us into perhaps final breakdown.

For this reason, any effort to impose a theological purpose on two thousand years of Galut is to deliberately misread all the signs. Jewish theology and the Jewish prayer book ruled out any mitigating characteristics of Galut. When they dealt with it, they expressed a single wish: "God, get us out of here so that we can resume our fit place in your scheme of things." Galut was barely tolerable because it was offset, in hope and in vision, by *geulah* ("redemption"). Remove the messianic hope and you remove all basis for persisting Jewish existence. In our day, no concern with Auschwitz can possibly have authenticity without comparable concern with Jerusalem and, of course, vice versa. They are historically linked. Without Jerusalem, the remnants of Auschwitz would have gone mad. Without Auschwitz, Jerusalem would not have risen. By this I mean that the world's callousness to Jewish suffering was sufficiently softened to permit Jerusalem. In the religious scheme of Judaism, there had to be Jerusalem after Auschwitz as there had to be Sinai after Pithom and Raamses.

Yet until the middle of the twentieth century, wasn't Jewish life in Galut authentic? Therefore, why can't American Jewish life be authentic? Where Jewish life was indeed authentic, it was due, paradoxically, to the fact that Jews knew they were living in Galut and were exerting all their moral power to resist its encroachment. Bent of *geulah,* and settling for nothing less, they established a communal and religious system intended to enable them to wait out the Galut. But this is only part of the story. Often enough, when waiting became unbearable, even the sacred community broke down in different times and places. No one who rhapsodizes over the shtetl can escape the grim and repellent realities of Shmarya Levin's hometown in *Childhood in Exile.* What saved such communities from the ultimate consequences of Galut was the redeeming hope held forth by Eretz Yisrael. Authenticity? It can no more be for either an impoverished Soviet Jewry or an opulent American Jewry totally devoid of Israel than there can be for a person taken in childhood from a mother. Therefore, the counsel offered that each community go it alone is a counsel of suicide (which is an option, but one that most Jews reject). Both Israelis who wish to break (or radically weaken) all ties with Galut and American Jews who would have us phase out connections with Israel really seek the end of the Jewish people. American Jewry, with a hard-core and Israel-connected exception, would peacefully dissolve, as Sephardic Jewry in the South has faded into the Presbyterian churches. Israeli Jewry, with a hard-core religiously impassioned exception, would become either a latter-day Sparta or another languid Lebanon.

Galut has no purpose. It is not a goal but a condition. Medieval and more recent Jewries made something luminous of that condition. They did not choose to venture on a world-mission or to be a light to the nations. Whatever they became to the world was process, not purpose. Similarly, having said what needs to be said about contemporary Galut, it must be added that it will continue indefinitely and that we will have to confront it as effectively and creatively as possible. For the first time in almost two millennia, the contours of Galut have changed. It is not absolute, since Israel modifies it. Theoretically and practically, a Jew in the West need no longer reside in Galut. He has an option not enjoyed by any Jew since the loss of Jewish sovereignty. But for a vast segment of Western Jewry, for all kinds of good and bad reasons, Galut continues, but in relationship with Israel.

Since 1948, the structure of Jewish life has changed from Galut to Galut-Israel. Formerly a unicum in history by virtue of total uprootedness, we are now another kind of unicum by virtue of our dual existence as a people, not only of West and East but a sovereign and a universal people at once, an amphibian people occupying land and also the ever-shifting seas of Galut, benign or malignant. This complicates life for us and is part of the world's new and vexing confrontation with the problem of Jewish peoplehood. The world is having a difficult time absorbing this new definition of peoplehood, and we are having a difficult time conveying its meaning. Aside from the political struggles raging around Israel, the secular world finds it painful to live with a people that insists on an asymmetrical conception of itself, just as the Christian world has difficulty reconciling itself to the return home of the Wandering Jew, doomed by God to eternal expulsion for a cosmic crime. This new image is the product of our history, not our theology, just as Bruno Bettelheim points out that part of the radical structure of the kibbutz is the product of original necessity. But this does not minimize the significance of what the Jewish people has become, a becoming which is far more revolutionary than anything achieved by alienated young Jews.

Yet while Israel in Galut and in the state is at the very center of world events, compelling the nations to confront the issues stemming from our existence, we must be modest about our claims to moral leadership. If light is brought to the nations, it is not by ourselves alone. Every people seeking life in the face of oppression and hostility is a light to the world. It is presumptuous for Jews, especially in Galut, to speak of "perfecting the world" when we know that world perfection cannot come from a prosperous, successful, "all-rightnik" Western Jewry, but only from the dispossessed and the betrayed. In this context, Israel is more universalist than we are, refusing to arrogate to itself a spurious mission which our very condition belies, but working as best it can with or against other nations in the struggle for a peaceful world. I do not suggest that we abandon the concept of *tikkun olam*, the perfection of the world, but that we do not betray that concept by merely bandying it about in our cabanas. Nor is that task the monopoly of the Jewish people.

Stress upon the centrality, but not the totality, of Israel does not suggest that Jewish existence in the state can be complete. When or where has it ever been complete? All we can say of the possibilities is that Jewish existence in the state can be more viable than anywhere else.

On a folk level, we are discovering with increasing clarity that Jewish knowledge and commitment are more readily acquired by our young people through visits to Israel than by any other means. Some may return from Israel as uncommitted as when they arrived, but, for the most part, Israel represents a dramatic turning point for them. Our schools simply cannot compare to the intensity of the Israel experience, and our instructors are wise in turning toward a systematic program along those lines. On the academic level, the mastery of Hebrew, and through it of our classical sources, is being radically accelerated by Israel's living culture. American Jewish life will be greatly enriched by this venture. The viability of Jewish life in Israel, with all its imperfections, lies in its comprehensiveness, while Galut Jewish life must always differentiate between itself and the overwhelming non-Jewish culture enveloping it. The incessant burden of winnowing out the Jewish from the non-Jewish is a neurotic exercise which serves to irritate, to alienate, to reduce the Jewish experience to games about Judaism, not necessarily in Judaism.

All this is not to suggest that the land or the state is the source of

Jewish viability. Neither land nor state is endowed with any special sanctity. They are the vessels within which the creative capacities of the people can be cultivated, the body within which the spirit of the community may have the opportunity to flourish. In a nation-obsessed world, we must be careful to distinguish between the mystique of the state itself and the powers, for good or ill, which can be released within that state. The primary category in Judaism is the people, but a classical condition for the people's well-being is the land.

The people Israel opposes Galut. The State of Israel makes inroads against Galut. So it must be. But Galut endures.

Can there ever be a true end to Galut? Not by the ingathering of all Jews to Israel, not by the disappearance of Jewish communities throughout the world. How then? By the elimination of tribal nationalism among all men, by the emergence of world government so that all men, wherever they might dwell, would enjoy two homes—their own lands and the world community. And the new Jewry, living both on its own soil and in the world, may yet point the way to this nobler existence for all humanity.

14

Religious Meanings in Jewish Secularism

Ever since the Exodus, the land of Israel, the history of Israel, and the people of Israel have been examined in religious terms. In our own time, all three have become secularized for both Jews and non-Jews, but the religious components of these three elements still have binding power. In terms of the immediacy of Jewish existence, the politics of land, current events, and people appear to predominate. But in long-range terms, as we try to envision the goals of Judaism, the moral and religious factors are indispensable to the continued existence of the people and its still unfolding life-style.

In Jewish tradition, the land of Israel, and particularly Jerusalem, are earthly counterparts of heavenly realities. We are told that Moses built the wilderness sanctuary from a design imparted to him by God. Jerusalem too is the product of a cosmic model. Thus, in Jewish tradition, place is invested with sanctity. So is the people, which is summoned to be holy and a kingdom of priests. As for Jewish history, it is informed with a sacred content that permeates all the biblical writ and the mass of Jewish literature down to modern times. In that context, Jewish history is the record of God's people, moving toward its land, flourishing or struggling within its land, expelled from its land, all within the cosmic design of the God who had brought that people into the covenant. All this is sufficiently familiar and serves only as background in our search for the religious implications of land, history, and people in a postexilic age.

The term *postexilic* aptly introduces us to the true dimensions of the land of Israel in recent and present Jewish experience. One cannot understand the attachment of even the most secularized Jew to the land without understanding the meaning of exile, Galut, which was the

Jewish people's lot for almost two millennia. To see the land in national terms alone is not necessarily to see it falsely; it is to take a shortcut, thus eliminating a major part of the road leading to the land. Jewish nationalism has a good deal in common with modern nationalism. It manifested itself with intensified vigor after the middle of the nineteenth century. It emerged, seething with fervor, from the caldron of European life. But to equate it with European nationalism is to ignore a substantial element which is missing elsewhere. For many emergent nations, the missing factor was sovereignty. For the Jewish people, the missing factor was place. However difficult the lot of oppressed nationals was in Europe, they were at home, even though strangers ruled over them (as today in Czechoslovakia). Grievous as their condition was, not they but their oppressors were the strangers. For the Jewish people, the essential element in their condition was total alienation from everything the ancestral land meant to them. Galut meant being torn out of the orbit of accustomed existence, with all the agonies that severance brought; indeed one rabbi referred to Galut as a breach in the order of the cosmos.

Jewish nationalism began, not in the nineteenth century, but on the day the Jewish people found itself expelled from its land. Then the whole dynamic of Jewish existence turned toward righting the moral imbalance and to restoring the people to its place. It was nationalistic in impulse but messianic in content. That is to say, the people looked to God rather than to human agents to restore their fortunes. Nevertheless, medieval Jewish history is full of examples of individual Jews and Jewish communities making their way over brigand-infested highways and pirate-plagued seas toward Palestine.

It would be an oversimplification to say that the flight from Galut was only a flight from persecution, though this was a most important factor. But Galut meant something more to many Jews; namely, spiritual alienation so long as they could not completely and freely share in the world into which they had been thrust. In monolithic Christian Europe, religious as well as cultural pluralism was heresy; and for Jews who clung to their faith, anything less than the unconditional fulfillment of Judaism was Galut. What they experienced, without verbalizing it in twentieth-century terms, was that no society and none of its individual members can achieve inner fulfillment when uprooted from their territory or cut off from contact with it. This is true of men and animals alike. The most striking example of this nonpolitical compulsion is the response of a group of thoroughly secularized Russian Jews in the early stages of the Zionist movement toward the end of the nineteenth century. The founder of political Zionism, Theodor Herzl, had been offered the territory of Uganda as an interim homeland for the oppressed Jews of Eastern Europe. By reason both of their secularism and of the desperate plight of the millions of Russian Jews they represented, it could have been assumed that the Zionist leaders would seize the opportunity thus offered. Yet they rejected it, insisting they could regard no place as their homeland except the land of Israel. In so doing they made a religious assertion, predicated upon a popular perception of the meaning of homelessness which was eventually to be interpreted in psychological-religious terms.

Interestingly enough, two secularist Jews were the earliest agents in isolating this factor. One was an Odessa physician, Leon Pinsker; the other a Viennese journalist, Theodor Herzl. Both men were as-similationists at the beginning of their careers; they were driven to their Zionist positions both by the realities of Jewish history and by the psychological consequences of those realities. Dr. Pinsker, writing in 1882, saw the Jewish people as hated and feared not for political or economic but for pathological reasons. Because the Jews were homeless, they were regarded as a fearsome ghost haunting the world, which was bent on exorcising and eliminating them. He said:

> Among the living nations of the earth the Jews occupy the position of a nation long since dead. . . . The world saw in this people the uncanny form of one of the dead walking among the living. . . . If the fear of ghosts is something inborn, and has a certain justification in psychic life of humanity, what wonder that it asserted itself powerfully at the sight of this dead and yet living nation? . . . Judeo-phobia is a form of demonopathy . . . a psychic aberration transmitted for two thousand years, and it is incurable.[1]

In linking anti-Semitism with the occult, with ghosts and demons, Dr. Pinsker opened up a new approach to the problem of anti-Semitism for which he has not been properly credited. Recently, however, his contribution has been extensively treated by Joshua Trachtenberg (in *The Devil and the Jews*) and by Norman Cohn (in *Warrant for Genocide*). Trachtenberg documents the thesis that from the early Middle Ages on, hatred of the Jew is related to a deep-seated theological and popular conviction that the Jew is literally in league with the devil. The continued existence of this conquered and exiled people was explained in terms of their alliance with the supernatural forces of darkness, which used Israel as the instrument of their malign plottings against humanity; that is, the ghostly people and the satanic hosts were joined in combat against the Christian world. Thus Israel was not an ordinary enemy; it was the ally of the archdemon himself, to overcome whom was the Christian's religious duty. Similarly, Cohn writes:

> The deadliest kind of anti-Semitism, the kind that results in massacre and attempted genocide, has little to do with real conflicts of interest between living people, or even with racial prejudice as such. At its heart lies the belief that Jews form a conspiratorial body set on ruining and then dominating the rest of mankind. And this belief is simply a modernized, secularized version of the popular medieval view of Jews as a league of sorcerers employed by Satan for the spiritual and physical ruination of Christendom.[2]

In the light of this "devil doctrine," it is no wonder that two of the most obsessed anti-Semites of our age, Hitler and Stalin, saw the Jewish people in conspiratorial and demonic terms and applied to them such sinister epithets as "rootless cosmopolitans" and "international Jewry."

If Dr. Pinsker gave us the first clue to the demonic factor in anti-Semitism, it was Theodor Herzl who stumbled upon a second. This was the theological importance of Jewish exile to Christian thought. Central to this understanding was the notion that Israel has been condemned by God Himself to suffer eternal wandering because of a dual sin: deicide and the rejection of Christ. Obviously, this idea had been basic to Christian thought for a long time, but Herzl quite accidentally brought it into the open. In January 1904 he went to the Vatican to intercede with Pope Piux X in behalf of a Jewish state in Palestine. He recorded the following conversation in his diary:

> [The Pope] answered: "We are unable to favor this movement. We cannot prevent the Jews from going to Jerusalem—but we could never sanction it. The ground of Jerusalem, if it were not always sacred, has been sanctified by the life of Jesus Christ. As the head of the Church I cannot answer you otherwise. The Jews have not recognized our Lord, therefore we cannot recognize the Jewish people. I know, it is disagreeable to see the Turks in possession of our Holy Places. We simply have to put up with it. But to sanction the Jewish wish to occupy these sites, that we cannot do."
>
> I said that we based our movement solely on the sufferings of the Jews, and wished to put aside all religious issues.
>
> "Yes, but we, but I as the head of the Catholic Church, cannot

do this. One of two things will likely happen. Either the Jews will retain their ancient faith and continue to await the Messiah who we believe has already appeared—in which case they are denying the divinity of Jesus and we cannot assist them. Or else they will go there with no religion whatever, and then we can have nothing at all to do with them.

"The Jewish faith was the foundation of our own, but it has been superseded by the teachings of Christ, and we cannot admit that it still enjoys any validity. The Jews who should have been the first to acknowledge Jesus Christ have not done so to this day."

But, Holy Father, the Jews are in a terrible plight. . . . We need a land for these harried people.

"Must it be Jerusalem?"

We are not asking for Jerusalem, but for Palestine—for only the secular land.

"We cannot be in favor of it."

Does Your Holiness know the situation of the Jews?

"Yes, from my days in Mantua, where there are Jews. I have always been in friendly relations with Jews. Only the other evening two Jews were here to see me. There are other bonds than those of religion: social intercourse, for example, and philanthropy. Such bonds we do not refuse to maintain with the Jews. Indeed we also pray for them, that their spirit see the light. This very day the Church is celebrating the feast of an unbeliever who became converted in a miraculous manner—on the road to Damascus. And so, if you come to Palestine and settle your people there, we will be ready with churches and priests to baptize all of you."[3]

Thus the first recorded theological objection to Zionism is a reaffirmation of the principle that Israel occupies, and must continue to occupy, the role of Cain, who killed his younger brother because God favored that brother. The wandering exile eventually emerges as a demonic figure. One remembers Augustine's linking of Cain with the building of the first city, the embodiment of everything that is evil in human society.

We come now to that juncture in history where the Jewish people has broken the two-thousand-year syndrome of Galut, has returned to its ancestral land and thereby shaken to the roots the Cain theory and all its implications. For those who adhere to that theory and have theological reservations about the State of Israel, its rebirth raises extensive issues. Within Catholicism a far-ranging reassessment of this question is taking place, a reassessment that diverges radically from the position of Pope Piux X. The fact is that if exile was an indispensable factor in generating the demonic myth of anti-Semitism, restoration is an indispensable factor in dissipating it, though like any plague, anti-Semitism will not soon or easily be eradicated.

The second religious element in contemporary Jewish existence lies in the uniqueness of Jewish history. The determinism generally operative in the rise and fall of civilizations has not applied to the Jewish people. Ingenious attempts have been made to prove that this people exists only as a fossil, but who can take such theories seriously after the emergence of the Jewish state? In contrasting Jewish history with that of other civilizations that have passed through the cycle of birth, maturity, and death, I refer not merely to the continuity of Jewish history, but rather to the fact that the Jewish people, as a covenant people, has passed through the historical orbit in cycle after cycle and still returned to the world as *the* people that traces its origins to Sinai. Somehow Israel has again and again emerged from death and undergone transfiguration. If Easter is the sign of the resurrected Christ, Passover is the sign of the resurrected Israel.

The paradigm for Jewish history is, of course, the Exodus, where a number of factors converge: Israel confronts power; Israel is on the threshold of death; Israel emerges from death. Israel experiences a moment of transcendent illumination which shapes its history for generations to come. Israel turns toward the land of promise as the means by which it hopes to attain its fulfillment. At several great turning points in Jewish history this paradigm has worked itself out, notably the Babylonian exile and the confrontation with Rome. Although the Roman episode led to destruction and exile, the survival of the people as a living community was made possible by their tenacious clinging to the messianic hope kept alive by their inflexible confidence in their ultimate restoration.

In our own day, the original paradigm is dwarfed by the awesome dimensions of Auschwitz and Jerusalem restored. I insist upon joining these two places, which represent in almost cosmic terms both the polarity of the Jewish experience in the twentieth century and the validity of the theme of death and transfiguration in Jewish history. We simply distort and desecrate Jewish history if we speak of Auschwitz alone. Whatever the oscillations of the political and military events in the Middle East, the creation of Israel—or, better, the reappearance of the Jewish commonwealth after two millennia of submergence—must challenge our religious sensibilities.

But we have to begin with the somber recognition that Auschwitz was not only a prelude to Jerusalem, but the event without which Jerusalem would not have taken place. I disavow the belief that God required Auschwitz as a precondition for Jerusalem; this would be the act not of a god but of a demon. But I affirm that men and nations were moved to allow Jerusalem only because they had consented to, and been implicated in, Auschwitz. In Auschwitz, which is of course the symbol of every death camp, every ghetto, every ditch where Jews tumbled into graves dug by their own hands, the Jewish people came face to face with annihilation. And in Auschwitz, as in Egypt, Babylon, and Rome, the Jewish people came up against the incarnation of power. At that moment in our history, the inexplicable element in the Jewish experience came to pass: the rebirth of the people. A legend has it that on the day the Temple in Jerusalem was destroyed, the Messiah was born. This is a metaphoric description of the simultaneous process of death and renewal which animates Jewish history.

Jerusalem is far more than a symbol of the creation of the State of Israel. It represents the rebirth of the entire Jewish people. But above all, it speaks of the resiliency of Jewish history, which follows its own unique course. While it is much too soon to speak definitively of the meaning of this moment, one can suggest that it has something to say to a Western world bedeviled by doubts about its own destiny, by a sense of insecurity heightened by its own deterministic theories on the rise and fall of empire. Just when the West is seized by this insecurity, Israel, like Joseph of old, rises from the pit and promises to enter upon a new existence. This is doubly remarkable in view of the traditional view of Judaism as crushed and debilitated. A famous medieval statue in the Strasbourg Cathedral depicts the Church as a strong and beautiful young woman standing triumphant over a feeble, crouching old crone symbolizing the Synagogue. Similar statues are to be seen in church after church in the Rhineland. Perhaps it was so often copied in the Middle Ages because of a need for reassurance that the Synagogue had really been vanquished, although the collective unconscious may have had reason to be unsure.

In this day, no historical event except Jerusalem could have rescued the Jewish people from the utter despair in the wake of Auschwitz. Auschwitz alone would have been impossible to bear. A vast volume of Holocaust and post-Holocaust literature has developed portraying the emergence of the Jewish people from its ordeal. Virtually every effort of the people was directed toward getting out of the European graveyard; and not that alone, but opening a road to the land of Israel. As soon as the death camps began to be liberated, the remaining energies of the last remnants were unleashed in an impassioned drive toward what was then Palestine. Had there been no Palestine, the ensuing moral break-down would have been unimaginable. Not only the remnants in Europe, but Jews all over the world, would have been engulfed in a spiritual chaos to overcome which would have taken centuries if not forever.

I cite a single corroborating incident. In the mid-1930s, the condition of the Jews in Poland was rapidly deteriorating. Government-inspired attacks upon the Jewish population, massive poverty, and the refusal of the British government to permit large-scale immigration to Palestine combined to create an intolerable situation. In 1936, when the World Jewish Congress met for its first, organizing session in Geneva, its officials were approached by representatives of Polish Jewish youth and told that hundreds of these young Jews were planning to surround the building where the Congress was being held and to commit suicide as an act of defiance against their lot and the silence of the world. They were dissuaded by the Congress leaders. But their plan revealed how deep was the sense of futility in Europe even before Auschwitz. The creation of Israel, as well as the prior longing for Israel, made life endurable for multitudes whose only alternative was self-destruction or madness.

Bruno Bettelheim, in *The Informed Heart,* tells us that only two categories of Jews were able to overcome the dehumanizing effects of the concentration camps in the earlier years of the Nazi tyranny: the utterly devout Hasidim, and the Zionists, who had been in training for migration to Palestine.[4] At first glance it would appear that these two groups could not possibly have anything in common. The Hasidim adhered to a pietistic eighteenth-century life-style which was the antithesis of the secularist, nationalist twentieth-century view of the Zionists. But on closer scrutiny it becomes apparent that both groups shared a common Jewish value: a messianic belief. Each clung to a specific aspect of Jewish messianism, and both aspects are legitimate and inherent in the tradition. The Hasidim, like their medieval ancestors, lived and died in the conviction that it was under supernatural circumstances that the Messiah would be sent forth by God to release His children. They were ready to wait, however long, for the advent of the Messiah. A report from the Holocaust symbolizes this patient waiting. It tells of a father holding his son at the edge of a pit into which they are soon to fall before Nazi bullets, and the father is pointing toward heaven.

This Hasidic view is in keeping with one tradition, which speaks of the Messiah tugging at his chains and pleading with God to let him go out into the world. But another tradition is that the Messiah would be a human descendant of King David and would appear in the midst of the historical process. Moses Maimonides cautioned the Jewish people not to expect the Messiah to be a supernatural being or to perform supernatural events; he would be a historical person bringing rescue to the people, restoration to its land, and a reign of justice and peace.

The Zionists, prompted by this second messianic view, transposed it into secular terms, which involved two radical changes: first, the Messiah's advent was not to be awaited but induced; second, the people, not any one individual, acted messianically. The first change, by the way, was not as radical as it may seem. During the Middle Ages some Jewish mystics engaged in occult practices by which they hoped to prod the Messiah into entering the world in their time. And the number of instances in which messianic pretenders, self-deceived or otherwise, were received by the Jewish community with frenzied joy would indicate with what desperate impatience Jews awaited their release. But however the Zionists transformed the messianic idea, they saw it as part of the authentic tradition of Judaism. The messianic expectation and its fulfillment, even if on the most precarious and tentative terms, was indispensable not only for the people's physical and political well-being, but for its rescue from moral collapse.

I do not wish to suggest that the creation of the State of Israel represents *the* fulfillment of the messianic dream. But I believe that the existence of the State of Israel is an absolute prerequisite to the fulfillment of that hope. Above all, Jerusalem is the historical necessity that makes Auschwitz, not comprehensible, not acceptable, but susceptible to being transcended by a living Jewish people. Jerusalem tells us not only that Jewish history continues, but that Jewish history is more than a tale told by an idiot. It awakens the consciousness of the Jew as one restored to the historical processes of his people. No other event has made the Jew as existentially aware of his identity and of his personal involvement in Jewish history as has Jerusalem. Auschwitz alone would have shattered this identity and reduced this involvement to that of a bit of debris flung along on the crest of an angry torrent. But Jerusalem gives the Jew an awareness that he is not altogether the creature of inexorable external forces.

Neither the Jew nor any other man anywhere can lay claim to total freedom. But for the Jew, just to have entered Jerusalem is an act of freedom denied him for two millennia, an act which tells him, even in these extremely contingent times for himself and the world, that redemption, however circumscribed, is possible.

Redemption, an essential aspect of the messianic hope, has never faded from the prayers and visions of the Jew. Jerusalem proves that it is not an impossible dream. And Jerusalem sharpens the consciousness of the Jew that he is part of the redemptive process. The Haggadah, the book out of which the Jew tells the story of Egyptian bondage and Exodus, states: "In every generation one must see himself as though he personally went forth from Egypt." Until this age, re-enactment of the Exodus was largely a fantasy return to the past, a wry play-acting, and at best a poignant hope. Today the reminder that present reality is compatible with the Exodus is an immediate reality. I can best describe the Jew's feelings about Jerusalem by citing the words of a teenager of my congregation on his return from Israel: "Whenever at our services, I would hear the words, 'We are standing within your gates, Jerusalem,' I would say, 'So what'; and then when I stood at the Western Wall, I suddenly realized, it's true, I'm really here."

Let us consider now the people Israel, which means the restoration of the covenant. Since political considerations are not germane here, the fact that covenant plays no role in politics is irrelevant. Yet it must be added that even among those who are not theologically oriented, the events of our time are viewed in terms of the people's renewed covenant with its scattered remnants. This requires an effort both to reunite the people and to understand what this people is in the light of these events.

We recall that three of the components of God's covenant with Israel were the making of a people, the rescue of that people from suffering, and restoration to the land. To understand what is occurring today, we must realize that in every critical experience the Jewish people has undergone changes which have transformed it and at the same time have kept it intact. Sinai, which is above all the point of Israel's origin, is the constant in this equation. If we ask what it is that unites Hebrew Bedouins of three millennia ago with today's suburban Jews, or Moroccan cave-dwellers with college-trained, secular professionals, we can only answer: A common origin, generated with such intensity in the Sinai wilderness that its vibrations continue to draw us toward each other.

It will be said, with considerable justification, that what really holds us Jews together is oppression. Yet if oppression were the only basis for our unity, Jews would have summoned the ingenuity (as many have) quietly to separate themselves and their children from the Jewish people. The most remarkable example of renewal is to be found in the Soviet Union. There a substantial portion of Jewry—not only members of the old, dying generation but many of the young—continues to insist upon its identification with the Jewish people. It may be true that large segments of Soviet Jewry are being assimilated into the mass, but tens of thousands refuse to be absorbed. They may not be able to define the term *Jew*, but they choose to share an existential relationship with a people which, despite disparities and incongruities, finds its historical origins so compelling that it cannot but cherish them. The uncovering of our beginnings in Israel and our renewed interest in the Sinai Peninsula have more than scholarly significance. The avid concern with archaeology is more than a national sport. A quest—still embryonic but burgeoning—is under way for our collective and psychic roots out of which our renewed and also our new identity will emerge.

But Jewish identity and covenant consciousness do not come out of ancient ruins alone. They come out of an awareness that the Jewish people may be on the threshold of a new and altogether different era in its existence, yet an era related to its prior history by circumstances out of which the new era erupted. By way of analogy, I cite what happened after the destruction of the Second Temple. While the people may not have fully absorbed the meaning of that destruction and of their own expulsion from their land, they became steadily aware that they were not only undergoing a massive change in life-style but were in a real sense becoming a different people (even as the desert tribes, upon entering Canaan, became a people). Perhaps the most significant change, aside from the historical transformation, was the metamorphosis of the Jews from a biblically to a rabbinically rooted people. Of course this was a very long process, which originated in Palestine while the Temple still stood. But the culmination of this process was hastened by destruction and exile, and it saved the Jewish people from annihilation. Had the people clung only to its temple, its cult, and its biblically prescribed society, it could not have endured, or it would have been reduced to the truly fossilized status of the Samaritans, who still adhere to a strictly biblical regimen.

Today the Jewish people enters upon an age into which it has been catapulted by a disaster no less monstrous than that which occurred over nineteen hundred years ago. Instead of being driven westward, it now turns eastward in vast numbers. Its institutions have been shattered, its communities destroyed, the framework within which it lived for centuries obliterated, and the texture known as rabbinic Judaism ripped apart. I am not suggesting the demise of rabbinic Judaism. I am suggesting that something new is unfolding, which will stand side by side with it. New institutions, new practices, new forms of Jewish living are opening up, particularly within Israel. The Israeli kibbutz, conceived and born early in this century, is a new development in Jewish life out of which a new kind of Jew has emerged. From one point of view, it represents a latter-day Qumran society in its stress on community; on sharing, and on a voluntaristic, uncoerced structure in which not profit but the enhancement of human existence may be achieved. From another point of view, it represents a peaceful revolution in Jewish life—one that many young people, seeking the new man in Cuba, regrettably overlook. As rabbinic law and belief held the far-flung Diaspora together the State of Israel serves as the unifying force today. It has contributed most toward the sense of covenant which animates Jewish life.

No event served better to drive that covenantal feeling to the surface than the peril that faced Israel before the Six-Day War broke out. Until Israel came into being, Galut was the only medium in which the people lived. It was a state of living beyond space, of occupying time but not territory, as Paul Tillich put it in an address. Now, by an act performed by themselves (and only ratified, not executed, by the United Nations), this people has become a unicum in the world, a people of territory and of Diaspora as well as of Galut. A people transcending land and living only in eternity finds itself almost overnight inhabiting its own territory and living, in its majority, beyond that territory. From a people that rejected its nonterritorial status, we have become a people that requires both homeland and dispersion.

This means that for the first time since the destruction, the people by an act of choice undertakes to live on two levels. Diaspora, provided it does not degenerate into captivity, is no longer a violation of the cosmic scheme. Yet both Diaspora and the State of Israel are bound to each other by a covenant of history, of danger, and of suffering. No one knows whether the convenant will withstand the tensions of distance and differing experiences. It did in ancient days, when the Diaspora and the Jewish Commonwealth were united in covenantal bonds. If it does withstand those tensions, then a new yet ancient Jewish people will have entered upon a new spiritual adventure, born out of both Auschwitz and Jerusalem.

15

Mi Yakum Yaakov—
How Can Jacob Endure?

Today the forbidden question is being asked with mounting urgency: *Mi Yakum Yaakov*—can the Jewish people survive?

We run the peril, not only of de-halakhizing Judaism, but of departicularizing the Jewish people. The issue may appear minuscule and unthreatening to some, but to others it is a cloud as big as a man's hand, foreboding a coming storm. This danger has haunted our people periodically in various guises. In a time when the question *Mi Yakum Yaakov?* becomes painfully legitimate, those of us who are committed to survival must again proclaim to those who would universalize Israel and Judaism out of existence, *Lo zeh ha-derekh*—this is not the way. We must recognize that to some elements in Jewish life and within the Reform movement and even within our Conference, the issue of Jewish existence is not an important question. Theologically, this means that for them the covenant, even if once valid, is canceled by Israel's choice, since God, who is at best in eclipse, has long since abdicated His own covenant role. Philosophically this means that Judaism truly realizes itself when it is diffused and absorbed as universally as possible, even to the point of the dissolution of the Jewish people. In 1895, Rabbi Elie Benamozegh, responding to Aime Palliere, a Catholic seeker in Judaism, wrote: "We Jews are carrying within ourselves the form of religion predestined ultimately for the whole human race, the one and only faith to which the Gentiles will also become subject." Benamozegh's statement poses the question whether in refracting this "form of religion" among the gentiles, the Jews as an identifiable entity could thereby become expendable. We should also pose the question whether Judaism can be truly viable without Jews practicing mitzvot and preserving the Torah.

151

Now that the State of Israel is an indisputable reality, now that we have empirically demonstrated the viability of particularism and universalism as embodied in the nation and in the Galut, we must seek a synthesis of both, rather than the liquidation of one by the other. We should be concerned about the danger of an alienation that would result in unbridled particularism on one hand and diluted, dejudaized universalism on the other. We must remind ourselves that despite current efforts to rewrite Jewish history, we are not and never were an ethnic entity alone, just as, in contrast to other attempts at rewriting our history, we are not and never were an ecclesia alone. We therefore cannot abandon our role, although it is no longer limited to us, of *tikkun olam*. But it must also be said that we are not so universalized that any differentiation between us and ethical humanism, however it may be impregnate with Jewish influence, is beyond discerning. Neither this nor the unreserved placing of the Jewish people at the unreciprocal service of humanity can be sustained, not only in terms of prudence, but in terms of morality. Both out of self-interest and out of the ethics of the sanctity of every person's and every group's existence, we cannot immolate ourselves for other causes, any more than Buddhist monks or Czech youths, who by their lights are as universalist as we, have immolated themselves for Soviet Jewry. Not everything edifying is necessarily to be equated with Judaism. Therefore our social, ethical concern must, wherever possible, be informed with the moral insights of our tradition. We should mandate our committees, such as Justice and Peace and others, to speak with the voice of Jewish authority, not in the idiom of their civil counterparts. Not everything which is embraced by the liberal world need be acceptable to us. A people mutilated by Auschwitz cannot accept zero population control as its norm. How can we reconcile the universal and the particular? By never allowing ourselves to forget the lessons of Hiroshima. By never allowing ourselves to forget the lessons of Auschwitz.

In the particularist context, the failure of the established Jewish agencies to be more alert to the social upheavals that engulf the Jewish community has helped spawn both the Jewish radical right and the Jewish radical left. Deplorably, consciousness of our poor was not born within the establishment but was thrust upon it, and the implications of social change have likewise been evaded too long by Jewish bodies. They should know what happens historically when a Jewish community finds itself maneuvered into the no-man's land between the poor and the powerful, each surging toward the other.

In our time, universalism takes on an especially distinctive form. It goes beyond the proliferation of Judaism into the world community and seeks to liberate the individual, Jew and non-Jew alike, from the restraints of his own culture and society. With the communications breakthrough all over the world, with the cultural revolution causing shock waves far beyond the borders of any nation, with the opening of moral and spiritual options in once monolithic societies, with the possible dawning of a new consciousness, the individual can now, theoretically at least, move from one culture to another and find a community of kindred spirits, likewise alienated from their native cultures. This, incidentally, is one of the deepest rationales for mixed marriage, religious and racial alike. We must begin by recognizing that individualism springs from the profound moral compulsions articulated by Buber, Kierkegaard, and others who clearly saw the advancing annihilation of the Single One before the relentless monster of technological and national collectivism. The issue has become the person as threatened by dehumanized abstractions—the state, the people, the economy. In the name of the abstraction, the person is destroyed physically and spiritually, so that a macabre representation of the future might show a computerized national or world government ruling from a depopulated capital over multitudes of depersonalized slaves. Individualism is therefore not an aberration but a legitimate hunger for freedom before it is too late. But it suffers from fatal flaws. Its basic flaw is that it has learned nothing from a past which also sought to liberate the person from his own ethnic and cultural bonds. Today's individualism was once embodied in the melting-pot theory, assimilation, emancipation, integration. These could not be sustained because formerly, at least, individuals, and the groups to which they gravitated, discovered to their sorrow that their fates could not be extricated from the fates of their primary communities.

The authentic issue is not whether the Single One can find completion within the Jewish community, but whether he is willing to seek it there, even if he must struggle together with other Single Ones to vanquish an inadequate Jewish community and reconstitute it. The issue is whether he is legitimately concerned with creating Jewish alternatives, Jewish counter-cultures, or whether he is bent on establishing alternatives to Judaism, cultures that run counter to Judaism and the Jewish people. If he uses terms like *Jewish, rabbi,* or *synagogue* as euphemisms for presiding at a rite de passage out of Judaism, integrity requires that he show his true credentials.

Such views of man and of the Jew are not new. All that is new is their protagonists, and their awareness of history is shallow. The archetypes for their celebration of the new man and the now man have always existed—in infamy. They existed in the messianic traducers of medieval Christendom and feudal Europe, documented in Norman Cohn's "Pursuit of the Millennium." They existed in the obscenity of *mitzvah habaah ba-averah* of the Sabbatian movement and in its catastrophic aftermath, the cult of Jacob Frank.

Zeh sefer toledot adam has validity only in conjunction with "I will establish my covenant between Me and you and your progeny for an everlasting covenant." We can radically redefine God, Israel, and Torah, but we cannot eliminate them in the name of Judaism that ceases to be, not only for us, but for the world we presume to enrich. Perhaps the most militant individualists in recent Jewish history were the Jewish Bundists in the early promise of the Russian Revolution. Their lofty expectations of release from Jewish tribalism into the world revolution, which would bring not only class-salvation but personal redemption, were quickly shattered by Soviet betrayal. When the moment of individual triumph appears at hand, the antithesis of ethnic consciousness comes into play. This does not necessarily reflect the resurgence of an evil counter-revolutionary force, but indicates the equally powerful human need for collective as well as personal identity. At the very moment when individualism asserts itself in some circles, individual religion is declining. A glance at what is happening to Unitarianism should suffice. True, the liberal pragmatic stress of ethical humanism is receding before a fierce kind of individualism, the mythic, the mystical, but this new phenomenon will not in itself prevent its own corruption and disintegration. Hasidism was Jewish individualism in the eighteenth century, and Jewish obscurantism in the nineteenth. But more important, the mythic and the mystical, like the rational, can function only within particular cultural structures. These structures are not invalidated but become indispensable wombs in which cosmic and collective myths are born. It is significant that while some segments of Christianity, in their search for survival, seek models in our biblical norms of community, some Jews prefer Paul, whose orderly, individualist religion, now languishing in a post-Christian world, allowed no distinctions between "Jew" and "Greek."

But, we are told, the new age offers greater promise than the past. What failed then will at last triumph tomorrow. To this, Heilbroner, in *The Future as History,* reponds:

> Taking into account the human condition as it now exists, the laggard slowness with which improvements in institutions are followed by improvements in "life," the blurred and ambiguous

fashion in which history passes from problem to problem, it is certain enough that the tenor of world history will remain much as it is for a long while to come.

Indeed, from the point of view of the West and especially of America, it may seem to be deteriorating. . . . Many of the tendencies of world history are likely to manifest themselves as a worsening of the outlook. We may well be tempted to interpret this growing intractability of the environment as the metamorphosis of progress into retrogression.[1]

More than any other community, we Jews should beware of speculating in futures. At the very best, we can employ current and often conflicting data to venture guesses, but the testimony of the past is more valid than futurism. If we are told that world socialism or world capitalism holds messianic promise for mankind, and for Jews, then we are warranted in responding that what promises messianism for some forebodes apocalypse for others. In 1917, Lincoln Steffens returned from the newly born Soviet Union and wrote "Seven Days That Shook the World," which began: "I have seen the future and its works." Therefore, we must warn against stripping the Jewish people of its collective entity, inducing a centrifugal fragmentation of the people into isolates in yet another catastrophic ransom to a dubious tomorrow which, by all precedent, could be as treacherous as all the tomorrows Jewish history has tragically encountered. Friedrich Heer, in *God's First Love*, warns us that a holocaust is being prepared in the Middle East.[2]

It is more than likely that what awaits us is not the dawning of individualism, when Jews will be able to go their way unmolested, but a night of anguish for the world and for the people of Israel, in which men will again draw together for collective and personal consolation, in which betrayed Jews will seek the comfort of the synagogue and of a chastened people. Individualists must confront the fact that many of our young, who with the keen vision of their youth sense tomorrow better than their elders, are banding together as Jews to reaffirm their commitment to Jewish existence and to the creation of new and identifiably Jewish structures, predicated on Jewish survival, not the dissolution of Jewish life either under the pretext that whatever is noble is Jewish or on the open assertion that Judaism is expendable. Making the fullest allowance for diversity in Jewish life, we must distinguish between those who are covenanted to the survival of the people and those who are using the Jewish enterprise as camouflage for dissolving Jewish life with the disarming appeal that the lonely and the rejected are more important than institutions. Judaism is not so diversified that even its dismantling becomes a legitimate option.

The real question is not, How will history unfold? but, How do we want to contribute to the shaping of history? Do we want to remain Jews, or do we want to obliterate our identity under the pretext of making all mankind authentically Jewish? In facing these questions, we may recognize that it is not speculation on the future but a failure of nerve, a failure of confidence in the merits of our Jewish enterprise. We may discover that futurism is not a science but a device for manipulating the future, and not necessarily along messianic lines. Nevertheless, we must contend with responsible judgments that humanity may be entering upon an age of a new consciousness, not only new economic and social modes. This may well be, but it is no warrant for believing that the emergent age, if it is to be a higher age, would be devoid of structures and societies, sustained both by ancient traditions and by their ultimate hopes. Were it to annihilate traditions and structures it would be an age of tyranny, not of freedom.

It is an awesome thing to insist upon remaining a Jew after Auschwitz. It was almost as awesome before Auschwitz. When, in his pre-Zionist period, Theodor Herzl contemplated suggesting to the Pope that he make it possible for the Jewish people to undergo mass apostacy and thereby rid itself once and for all of its torment, he was at that moment saying more honestly than others now say, that Jewish life is not worth suffering for. But he soon abandoned his scheme. What impelled him to do so, in favor of his Zionist vision? Certainly the collective genius of the Jewish people could have found a more effective way of overcoming the agony of our existence. It is not enough to say that the world would not have allowed us to find such a way. If we had acquiesced to the post-French Revolutionary formula, "For the Jews as individuals, everything; to the Jews as a people, nothing," we would have opened the gates to our eventual liberation from history. Jews of the past in multitudes, and Jews of our time in escalating numbers, have found those gates unlocked. Yet we persist, and it is not only because we want to deny Hitler his victory. I do not think this is what our colleague, Emil Fackenheim, has in mind. It is rather that by giving up, we confess that the universe and the world are forever in the hands of the powers of darkness. But we renounce this confession and stake our lives on the faith that this is not so. Therefore we choose life. Therefore we choose life for our people. Therefore we are commanded to fulfill the greatest mitzvah of our generation, the mitzvah of Jewish survival. Therefore we must remember and not let the world forget. If it forgets, if we cease to be, then there can never be a day when God shall be one and His name one.

16

Israel and Galut:
The Unresolved Encounter

Shalom, Zalman,

For more than forty-five years, as fellow students and fellow teachers in Cleveland, in our many encounters in the United States, in Palestine, and in Israel, we have carried on scores of conversations about the relationship of the Galut to a potential Jewish state and then to a state which has become a reality in our time. (I use the term *Galut* because it identifies an existential condition for the Jewish people, which, even in the most secure of its communities, feels the pangs of remembered agony, and dreads, even unconsciously, its reoccurrence. We felt Galut in May of 1967, and we may soon feel it again.) Now, at the Centennial of the Union of American Hebrew Congregations, to which you have contributed of your own wisdom, this issue is advanced with mounting urgency.

It is not likely that this discussion could have found its way to the head of the Union's agenda were it not for two anniversaries. Without them, both the character and the constituency of this gathering would have been out of a different age. The first anniversary is Israel's twenty-five years of statehood. The second, without which Israel's birth would have been problematic, is the thirty-fifth Yahrzeit, almost to the very day, of Kristalnacht, that terrifying overture to the Holocaust. I speak neither moralistically nor theologically, but out of a detached historical conviction that had there been no Kristalnacht, with its Holocaust aftermath, there would be no Jewish state. The world would not have allowed it. The Jewish people would not have stormed humanity's conscience, would not have violated blockades for it. The Jewish people, not the United Nations, gave birth to the State of Israel, although the world can, as it has tried to do, make Israel's situation precarious. The United Nations ratified what the Jewish people consummated out of its agony, and out of a monstrous sense of guilt felt by the Western world. There has never been an ordeal like that of the Holocaust. There has never been a deliverance like that which we have witnessed. Israel had to come into being. For the sake of our lives and our souls, it must remain in being. If ever a new Writ is added to the spiritual continuum of our people, it will tell of wonders and the contraction into brief decades of what the Exodus and the occupation of the land under Joshua and the Judges could not achieve in many generations. Of course there were Sinai and the Torah and the covenant, and these components are absent in Israel's most recent prodigies. I will deal with this later. For the moment, let the wonder speak for itself, although it requires no rehearsing in this particular setting. Yet I insist on mentioning it here because we have come upon a time when Jews who are critical or dissenting out of a passionate commitment to the Jewish people and its mightiest achievement in this age, the State of Israel, risk charges of heresy. Moreover, I make this comment by way of disassociating myself from those Jews who, both by deed and word, have succumbed to bitterness and hopelessness about Israel, adopting the hostile epithet of "Israeli imperialism, aggression, and oppression." They are disciples of Spengler, who wrote: "Vespasian's War, directed against Judea, was a liberation of Jewry. It ended both the claim of the people of this petty district to be a genuine nation, and the pretensions of their bald spirituality to equivalence with the soul-life of the whole."[1]

We must begin our discussion with the recognition that no force in the world plays more perverse tricks than history. And the Jewish people of our day has felt the fury of those tricks again and again. Ahad Ha-Am and Theodor Herzl projected constrasting programs for the Jewish people's restoration to its land. Ahad Ha-Am wanted a slow, selective process of the moral and spiritual recycling of Jews before they could become qualified to settle in Israel. The goal was the inner transformation of the people, and only those Jews were to go to the new land who had already undergone that transformation. Through them, other Jews, purged of the corruption of the Galut, would follow. But the Holocaust put an end to the vision. Theodor Herzl, who saw the untenability of the Galut, contemplated an orderly withdrawal of the Jews from Europe. But, granting even the acquiescence of masses of Jews (an acquiescence which did not exist), the withdrawal never materialized, and the Holocaust destroyed any hopes for a systematic departure. Ahad Ha-Am and Herzl were not the only ones to be overwhelmed by the malevolence of history. Shimon Dubnow dreamed of autonomous Jewish communities which could exist as self-contained nationality groups in Eastern Europe, but the dreamer was swallowed up in a Baltic concentration camp. Following the First World War, solemn treaties were drawn up guaranteeing the Jews of Poland, Rumania, and other lands full minority rights. Yet, even before the rise of Hitler, those treaties dissolved into a night of terror for East-European Jews. These, then, were some of the malign tricks in history's political arsenal.

But there is entrapment and a perverse trick on the psychological level as well. Precisely at the moment when statehood emerged, a relapse in the will of the Jewish people to live occurred. We are certainly aware of the massive adrenaline which charged into our people with the birth of the state. It is superfluous to dwell on that. But in our ecstasy, which is beginning to abate, we hardly noticed that for large numbers of Jews in the Western world, the will to remain Jews either coincided with, or was a consequence of, the rise of Israel. I am fully aware that assimilation has been advancing ever since the Emancipation, and that we should not identify the State of Israel with that process. But there is a new component, which statehood added to the process. It was best articulated by Arthur Koestler, who, after Israel came into being, said in effect that now that there is a Jewish homeland, a Jew could make a free choice to be or not to be a Jew. We must not overlook this unconscious motivation on the part of large numbers of young Jews, for whom Israel is not a source of identity but a valid justification for severing or phasing out identity. I state this not for judgmental reasons. But let it be understood that if there is to be a Jewish state, which means a place where Jews can, supposedly, determine their destinies at last, then it must follow that such a state also can release Jews, even in Israel, from pursuing their heretofore coerced destinies as Jews. What more dramatic evidence than this—that from 1966 to 1972, precisely during the post–Six-Day War period, one out of every three American Jews intermarried compared with one out of six from 1961 to 1965.

The third trick by history is ideological. Zionism came into being, in part, as a consequence of the great nationalistic explosions which burst upon Europe and reached their climax in 1848, just one hundred years before the birth of the State of Israel. When I speak of nationalism in this context, I refer to nationalism as an ideal, not necessarily as a reality. Its European exponents saw it as an embodiment of a higher religion and looked toward its fruition as a major step toward a nobler human condition. Before the corruption of nationalism in the mid-nineteenth century, it aspired to keep governmental power in check and to achieve civil rights.[2] For Herder, nationalism was a spiritual concept, based upon the idea of *Volk,* which was rooted not in rational political goals but in the "unconscious development of the people" which he called the *Volkgeist*. Fichte summoned his people not only to national rebirth but to cultural leadership in the world.

Today, we are confronted, not only in the case of Jewish nationalism but of all new national movements, with a current of political and philosophic thought that can be called postnational. I do not suggest the cooling of national ardor. Its intensity requires no elaboration. But at least some of those who scout out unknown and forbidden terrain, are already living beyond nationalism in the post-Hiroshima age. This is true in Israel as well as in other places in the world. I am not arguing the merits of this development. I simply cite the irony of the emergence of Jewish statehood at a time when nationalism, as a philosophic construct, has become problematic. Louis Snyder refers to nationalism as an "obsolete phenomenon."[3] Harold Laski asks: "Does not the mere selfishness of ensuring our own survival compel us to think in different terms?"[4] Erich Fromm writes: "This incestuous fixation not only poisons the relationship of the individual to the stranger but to the members of his own clan and to himself."[5] Hans Morgenthau says: "The Nation-State has been rendered obsolete to the nuclear revolution in the same way in which feudalism was made obsolete 200 years ago by the first industrial revolution."[6] Although nationalism appears to be stronger than ever, a close look indicates, first, that this is true chiefly of newly created or liberated nations, and second, that its triumphalism and arrogance have been dissipated among older powers. Therefore Barbara Ward tells us that nationalism cannot be "the active principle of a new social order . . . wide enough to match a world made scientifically and technologically one."[7]

Finally, for Americans history has recently dealt a severe moral blow. It might be called the illusion of constitutional immunity. More than anything else, Watergate has compellingly demonstrated the fragility of constitutional guarantees, which ultimately are only as secure as the persons who administer them. I am fully aware that, when finally alerted, the democratic process came to the rescue, and that there seems to be a new sense of moral urgency in the land. But we succumb to euphoria if we fail to see how close our nation came to entering upon dictatorship with barely a whimper from the electorate. It will be said that this was a freakish situation from which America is recovering with remarkable vigor. Such optimism is not yet warranted. To the contrary, a nation barely recovered from the plague of McCarthyism, and falling into this hideous relapse, is hardly out of danger. This alone weakens the argument for the singularity of America. There is no objective way of knowing whether the nation will recover. Perhaps it is the fate of democracy to be fragile and evanescent. This has a special bearing upon American Jewry. A nation so sorely beset by revelations of betrayal in the highest places, of the fragility and near-shattering of the democratic structure, of political and economic future-fears, is a nation where Jews must abandon the illusion of an America that is intrinsically different.

The Watergate crisis will continue to agitate America long after the hearings are over and the judgments handed down. Unless we are exceedingly lucky, America will be torn by internal conflict. It would be illusory to believe that the forces that brought the nation to the brink of dictatorship will subside into silence and acquiescence. Let no one think that the repressive political morality proudly embraced by some will vanish. Unlike liberals whose sense of outrage is not matched by perseverance, the temporarily frustrated plotters of democracy's overthrow will bide their time and make other assaults. Like the dormant carriers of pestilence in Camus's *Plague,* they will fester in silence and emerge again to resume their ravages upon a steadily weakened body politic, undermined by the excesses of the Palmer raids, the Sacco-Vanzetti case, McCarthyism, My Lai, and the multiple warhead known as Watergate. Thus, divisions and recriminations are to be expected, splitting the nation and challenging its future. The implications of this for American Jewry should not escape us. For the bewildered and the lost, whose vision of an undefeated and inviolate America has been the one sustaining force in their lives, an enraged witch-hunt could well emerge in which Jewish culprits could again become a necessity. No nation, awash in the flood of military debacle, corruption reaching into the highest places, and a faltering economy, is immune to the possibility of resurgent anti-Semitism. Perhaps this is history's dirtiest trick of all—a reminder to Jews that neither constitutions nor political institutions are in themselves protection against the ever-present, though often latent, demonic image of the Jew, an image aroused whenever a society is caught in a time of disaster. This image can become magnified should a shift of attitude toward Israel take place. This shift, indicated by growing hostility to Israel and to Jews in various quarters, is a source of concern to competent observers. In the context of our discussion, it is appalling how insensitive otherwise discerning Israelis are to the implications of Watergate.

Thus, in assessing our relations with Israel, there are no absolutes. Any preconceptions which Zionists, Israelis, and American Jews may have nurtured have been shattered repeatedly, and we must therefore attempt an assessment on an altogether different set of premises. The first, and for the moment it may be a source of vindication for some Israelis as well as some American Zionists, is that past history (and no one can speak of future history) is on the side of Jewish apprehensions. By apprehension I do not mean hopelessness, but rather the sober understanding that it is better to confront history for what it is than for what we wish it to be. Jewish history speaks of tentativeness and contingency. So does life, of course, but Jewish history is the paradigm, in its starkest form, of the tentativeness and contingency of the human condition. We American Jews do not appreciate this approach to our history because we would rather live as though we had discovered the clue to the uncontingent life. But in the context of relationship to the physical and cultural source of our being, contingency has been made manifest not only by disaster but by erosion. Apprehension is engendered not by the facts of oppression and catastrophe. If we were to contend with that only, we could at least fight on a single front. But apprehension derives from the knowledge that in many sectors of our existence, where oppression abates, dissolution and the weakening of the will to live, intervene. We need not go all the way back to ancient Alexandria. We can cite some pre-Hitler Jewries where the pace of assimilation was intense. We can cite American Jewry, where the metabolic process reflects growth and building-up, but, also, massive disintegration and breaking down. Thus, many factors exist which do not hold forth much promise for the continuation of the Galut. For those of us who wish this continuation, this prospect is alarming. This should arouse even greater alarm for Israel because its future as a state is affected. Even more, its future as a Jewish state is affected.

Because of historical reality, the Jewish response cannot be authentic unless, in addition to contending with history, a mandate which our tradition puts upon us, we must strive to overcome history with messianism.

Another premise is that in confronting one another, we must recognize that certain terms should be redefined in light of events which must draw Israel and Galut into an inseparable unity. One such term is the "centrality of Israel." I affirm the moral, psychological and spiritual centrality of Israel. Nothing has so aroused historical consciousness, and hence the potentiality for covenant consciousness, as Zionism. The transformation of awareness of our past from an attenuated textbook tie with our history to a living reunion with it is a precondition for the rebirth of the people's spirit. For American Jewry, Israel has reestablished the awareness of the people's proximity to its history and civilization. Jewish worship in America has been given vitality by Israeli culture, which affects our religious life from both religious and so-called secular sources. Summers and years of study in Israel prove more effective than our own formal education. A comparison of the state of our culture before and after the creation of Israel would be embarrassingly instructive. To assign total spiritual autonomy to American Jewry would only hasten the de-Judaizing process. The Shoah has undoubtedly played a major part in the awakening, but the Shoah alone, without the redemptive quality of Israel, might have given us nothing but despair.

Israel has given Galut Jews an existential response to the land, a response which perceives Israel and its spirit more authentically than may be reflected by the externals of Israel's culture and our own. It has given us cultural, psychological, and moral strength. It has reinforced our will to live and to labor on behalf of our fellow Jews. It has helped make us Jews again. It has galvanized us in the struggle to survive. In its ordeal, it consumes virtually all of our concern and possesses our beings. But in the one area of the determination of our internal affairs it is not central, and we must remain autonomous, even though we would be well advised, as would Israel, to retain a strong consultant relationship. Thus, having asserted Israel's overwhelming and encompassing place in our lives I confine myself solely to the question of political centrality. The peril confronting Israel demands not political centrality but the political unity of the entire Jewish people. I urge, not the contraction of political organization, but its extension, consonant with the needs of a people both landed and dispersed.

The times are too perilous to warrant anything but a relationship of fullest interdependence—each community bound to the other, yet acknowledging the initiative of the other in its own inner life. As long as the Galut is viable it must possess its own internal political structure, and it must be encouraged to share more deeply in the internal processes of Israel. The Galut and Israel bear mutual vulnerability, and they must therefore be mutually allied. Obviously, Israel alone must determine ultimate issues affecting its existence and security—the issues of war and of borders, just as the Galut must enjoy its own special areas of autonomy. But in other spheres, the principle of bilateralism should be advanced. This is not for the sake of diminishing Israel's political strength but rather of enhancing it through inducing the political growth of its only sure ally, the Galut. Despite its achievements, American Jewry is a politically underdeveloped area, led by individuals, not mass movements. Before Israel came into being, the bilateral principle in which the Yishuv and the Galut collaborated, did obtain on the grounds that the Yishuv was too insecure for it to assume power exclusively. When the State of Israel came into being, there was a transference of power from the Zionist movement in the Galut, especially from American Zionism, on the premise that if the state had not yet attained full security, the attainment was nevertheless imminent. Today that premise has proved to be premature. Consequently, the Galut (again, especially American Jewry) must turn its energies toward qualifying itself to play a vigorous and intimate bilateral role which currently it neither possesses nor is qualified for. This means the creation of a truly democratic, representative body which would speak for all the survivalist elements in our communities. To a limited extent, world Jewish and Zionist agencies identify themselves as embodying this objective, but their representative character is limited, their political role circumscribed, and in certain instances, they are extensions of Israeli policy rather than of Galut-Israel political interaction.

The only authentic centrality in these intimidating times is that of the Jewish people. Societies are central only when they can relate creatively or even domineeringly to a periphery. But if the periphery is lost, whether by reason of destruction, or disintegration, or alienation, or defection, the center ceases to be a center and becomes an isolate. The British Empire, or more latterly the British Commonwealth, is an unhappy validation of this. England as the center of an English-speaking commonwealth is today a fatuity. England once had colonies. They rebelled because they were colonies. England also had a far-flung Diaspora whose language, culture, identity, sense of history, were once no less binding to the center than the diverse civilizations of the Jewish Galut are to Israel. (Again, I deliberately omit reference to Torah and covenant, which the commonwealth did not possess and for want of which it dissolved at last. And isn't this the point, that the universal Jewish commonwealth is in danger of dissolving for similar reasons?) Now England stands virtually alone, shorn of the last shreds of its centrality, seeking union with neighbors of other cultures, languages, and traditions. Whatever the reasons, estrangement between center and periphery has made political centrality an anachronism.

A center has certain characteristics. It may be nourished by its satellites; it may nourish them; they may nourish one another; it may exercise moral domination over them; it may refuse to tolerate parity with them; all these factors may interplay. But at this juncture in history, at a time of decolonization, of the break-up of small states into smaller states of north and south or east and west, nothing validates the concept of centrality except consent, and if consent is not forthcoming, centrality is no more compelling than the British Crown.

As the twenty-first century approaches, even Israel cannot command centrality. If dissolving Diaspora communities or reluctant Diaspora communities fight for their existence as viable Jewries, partly because the very stress on centrality has made them invidious in their own eyes, then the centrality of Israel will be nothing but a myth, without even the redeeming remembrance of the myth by dying Jewish communities. Whoever speaks of centrality and relationship simultaneously cancels one out with the other. Where there is insistence upon centrality, there can be no true relationship. Centrality at worst is authoritarian, at best, paternalistic. Centrality excludes encounter. Central excludes diversity and dissent. It must by definition demand compliance and uniformity. By this I do not mean that it is Israel's "fault," any more than it is the "fault" of a gifted child who excels his siblings. But if no regard is given to this potentially dangerous relationship the siblings will develop contempt for themselves, will shrivel and diminish in their growth.

Whatever the relationships of free Diasporas may have been with Zion in the past, and there is good evidence that some of them clung to their own autonomy, the dependency factor does not exist in those Diasporas which are still free. Let me qualify. First, I do not challenge the torrential moral force which has burst out of Israel to the Galut. Second, it is clearly beyond dispute that endangered communities must look to Israel for help. It is also possible, in terms of my apprehensive view of Jewish history, that the political fortunes of any Diaspora community can change, or else such a Diaspora might dissolve over a period of time. Likewise, when Israel is in mortal danger it unquestionably occupies the center of our attention. But when a community like American Jewry is struggling to preserve itself politically and to save itself spiritually—yes, with Israeli help—such a community must have a sense of its own inherent strength, or it will face disintegration.

The question of the nature of Jewish sovereignty and its relationship to the people was not at all simplistic in our history, and deep passions, deep divisions, wracked the people in its own national home. What can we extrapolate from that issue for our own time? I see it as the issue of whether we are ultimately a nation or a people. The resolution of this issue will determine whether the state will attempt to shape the existence of the people or whether it will regard itself and conform to its self-awareness as an instrument of the people. Has the goal of the Jewish people been the creation of a state or has it been the redemption of the people through the creation of the state? Let us not answer too impulsively. We must never allow ourselves to forget that statehood was indispensable to the physical, primal rescue of the Jews. Nor must we forget that the state is indispensable to the protection and security of its inhabitants. But we must also remember that when we say this, we are discussing strategy, not the goals of a people. Those Russian delegates to the Sixth Zionist Congress in 1903, who refused Herzl's proposal of Uganda as a temporary way-station for oppressed Jews, understood the distinction. They understood it with the blood and tears of their children and their fathers. Yet they wanted something more than a place of refuge. These were the Jews from whose midst the Ahad Ha-Ams and the Bialiks had sprung. Thus, despite efforts to rewrite Jewish history as though it were one-dimensionally the record of a nation in exile, the Jewish people as the repository of the hope for national restoration is the primary structural component in Jewish life. To reduce that people to an instrument of the state, and even more, to seal its verdict by proclaiming its tentativeness and its solitary hope in packing its baggage, is to distort the Jewish state and to destroy the Jewish people. If the people as it now exists in the Galut is thus subordinate to the state, what would become of that people once it were totally swallowed up within the state?

What is the distinction between people and state? The state is an apparatus that must subsume morality to self-interest. The state is not a state if power is not its primary concern, certainly in the hour and place in which Israel finds itself. The Jewish people must concern itself with all that—and more. The "more" is the messianic component out of which the idea of the state emerged, but only as a prelude to more transcendent goals. As I have indicated, the lot of the people is not only to be in tension with the state, but also to be inextricably bound up with it. It is even more certain that if the people is successfully appropriated by the state, its last hope for renewal will have been stifled, and with it the last best hope of the state as well.

The people has always overflowed the borders of Israel, not only under compulsion but of its own free will. It has been suggested that if the entire people had lived in its land during the rebellion against Rome, the Jewish state could never have been destroyed. This is dubious, no less dubious than speculation that if a minority of zealots had not rebelled against Rome, an important measure of Jewish sovereignty might have remained. But the fact is that Jews, under duress and otherwise, have been a Galut people for millennia, and have become de facto a universal community which makes its own unique claim upon the world and the State of Israel. I do not suggest that Jews must cling to lands of persecution to prove this point, or that aliyah from the free world should not be encouraged. I do suggest that wherever Jews live under freedom, it is the obligation of their leaders and of Israelis to recognize this as a condition whose continuity should be supported from within and from without. I am speaking psychologically. It is unacceptable that any free Jewish community should be told that it is a wayfarer. A people that is encouraged to pack its baggage is condemned to premature self-annihilation. Jews here and in Israel deny this, but their message comes through with telling clarity. Nowhere, for example, does the Jerusalem Program of the World Zionist Organization speak of the need for the continuity of the Jewish people in a relationship of mutuality with Israel. Note that I do not say parity, because as long as our children continue to be educated by Israeli teachers, parity is as empty a term as centrality. But I would reinforce mutuality with the term interdependence, being convinced that neither community can long endure without the other. The outspoken opponent of the Galut, Yaakov Klatzkin (1882–1948), wrote: "The Galut does not deserve to survive. . . . The *Galut* has a right to life for the sake of liberation from the *Galut*. . . . without the goal of a homeland, the Galut is . . . not worth keeping alive."[8]

This is an honest position, which most Galut Jews would oppose. It would be incumbent upon Jewish leaders here and in Israel to reject it formally and just as honestly. The right of the Jewish people to live as a people in the world has been established. I must again stress that I am not discussing the contingencies of history, which could overnight make Jewish life untenable, and for that matter could in the process pose awesome threats to Israel. But our claim to universality is unassailable—in Jewish terms. I do not propagate the "mission of Israel" theory, but it did not originate within the Reform movement. Nor do I cite the following for any reason other than to indicate that no later than the fourth century, the Galut was regarded as legitimate Jewish turf. Said Rabbi Elazar: "God exiled Israel so that converts could join them." This was by way of answering the charge that God had humiliated Israel and replaced it with Christianity. Said Rabbi Pinchas (at the end of the fourth century) in God's name: "If you do not declare My Name among the nations, I will punish you."

As a universal community which encompasses Israel, our greatest triumph and our profoundest consolation, we are obsessively but properly preoccupied with our identity and with the rediscovery of the values that can make us Jews in more than a superficially ethnic sense. It is no small matter that when a group of Reform rabbis from America and

Israel met with leaders of the kibbutz movement in 1971 and again in July 1973, the hunger for Jewish values transcended all other considerations. They and we encountered one another in a common recognition that nationhood alone will not produce or uncover those values.

For some time Mordecai Kaplan has been urging that the Jewish people proclaim its universal character in a formal manner. He has suggested that we once more enter into covenant by way of declaring our common bonds as a worldwide community, united in what the late Kurt Lewin called our common fate and our common destiny. The covenant of Sinai was the model covenant, but not the only one. It has been renewed throughout our history in order to meet new challenges to our existence. This is not the place to discuss the implementation of such a proposal, but rather the need to declare to the world and to ourselves that we intend to persist as a world community in an age when our presence in the world summons humanity to peer beyond national fortresses. I do not speak of abstract and even fatuous universalism. Universal man needs territory to love and on which to tread. But he must be a global man also.

Let me now attempt to make empirical applications of my theoretical comments. First, we Diaspora Jews and you Israelis have offended against one another, because of the thesis of political centrality and primacy. We have used one another rather than engaged in true encounter. How have we used one another? American Jewish leaders, acquiescing to the doctrine that there is no real future for the Galut, have made a surrogate religion of Israel. This is exploitation of Israel because it cannot sustain such an image and must inevitably suffer from the ensuing and unwarranted disenchantment. Making Israel, not a compelling value in itself but *the* value, and even more, a replacement for other values, reduces Jewish life in Galut to a living acknowledgement that we are morally and spiritually spent, that we have no future, that we live by the grace of the kidney machine called Israel.

The second empirical application of my thesis is that the American Jewish community, in order to enter into authentic relationship with Israel, must reorganize itself. For the indeterminate future, the capacity and will of the Jewish people to survive will be put to a supreme test. Nothing else on the Jewish agenda must be allowed to preempt this consideration. In light of most recent events, a far-ranging restructuring of organized Jewish life in America has become mandatory. In the earliest days of the crisis, perceptive Jews became aware that not only the future of Israel but the future of American Jewry was in jeopardy. Had Israel gone down to defeat, we would have suffered both the bitterness of overt anti-Semitism and such a tidal wave of despair that the beginning of the end of the Jewish people could have set in. Were organized Jewish life to go back to its prewar operations, to resume business as usual—saying that American Jewry can always be counted upon in time of trouble—it would be willfully to expose American Jewry to round after round of disaster for which it will never be prepared and from which it will emerge with diminishing strength and diminishing material and human resources. American Jews responded magnificently to the present crisis, and so did our leadership, but we tend to overlook the fact that only a small segment of American Jewry was engaged in the struggle. We have entered upon a new era in our American experience. The euphoric and arrogant days of "we've got it made" are over. Even before the Day of Judgment War, the time of our ascendancy was over, but organized Jewish life continued to be manipulated as though nothing fundamental and irreversible had happened. The time for examining our own inadequacies as a community, the inadequacies of our leadership and some of its assumptions, which could have had catastrophic consequences, is at hand. We were caught psychologically unprepared by the Yom Kippur onslaught. In large measure, a mood of excessive confidence, of perilous hubris, accompanied by the discrediting of those who challenged that mood, had been generated by our leadership, which, with all its devotion to its tasks, had failed us in crucial areas. Jewish leadership in America perceived its role to be uncritical acquiescence to the doctrine of Israel's political centrality with all the specific applications and dangers of such a doctrine. American Jewish leadership had resisted efforts to move it from a passive and outer-directed agent to a resourceful and inner-directed interactor with the State of Israel. This has been damaging to both American Jewry and to Israel. The tenacity with which Jewish leadership has clung to this role has inhibited the development of great sources of human energy, such as the academic community. It has also inhibited the political growth and maturity of American Jewry. Yet no effort has been made to hold this leadership accountable.

The Jewish communal structure is archaic, even if it is capable of arousing itself in time of impending disaster, as a ravaged body can still respond to external danger. The time has come for American Jews to dare to reexamine their assumptions and radically to rebuild the structure of the Jewish community. I suggest four courses of action.

First, we must demand a greater degree of coordination among all Israel-oriented bodies. American Jewry must warn that we will not tolerate an adversary relationship among them. The initial fighting for position between the United Jewish Appeal and Bonds for Israel was an unmitigated scandal.

Second, the studied relegation of the American synagogue to the periphery by the great communal agencies must come to an end. For too long, the American synagogue has been regarded and treated as expendable in a Jewish world where the real issues of Jewish existence were being confronted with total disregard for the synagogue. This downgrading, in which laity and rabbinate acquiesced, has contributed to the weakening of Jewish life in America, and to the dismantling of the moral infrastructure of our people. If I were a Federation leader, lay or professional, or if I were an Israeli leader, I would be deeply worried about the devaluation of the American synagogue, because their institutions, which are also ours, are anchored to that American synagogue. In the process of making Israel our displacement, American leadership must of necessity diminish in moral and intellectual stature as it subordinates itself. Where there were once giants in the rabbinate and among the laity, there are generally unimpressive functionaries who too often inadequately occupy places once held by the great as well as the mighty. We might reluctantly settle for this period of sterility if we did not also have to contend with the corrupting of Jewish life in which men who discredit us, tactics which shame us, honorees who disgrace us, were not the inevitable consequence of the deprecating attitude toward Galut. Can we really hope to educate and edify our young in such a moral environment? Suddenly, with the shattering awareness that Israel's ordeal has thrust upon us, the synagogue emerges as the primary instrument for arousing the Jewish will to live, to seek community in a bleak and unfriendly world and, yes, to marshal powerful forces for the defense of the State of Israel. If, God forbid, Israel had suffered defeat in the treacherous attack upon her, what compensatory moral and emotional strength would American Jewry have possessed in order to survive? What resources to face the unthinkable calamity beyond which an unprepared community might have seen only its onrushing end? Never again can the so-called secular agencies in Jewish life treat the synagogue with condescension after the role it played throughout the war. No other institution in Jewish life was mobilized as rapidly and effectively. Now it must turn to those agencies, particularly the local and national federations, and insist that the time of false distinctions between secular and religious is over, that the time of excluding the synagogue from great decision-making processes is over, that the time of using the synagogue but refusing to consult with it as an equal, is over.

Third, and a logical derivative of the first two points, is that the time has come for American Jewry to become a community, no longer a chaotic jumble of discordant entities. The closest we have come to this is the Conference of Presidents of National Organizations, but that is no longer nearly good enough. Even in prewar days this body was an inadequate instrument, fighting stubbornly to thwart any efforts to make it something other than the agency for promoting the premise that it served Israel best by listening but not by interacting or initiating meaningful conversation. By adhering to this position, by failing to confront issues from an independent perspective, it developed a strategy of rigidity instead of the creative openness the times demand. It served manfully during the crisis, but Jewish life requires a structure not only for coping with crisis, but for confronting the day-to-day realities of Jewish existence during a kind of adversity which could become normality. Essentially, some of us have been requesting that the Presidents' Conference expand from its present role of receiving information and responding to it, or hearing Israel's concerns and acting upon them, also to conveying American Jewry's concerns to Israel and urging Israel's sensitivity to those concerns. We have therefore been requesting dialogue. We have been requesting true relationship instead of one-sided centrality. We have been rejecting what is essentially a passive role on the part of American Jewish leaders. We have been urging the creation of a channel through which our concerns could be communicated, outside the glare of the media, to Israelis, official and unofficial, in which there would be true brotherly encounter. As long as national Jewish bodies continue to perceive themselves as dependent instruments of political centrality, such a process will not come into being, our capability for action will be strangulated, and our enormous human resources, waiting to be activated, will be aborted.

This shattering moment demands that American Jewry move forward to a stronger kind of unity, to ever more confident discourse with Israel, a discourse we have earned in Israel's hour of danger and in our own. We cannot be content with the built-in limitations of the Presidents' Conference. Now, more than ever before, we must envision and require a representative assembly, encompassing not only presidents but elected delegates from the entire spectrum of American Jewry, to deliberate and to act on the issues of our people's survival—in Israel, in the Soviet Union, in the United States. To resist this course of action following our people's most recent ordeal is to be willfully blind. It is to fail to realize that we shall be living with crisis for an indeterminate period. I hope the Reform movement will demand that American Jewry come of age and constitute itself, as a true community, as a true Kehillah, as a true Kelal Yisrael. We are inadequately equipped to confront the challenges of existence, both in peace and in war. The future of American Jewry is not so assuring that it can afford to ignore the warning of the present moment, bursting from Egypt and Russia and the oil fields of Arabia.

Fourth, we cannot indulge in the luxury of separatist religious regimes on the American Jewish scene. If political and fiscal collaboration is indispensable for physical survival, religious collaboration is indispensable for moral survival. Our seminaries, our unions of congregations, cur rabbinical bodies, must enter into the most intense relationships with one another, because the climate and the mood of Yavneh are at hand, and we compete with one another at the peril of the existence of our people.

I recognize fully that Israel is a sovereign state which must make its own political decisions and enjoy or suffer their consequences. I am also convinced that we cannot and should not attempt to define Israel's geographical borders. But if my thesis is correct that Israel is part of the greater Israel, the Jewish people, then we have both a right and a responsibility to voice our judgments on issues which are clearly moral and clearly transcend issues of national security. American Jews will and should make judgments, as do their Israeli counterparts—and these judgments will have an ultimate, if not immediate, bearing on the depth of our relationships. These issues will also help determine whether Israel will endure as a *Jewish* state. At the same time, the judgments of the Galut will be honest only if it sees Israel's actions as increasingly outraged and besieged responses to the treachery of the Arab nations, the venality of the United Nations, the bending of the international conscience to oil blackmail, the isolation of the Jews—on the playing fields of Moscow and in the chambers of a Security Council straight out of Kafka. Those who refuse to see this and to act on this are not qualified to make moral judgments.

Israel is in the grip of a terrible dilemma. Had Israel abandoned its policy of firmness in favor of conciliation, there is no objective indication that the ultimate goals and the immediate terror of its enemies would have been dissipated. Nothing could have made this more clear to many of us than the declaration in 1970 by the Israel Revolutionary Action Committee that "the final goal is the creation of a Socialist, revolutionary Middle East."[9] Nothing could make this more clear than the attack on Israel on Yom Kippur.

If our relationships are to be enduring, the concept of bilateralism, of interdependence and mutual accountability, will have to be invoked. We have never been more dependent on one another than we are now. On Yom Kippur we could not have survived without one another. American Jews should be accountable to Israel for the quality of our Jewish life, which is often shallow and uninformed, and sometimes vulgar. And the Israel community should consider itself accountable to world Jewry for its own priorities, which will be scrutinized when Israel finds surcease, and to which Abba Eban alluded in a famous speech in Haifa. A way must be found for mutual discourse, predicated on liberating American Jewry from its tatus of acquiescence, accepted by some, rejected by others.

A logical consequence of our interdependence with Israel is that while preserving our own identity as a Galut community, we must also encourage aliyah. We cannot pass judgment upon Israel without sharing in its struggles. Otherwise we are no less paternalistic than Israel. But if we are to be open to aliyah, then Israel must seriously confront those conditions in its economy and social system that make for a higher degree of emigration by Americans than by people from any other country of origin. A special factor for Reform Jews is the outright hostility manifested toward us, individually and as a movement, by the religious establishment, which openly proclaims that we have no rights in Israel and then invites us to come to Israel if we want to make changes. As long as this hostility exists, as long as some Americans presently in Israel live under the cloud of Jewish and halakhic illegitimacy, then Israel, not we, will be hampering aliyah. Following American Jewry's most recent response to Israel's jeopardy, who dares to imperil Jewish unity by saying to us that we are inauthentic Jews? Who dares to imperil our unity by saying that our rabbis are not rabbis, our conversions are not conversions, our children are not Jews?

Will aliyah not drain us of our most gifted leaders and our most promising youth? It will if we fail to cultivate our spiritual and intellectual resources as assiduously as we should. Even without aliyah we will decline through euphoric sloth. But with Israel's help, we can regenerate ourselves and replenish our ranks through exertions which we are only beginning to make, such as the first-year program at our Jerusalem school, our camp activities, and the growing numbers of our teenagers on summer pilgrimages to Israel.

In encouraging aliyah we must not reduce our zeal for participating in the struggle to bring America back from the brink of the abyss. We must do this because of our moral concern and also because our future in America depends on the soundness of the democratic process. As long as the possibility remains for restoring that process, we hasten its destruction if we assume that all is lost, that America's decline and fall are inevitable. Thus, on the two fronts of aliyah and the commitment to a reborn America, heroic spiritual measures will have to be taken. This involves great risks. I will cite only one. How far can we go in being a prophetic people in Galut, under unfriendly conditions? When the prophets whom we invoke prophesied to wicked regimes, it was in their own land, not in Galut. Should American Jewry approach a point of danger, we will have to turn inward in self-defense. But that point is not so near that we can opt out of our moral duties, by whose neglect we bring on the point of danger.

For what, ultimately, should we strive? A state of Jews, or a Jewish state? A total ingathering, with the Galut falling away like a spent rocket booster? If this is all, then should we not be assiduously encouraging aliyah for some, and painless assimilation for the rest? We must not evade the issue by euphoric reconcilation to Israel as a state like other states. If that is what it must become, it will be only because it is willing to loosen its ties with the Galut, whose very existence and viability prevent Israel from being like all the nations. Our dreams are unquestionably not reality. But we must not reject the messianic vision imbedded in the dream. Otherwise we are tied to raw nationalism, which a new generation will reject, except through the hostility of the world, God forbid.

I have come full circle back to one of my premises—we are a people which has given rise to a state. That peoplehood alone gives *Jewish* validity to the state. When Israel's Supreme Court recently upheld the decision of a kibbutznik, Yeshaya Shyk, not to register as a Jew but only as an Israeli, on the grounds that he was a cosmopolitan and not a Jew, it may have rendered a sound libertarian judgment, but one which could strike at the roots of the Jewish people. Clearly, no one can be compelled to remain a Jew, but in this case the choice was not between Jewishness and cosmopolitanism, whatever that may be, but between Jewishness and Israeliness. The Supreme Court validated that distinction and theoretically made it possible for Israelism to replace Judaism.

I believe that the Jewish people stands at the threshold of an epoch in which it will undergo yet another mutation, as it did during the Exodus, the Babylonian captivity, the rabbinic period, and the period of the destruction of the Second Commonwealth, when we entered upon millennial exile. All these were mutations within the permissible boundaries of the people as it understood and applied its relationship to its God, its Torah, its unbreakable covenant, its belief in messianism, which defied all of history's dirty tricks. But there were other mutations in which the boundaries were wiped out. These were the Christian mutation in which the name Israel was misappropriated, the Karaite mutation in which Torah was stifled, the Shabbatian mutation in which the covenant and the Messiah were rendered obscene. A new mutation in which the state would become identical with the people would endanger the future of this covenant community. But there are also forces at work to preserve it. The commingling communities in Israel are literally transforming the physical being of the people, even as the axis of Jewish existence has shifted back to the land of our origins. But something deeper has begun to shape this people. It is our resurrection from Auschwitz at the moment when Western civilization lay dying. It is the complex religious civilization of the people Israel, which, however it construes that moment, is sustained by memories of Sinai; by the cords of the covenant, which quicken the hearts of unknowing Jews in Russia; by a Torah which speaks in disparate tongues, but nevertheless continues to speak; by a God who, worshipped or rejected, brought us to this time when He was heard to say at the Sea of Reeds, and says again: "Tell the People of Israel to go forward."

The State of Israel represents the climax of the death of our people at Auschwitz and then its transfiguration. We and you cannot ignore our responsibility in preserving the moral implications of that resurrection. Otherwise we reduce the miracle to another fantastic and even incredible feat of power alone. But, as our Tanakh tells us: "God was not in the fire."[10]

Zalman, not too much time is left to keep the Zionist vision alive.

Reprise:
Warsaw—1943

B'RESHIET

At first we defended ourselves with Torah
When they sealed us up within those walls.
We knew the adversary well and cherished no hopes
That like endless unspeakable masters before them
They would plunder us of everything but life.
But we waited for the trumpet of salvation
Hoping that it must sound somehow from beyond those walls.
Meanwhile, half-trustingly we waited, and like our fathers
Found both shelter and long-suffering in Torah.
A thousand houses, fetid with death and living decay
Became school houses, lyceums, and concert halls.
To vault those constricting barricades,
To defeat the agony of living, by stealth we brought from hiding
Our only contraband—our added soul,
And tasting of it greedily, we desisted before its flavor crazed us,
And hoarded it for days more bitter still.
Word would filter through the Ghetto—
The Yahrzeit of Peretz approaches.
Then overnight Peretz would be read, memorialized,
Declaimed, dramatized, sung
And through him we would descend into a deeper level
The world of Levi Yitzchok the comforter, Nachman the teller of tales
That bring you to the throne of Mercy itself—
The world of Israel Baal Shem Tov, by whose childish wisdom
An age drew back from the brink of madness.
Through them we descended to yet another level
And yet another until we stood in the very corridors
From which the imprisoned soul of the Universe,
Cries out in Eicho-tones to be released.
Thus we subsisted on the fare of which our fathers partook

But with lesser relish, for theirs was a confidence
  transcending death itself
And ours but a hope, diluted in doubt, and overcast
By a shadow before whose monstrous image
Even our Fathers would have trembled.

SH'MOT

So your name, Zundel, has been called up too,
Are you not honored by the attention they bestow on us?
They think they deceive us, and I think I deceive my Chanah.
It is a secret held together by terror's quivering sinews
But as apparent as your startled eyes.
I sense a moan welling up from your soul
And imploring your lips. Stifle it and grieve in silence.
They have had their will upon us—
Our homes gutted, our beloved violated and destroyed.
Their mark is on all that we called ours.
But they must not engrave fear upon our faces,
For they desire to see upon us, haters of idolatry,
  the imprint of their God,
Their great God Dread, whose horrid visage they would stamp
On every serene brow. Their great God Dread,
Sired by Hate and conceived by Frenzy,
Yet they alone worship him most awfully.
In the secret places of their loneliness
His image comes between them and their lustful reveries.
His image covers them like a black cloud.
When they lead us hence, knowing as the terror-ridden so truly know
That they shall walk this same familiar path some day,
Our unheard footsteps keeping time with theirs.
Our Exodus begins. Theirs waits, and in their spuriously impassive eyes
Their great God Dread cries out "Not yet, not yet."

VAYIKRA

I, Moishe the melamed, call to You, Ribono shel Olom.
Well may You say "Shehecheyonu" that I speak to You at last
For You know that all has not been well between us.
You gave me understanding and thereby confounded Yourself.
For how could my understanding justify Your ways?
Better that You had made me a fool,

Less self-afflicting and less rebellious against You.
I judged You once, and having judged You,
   ceased pondering on Your deeds.
Yes, You were an all-seeing eye. That I granted.
But You were, I knew, an impotent eye,
   mounted upon a senseless device
Whose insane movements, once begun, could not be stopped,
And never stopping, dragged a mangled Eternity between its wheels.
Your children passed before You like a flock.
You counted and recorded them in Your book.
The tortured in this column. The buried alive in that column.
Division of labor. You kept the books. The machine devoured.
Therefore, all-knowing One, You knew why my heart
   was not in my teaching.
I mastered the art of absorption in a poem by Avigdor Ha'Meiri
While teaching children God-eulogizing Haftoros.
I had no patience for "God is my strength and my refuge."
Lest my divorcement from you ensnare the children's souls,
I taught them the Hebrew, the chant, the prophets' times.
It was for You to do the rest.
If You could not entice them to know You, how could I?
So it went, and my heart hardened against You with each passing day.
The more I recognized that You were, the less I learned that You cared.
I would die, I said, defying you. Were a single Jew in Warsaw
To arouse the World, not by magnifying You, but rejecting You,
The myth of the compassionate God would perish with me.
Then, if men must be slaves, let them not be thrall
   to a fraudulent Chaos.

But now I call to You, Ribono shel Olom,
Like my rebellious father and my defiant grandfather,
Who learned that revolt is the interlude between
   searching and submission.
Who has not spurned You does not know You.
I know You, now. You are my fellow captive,
Cast down and afflicted and despised with me.
You have been exiled to this place with me. Driven
   from the hearts of men,
Your last refuge is this dwelling place of death.
Tomorrow we shall sally forth with You.
You may die here with us. Tomorrow you may perish with us,
In Synagogue or school or on the barricades.

When we die, and should the world take little note
Or look aghast in proper consternation and then move on,
You will be dead, and many ages will come and go before You live again.
If you are banished from the human soul, Your place in heaven is empty.
Everything is in Your hands except the reverence for You.
When men cast that aside, then it is Satan who banishes God to Hell.
And this is Hell, where at bay before the minions of Nothing,
    You make Your last stand.
I am ready. Not that I do not fear. Adonoi Li V'lo Iro?
The martyrs going forth to meet death in joy? Perhaps this saint or that,
The rest went with dragging step and chattering teeth. In
    this their glory,
That fearing they advanced, intransigence overpowering dread.

Now that You occupy the depths with me, I know You well.
I know, too, why the tots I have instructed first
    knew You through Vayikra,
That wearisome text of priestly ministrations and domicilic leprosies.
Vayikra is the book of sanctification, adjuring him who will hear
To make himself holy for the climactic moments of his life,
To be in readiness for the blow that must fall,
To garb himself in the vestments of martyrdom,
To fulfill the rites of disembodying the soul,
To hear at last the final decree—Kedoshim Tiheyu,
Martyrs you shall be.
L'cho dodi, come my Friend,
My wounded, rejected Friend, sheltered only by the
    wretched and the doomed.
We go to look into the fearsome face of the great Emptiness,
The soul-turned-monster which efficient men stripped of you.
Though we are dying I am not reconciled,
For if these who are no longer men look just like me,
Perhaps they feel no aching loss of You, since the demon
Who rides the void within them, must look like You.

BEMIDBAR

The Wilderness closed in upon them. For once,
    pagan blood flowed on Pesach.
The war with Amalek! The war of the embattled dreamers,
Zionists, socialists, Talmudists.
Zivion, one of the dispatch boys, has gone mad.

From barricade to barricade he rushes messages.
But he is mad. For he is thinking abstractly in the midst of battle.
An automaton-mentor has taken over Zivion's tasks
While fugitive, half-clad reveries run messages
      on the streets of his own soul:
Vengeance, vengeance, for us who are to die.
Let them not seek revenge who have not been aggrieved.
It will be spent with us, nor pollute the dainty souls
Of those who knowing not compassion, can know no bitterness.
Which is more loathesome in the eyes of God? The
      dark and soul-consuming
Will of a bereaved father on his son's assassin,
Or the sanctimonious turning of the eyes from the assassination
Three million times compounded by a world too
      prayerfully stunned to move.
Hate evil, not the evil-doer. Perish sin and not the sinner.
If I find a Nazi, I will teach him Midrash.
"Come, sinner, it is your sin I despise but not you
      nor your immortal soul,
For are we not all wanting in the eyes of God?
Therefore let me slay you lovingly and dispatch you with a blessing."
When we are done in Warsaw, all will be consumed—
We, the foe, our hate and our revenge.
Revenge does not spread like a plague.
It is engendered like a monstrosity, child of perverted justice.
Let them who profess to abhor it dare to kill it with one act of kindness.
Come, Zivion, this question has no meaning for you who are to die.
Let the world wrestle with it. I alone must grapple with this—

Is there meaning in my death and in these many, many deaths?
Why do we die? For us this is no war of survival.
In either case we are finished. Then why do we die?
They say there is nothing in life without its repercussions.
Even a missing penny somehow affects the world's money markets.
Yes, a missing penny. But are 50,000 Zivions worth a penny?
All theories are true, but not when applied to the Zivions,
A people is a people, but Zivion's people is a not-people.
A Nazi-victim is a victim but Zivion is a vacuum.
The oppressed must be defended, but Zivion is not oppressed.
Soon he will be non-existent. Therefore sub specie aternitatis
      he *is* non-existent.

Therefore, how can the non-existent, especially if not
     oppressed, be defended?
So what meaning, what repercussions are you talking about?
About an unknown man in a sound-proof chamber choking to death?
What difference to anyone, including himself, after he dies?
Well, Zivion, what now? I will tell you. You are mistaken,
Not because you are in error but because you are on the wrong track.
Compassion cannot stir the uncompassionate, nor desire the eunuch.

What if the choice of utter extinction, or a gilgul
In the form of a Nazi were given to me?
I would take the former, knowing well that I surrender eternal life.
For if Satan is anti-Christ, the Nazi is anti-Man.
By devices revealing supreme intelligence,
     by the rarest gifts of the mind,
He has contrived to alter his very essence, becoming other than a man.
Through a feat, generations long, requiring sciences, arts, devotion,
He has annulled the process of millennia and restored
     himself to sub-antiquity,
A man, self-demoted to a monster, the Golem spirit resurgent.
Unlike other hunters of men, he alone, unleashing
     panthers upon the world,
Did not run for shelter until they dropped harmless
     and heavy with prey,
But ran, naked and exultant before the pack which
     knew him as their own.
I would not be a Nazi, and accepting life from him,
Become, however distantly, kin to him.
Thus my defiance and my death are for the Zivions, circumcised and not,
Who looking upon the face of the foe, recognize Adam's brother,
Unapprehended, hunted by God Who once forgot to breathe upon him.
My death is for the Zivions who say "Boruch Ato Adonoi
     Shelo Osani Nazi."
"Blessed is the God Who did not make me a Nazi."

D'VARIM

Words! After the silence of death closed down upon the Ghetto
A squad of conquerors entering the gutted secret radio station
Heard words! The wires were torn, the radio smashed,
     the announcer's jaw torn away.
But words, falling like the last drops of a spent thunder-shower

Rumbled and wandered around the room:
Listen, you heavens, and I will speak. If men will not
    harken, the heavens will.
Let not the world be troubled, for its task is done.
Let not its spirit suffer mortification, nor its conscience be stricken,
For we are no more and stand not in need of help.
Patience is its own reward. The long-suffering with which
    you bore our agony
Has brought you compensation. In waiting was your salvation.
Now of another realm, we no longer understand the tongues and rites
With which you mustered sacraments, mystical ethics,
Doleful dirges, lugubrious laments to seal our document of doom.
Was yours a higher fetishism? (The savage, anthropologist's delight,
Stabbed dummies of his enemies and thus wished them dead.)
You, higher-minded, adorned and medaled us with invocations,
Wishing us life. This fatal hiatus between the wish and the deed
You dared not trespass for that was Caesar's,
    Nor did our brothers trespass it, for in boundless gratitude to you
For your solicitude, they dared not overstep courtesy's bounds.
Courtesy, propriety, at all costs must you be preserved.
In peaceful interchange of pious thoughts about God's grace,
    the healing qualities of prayer,
Who rudely talked of us, like a huckster, shouting
    down a chamber concert,
Met the rebuff of awkward silence and deftly altered comments.
But we are not chagrined. From our vantage point we know
    that days will come when celebrated societies
Will jostle for the honor of testifying to your courage and intercession.
A thousand divines, wise men, statesmen, teachers signed their names!
There was a day on which many voices said, Alas!
And in some footnote, buried like a helot in a dungeon,
The names of twos or threes who said, "Our hands will not be clean,
Our tongues will stammer until this deed is undone."
We are the ten, the last minyon, who stood upon the roof top.
We stood alone, looking beyond the ruins of this land.
We have seen a vision of a land far off.
Listen, our brothers who survive. This is our last testament to you.
When you go up to the land, as you surely will,
Go to the Negev, that scorched and desolate waste of the southland,
The land abandoned by man and God,
The land made sterile and terrible to dwell upon,

The land, ruined and bleak, even as this Ghetto is now ruined and bleak,
Scorched and desolate, awesome even to the brutes who stalk it.
Build houses there, with beams and stone brought from here.
Build schools there, with torn texts salvaged from here.
Build synagogues there, with desecrated scrolls brought hence,
And call your settlement—Ghetto Warsaw,
Plant our wounds and our martyrdom in the unyielding soil
Until it tremble and surrender to you.

Notes

FOR ZION'S SAKE

1 Taanit 5b.

2 Jer. 32:1–14.

3 Cahana, *Antologia Yisraelit* (Warsaw, 1922), 1:40.

4 Solomon ibn Gabirol, *Poems* (Philadelphia, 1923), pp. 20–23, 28, 29, 31–33.

5 Solomon Zeitlin, *Maimonides* (New York, 1935), p. 85.

6 Salo W. Baron, *A Social and Religious History of the Jews* (New York, 1937), 2:79.

7 Hasdai Crescas, *Or Adonai* (Vienna, 1860), p. 81.

8 Joseph Albo, *Sefer ha-Ikkarim* (Philadelphia, 1930), 4:424.

9 Alexander Marx and Max L. Margolis, *History of the Jewish People* (Philadelphia, 1927), pp. 517–18.

10 Heinrich Graetz, *History of the Jews* (Philadelphia, 1891), 1:32–33.

11 S. A. Horodetzky, *Leaders of Chassidism* (London, 1928), pp. 85–87.

12 Yehezkel Kaufmann, *Golah ve-Nekhar* (Tel Aviv, 1929–30), 1:463.

13 Judah Ha-Levi, *Sefer ha-Kuzari* (Vilna, 1905), pt. 2.

14 Moses Mendelssohn, *Gesammelte Schriften* (Berlin, 1929–32), 5:494; *Or le-Nesivah.*

15 Kayserling, *Moses Mendelssohn* (Leipzig, 1888), pp. 30–32.

16 Sh. D. Luzzatto, *Kinor Naim* (Padua, 1879), p. 64.

17 De Ligne, *Memoires et Mélanges* (Paris, 1827), 2:30, 32, 41, 46; Hartley, *Observations on Man* (London, 1801), 2:373–75; Shaftesbury, *Diaries* (1838).

18 Hayes, *Political and Social History of Modern Europe* (New York, 1929), 2:65.

19 Georg Wilhelm Hegel, *Philosophy of History* (New York, 1900), pp. 8–11, 16–23, 37–39.

20 Nachman Krochmal, *Moreh Nevukhei ha-Zeman* (Lemberg, 1863), p. 22.

21 Peretz Smolenskin, *Maamarim* (Jerusalem, 1925), 2:192–93.

22 Moses Lilienblum, *Kal Kitve* (Odessa, 1912), 3:86–89.

23 Ahad Ha-Am, *Al Perashat Derakhim* (Berlin, 1930), 3:91.

24 Ibid., 2:156–62.

25 *Encyclopedia of the Social Sciences* (New York, 1937), 7:529.

26 Kaufmann, *Golah ve-Nekhar,* 2:22–23.

27 Ibid., pp. 197–98.

28 Jer. 31:12.

29 Reinhold Niebuhr, *Moral Man and Immoral Society* (New York, 1934), p. 263.

30 *Kuzari,* pt. 2, pp. 129–30.

31 J. Sarachek, *Don Isaac Abravanel* (New York, 1938), p. 165.

32 Traditional Prayer Book.

33 Letter of Executive Committee of American Council for Judaism, March 1, 1943.

34 Isa. 5:8.

35 Jer. 20:7.

36 Letter of Executive Committee of American Council for Judaism, March 1, 1943.

37 *Jewish Daily Bulletin,* November 6, 1929.

38 Letter of Executive Committee of American Council for Judaism, March 1, 1943.

39 Hayim Nahman Bialik, *Devarim She-be-al Peh* (Tel Aviv, 1935), 1:55.

40 Jer. 32:42–44.

THE TWOFOLD TASK OF ZIONISM

1 *He-Atid* (Berlin, 1923).

2 Yehezkel Kaufmann, *Golah ve-Nekhar* (Tel Aviv, 1929–30), 2:194, 198–99.

3 Salo W. Baron, *Religious and Cultural History of the Jews* (New York, 1937), 2:217–18.

4 Hayim Nahman Bialik, *Devarim She-be-al Peh* (Tel Aviv, 1935), 1:54.

THE STATE OF ISRAEL: ITS MORAL IMPLICATIONS

1 G. F. Abbott, *Israel in Europe,* (New York, 1970), p. 533

2 Kautsky, *Are the Jews a Race?* (New York, 1926), pp. 246–47.

3 See Krochmal's *Moreh Nevukhei ha-Zeman* (Lemberg, 1851).

4 In Mordecai Zeev Feierberg, *L'An* (New York, 1927).

THE UNIQUENESS OF JUDAISM

1 Jer. 2:6, 8.

2 *Summa Theologica* 1. 23. 5.

3 Avodah Zarah 5ª

4 Baba Metzia 59b.

5 Ibid.

6 Ibid.

7 Ibid.

8 Yoma 86a.

9 Mishnah Sanhedrin 4:5.

10 Jer. 5:1.

11 Berakhot 33b.

12 Lev. 18:5.

THE CHOSEN PEOPLE

1 Deut. 18:5.
2 Deut. 21:5.
3 Exod. 19:6.
4 Isa. 42:6–7.
5 Amos 3:1–2.
6 Num. 23:21–22.
7 Num. 23:9.
8 Abudarham
9 Saadia
10 Orbach, *Amudei ha-Mahshavah ha-Yisraelit* (Jerusalem, 1955), p. 199.
11 *Kuzari* (London, 1946), p. 33.
12 *Amudei ha-Mahshavah ha-Yisraelit*, p. 213.
13 *Kuzari*, pp. 126–29.

ISRAEL: THE MEETING OF PROPHECY AND POWER

1 Kaufmann, *Toledot ha-Emunah ha-Yisraelit* (Tel Aviv, 1952), 4:181.
2 2 Chron. 26:15 ff.
3 2 Chron. 28:9 ff.
4 Johs. Pedersen, *Israel* (Copenhagen, 1926), sec. 3, p. 91.
5 Gerald von Rad, *Old Testament Theology* (New York, 1962), 1:90.
6 Ezek. 20:36–37.
7 Sukkah 27b.
8 2 Kings 19:31.
9 Isa. 2:3.
10 Judah Ha-Levi, *Kuzari* (East-West ed., 1946), p. 212.
11 *Midrash Zuta, Shir ha-Shirim* (ed. Buber), p. 2.
12 *Laws* 942.
13 Oscar Cullman, *The State in the New Testament* (New York, 1956), p. 70.
14 Ibid., p. 65.
15 Ibid., p. 58.
16 Rudolf Bultmann, *Theology of the New Testament* (New York, 1955), 2:31–32.
17 Muller, *Freedom in the Western World* (New York, 1966), pp. 98–100.
18 *She'elot u-Teshuvot Maharam b. R. Barukh* (Budapest, 1895).
19 Adret, 6:149.
20 Hegel, *Philosophy of History* (New York, 1944), p. 422.
21 Barth, *Community, State, and Church* (New York, 1960), p. 125.
22 Dubnow, *Nationalism and History* (Philadelphia, 1958), p. 247.

23 Rawidowicz, *Schriften* (Buenos Aires, 1962), p. 343.

24 Ibid., p. 274.

25 Ezek. 20:32–33.

ISRAEL AND CHRISTIAN CONSCIENCE

1 Harry A. Wolfson, *Philo* (Cambridge, Mass., 1947), 2:407.

2 *Mishneh Torah, Hilkhot Melakhim,* chap. 12.

3 *Perush ha-Torah,* on Lekh Lekha.

4 Avraham Yaari, *Igrot Eretz Yisrael* (Ramat Gan, 1971).

5 Heinrich Graetz, *History of the Jews* (Philadelphia, 1894), 3:637.

6 In addendum of Hebrew translation of Graetz, *History of the Jews,* by Shaul Pinchas Rabinovitz (Warsaw, 1893–1912).

7 *Perush ha-Mishnayot, Sanhedrin,* chap. 1.

8 Third Letter.

9 *Kuzari,* trans. Hartwig Hirschfeld (New York, 1927), pp. 78–79.

THE RELIGIOUS DIMENSIONS OF ISRAEL

1 *Netzah Israel* (Tel Aviv, 1964), pp. 26, 81.

ALL ISRAEL'S SEARCH FOR IDENTITY

1 Ps. 55:13–15.

2 Peretz Smolenskin, *Maamarim* (Jerusalem, 1925), 3:18–19.

3 Trans. Ruth Finer Mintz, in *Modern Hebrew Poetry* (Berkeley, 1966), p. 90.

4 Georges Friedmann, *The End of the Jewish People?* (New York, 1967).

5 Hayim Hazaz, in *Israeli Stories* (New York, 1962).

6 Gordon, *Kitve A. D. Gordon* (Jerusalem, 1951), 2:53–55.

7 Ibid.

8 Sh. Shalom, *Kol Shiray* (Tel Aviv, 1966); trans. D. Polish.

9 From a poem by Yehudah Karni in Penuel and Ukhmani, *An Anthology of Modern Hebrew Poetry* (Jerusalem, 1966), 1:130.

PHARISAISM AND POLITICAL SOVEREIGNTY

1 Abraham Schalit, *Hordos ha-Melekh* (Jerusalem, 1960).

2 Ibid., p. 254.

3 Ibid., p. 258.

4 Ibid., p. 260.

5 Matt. 24:2.

6 Ps. Sol. 17:21.

7 *Wars of the Jews* 2, chaps. 16, 17

8   Baron, *A Social and Religious History of the Jews* (New York, 1937), 1:184.

9   Klausner, *The Messianic Idea in Israel* (London, 1956), p. 399.

10 *Wars of the Jews* 2. 16.

11 Rom. 13:1 ff.

12 Berakhot 58a. See also *Genesis Rabbah* 9:13.

13 Avodah Zarah 18a.

14 Midrash to Ps. 14.

15 *Deut. Rabbah* 5.

16 *Mekhilta,* Jethro 20.

17 *Pesikta Zutarta,* Balak.

18 *Midrash Shoher Tov* to Ps. 27.

19 Ibid., 302.

20 *Otiot d'R. Akiba* 1.

SOME MEDIEVAL THINKERS ON THE JEWISH KING

1   *Mishneh Torah, Hilkhot Melakhim* 1:1.

2   Ibid., 1:2.

3   Ibid., 2:5.

4   Ibid., 3:9.

5   Ibid., 2:4.

6   Ibid., 4:10.

7   Ibid., 11:3, 12:17.

8   Ibid., 11:4.

9   Ibid., 12:5.

10 *Kuzari* 2.24.

11 Ibid., 2.15–23.

12 Ibid., 2.14.

13 *Perush ha-Torah* (Warsaw, 1862), Lekh Lekha.

14 Ibid., Vayera.

15 Ibid., Mishpatim.

16 Ibid., 1 Sam., chap. 16, p. 101.

17 Ibid., 1 Sam. 8, p. 91b.

18 Ibid., p. 3b.

19 Ibid., p. 93b.

20 1 Sam. 8:11.

21 *Politics,* bk. 5, chap. 10, p. 167.

22 *Perush ha-Torah,* Judg., p. 372.

ARE WE IN EXILE?

1 Albert Camus, *The Plague* (New York, 1948), p. 278.

2 Walter Miller, Jr., *Canticle for Leibowitz* (New York, 1969).

RELIGIOUS MEANINGS IN JEWISH SECULARISM

1 Pinsker, *Auto-Emancipation* (New York, 1935), p. 7.

2 Cohn, *Warrant for Genocide* (New York, 1969), p. 16.

3 *The Diaries of Theodor Herzl* (New York, 1956), pp. 427–30.

4 Bettelheim, *The Informed Heart* (Glencoe, Ill., 1960), pp. 256–64, 281.

MI YAKUM YAAKOV—HOW CAN JACOB ENDURE?

1 Robert L. Heilbroner, *The Future as History* (New York, 1959), p. 205.

2 Heer, *God's First Love* (New York, 1970).

ISRAEL AND GALUT: THE UNRESOLVED ENCOUNTER

1 Oswald Spengler, *Decline of the West* (New York, 1932), 2:210.

2 Hans Kohn, *Nationalism: Its Meaning and History* (1965), p. 29.

3 Snyder, *The New Nationalism* (Ithaca, N.Y., 1968), p. 357.

4 Laski, "Nationalism and the Future of Civilization," in *The Danger of Being a Gentleman and Other Essays* (New York, 1940), p. 43.

5 Fromm, *The Sane Society* (New York, 1955), p. 58.

6 Morgenthau, *At Pacem in Terris* (New York, 1965).

7 Ward, *Nationalism and Ideology* (New York, 1966), p. 58.

8 Klatzkin, *Boundaries,* in *The Zionist Idea,* ed. Arthur Hertzberg (New York, 1959), p. 325.

9 *National Liberation Fronts,* p. 142.

10 1 Kings 19:12.

INDEX

Abbott, G. F., 25
Abd-ur Rahman III, 2
Abraham, 32, 43, 46, 48, 49, 54, 80, 111, 126 *see also* Covenant, Israel's with God and Abraham
Abrahamitic perception, 31, 32
Abravanel, Don Isaac, 7, 73, 74, 123-130 *passim*
Adam, 14
African Jewry, 21
Agnon, Samuel Joseph, 76, 103
Agrippa, 119
Ahad, Ha-Am, 4, 15, 33, 64, 65, 74, 90, 113, 158, 166
Aharit ha-Yamim, 38
Ahasuerus, 25
Akiba, Rabbi, 37, 118, 119, 121
Albo, Joseph, 2
Alenu, 50
Aliyah, 173, 174
Almohades in Spain, 33
Alsace-Lorraine, Jews of, 16
Am Olam, 105
Amalek, 123
America, and admittance of refugees, 17
America, as a nationalist, 6
American Catholics, 109, 110
American Council for Judaism, 6
American history, recent, 160-161
American Jewry, 9-10, 22, 27, 67, 92, 93, 96, 99, 110, 132-137 *passim,* 159, 161-164 *passim,* 168-174 *passim*
American Jews of foreign extraction, 109-110
American Lutherans, 109
American Protestants, 110
American Reform Judaism, 112
American Zionists, 162
Americans living in Israel, 173
America's Black issue, 132-133
Amos, 44, 46, 50
Amsterdam Council, 78, 80, 81, 86

Ani (A. D. Gordon), 90, 104
Anti-nationalists, 6, 7, 8
Antiochus, tyrrany of, 116
Anti-Semitism, 9, 22, 69, 70, 77-85 *passim,* 98, 102, 133, 141, 142, 161, 169
Anti-Zionists, 1-14 *passim,* 16, 18, 23, 143
Aquinas, Thomas, 33, 127
Arab Christians, 78
Arab-Israeli war (1967), 78, 90, 96, 97, 99, 101, 103, 112, 113, 150, 169, 172
Arab-Jewish federation, possibilities of, 113
Arab nations, treachery of, 172
Arab-refugee problem, 86
Arab world, 30, 77, 80
Arabian desert, Western, wandering shepherds of, 21
Arabs, problem of the, from inception of Zionist movement, 113
Are the Jews a Race? (K. Kautsky), 25
Are we in exile, 131-38 *see also* Exile, Jewish
Aristotle, and Aristotelian concept, 33, 125, 127, 129
Armleder pogroms, 12
Assimilation, Jewish, 5
Augustine, 7, 143
Auschwitz, 54, 69, 83, 86, 91, 92, 106, 107, 132-135 *passim,* 144, 145, 146, 147, 150, 152, 156, 175
"Auto-emancipation," 86
Avelei-Zion, 1
Avodah, 40

Babel, generation of, 38
Babylonian captivity, 174
Babylonian diaspora, 96
Babylonian exile, 144
Balaam, 46, 51
Balfour Declaration, 14
Baltic concentration camp, 159
Bar Kokhba, 119, 121, 124
Barcelona, Jewry in, 87

Baron, Salo Wittmayer, 118
Barth, Karl, 7, 62
Basle, political covenant of, 67
Batavian Assembly, 16
Bedouins, Hebrew, 148
Behirah (selection), 44, 55
Bellows, Saul, 92
BEMIDBAR (Warsaw 1943), 179-181
Benamozegh, Rabbi Elie, 151
Ben-Gurion, David, 32
Benjamin, land of, 14
Benjamin, tribe of, 58
Bennett, John C., 84
Ben Zvi Library of the Hebrew University, 105
Berab, Jacob, 74
Bertinoro, Obadiah of, 73, 74
Bettelheim, Bruno, 136, 146
Bialik, Hayim Nahman, 21
Bible, 1, 31, 32, 36, 38
Biblical Judaism, 110
Black Community issue in America, 132-133
Bonds for Israel, 170
Book of Chronicles, 14
Book of Daniel, 115
Brandeis, Louis Dembitz, 10-11
B'RESHIET (Warsaw 1943), 176-177
Brit milah, 54
British Empire (Commonwealth), 164
British Empire, withdrawal of, from Palestine, 25
Buber, Martin, 15, 54, 106, 113, 153
Buddhism, 69, 152
Bukharians, 7-8
Bundists, Jewish, 154

Cain, mark of, fall of, and role of, 38, 70, 143
Camus, Albert, 133, 161
Canaan and Canaanites, 49, 72, 149
Canticle for Leibowitz (W. Miller, Jr.), 133
Catholics, American, 109, 110
Cave-dwellers, Moroccan, 148
Central Conference of American Rabbis, viii
Centrality, 164, 165
Chaldees, Ur of the, 21
Childhood in Exile (S. Levin), 135
Chmielnitzki massacres, 92
Chosen People, the, 41-55

Christ, *see* Jesus, Jewish rejection of
"Christian Approach to the Jews," World Council report on, 78-80
Christian Century, publications of, viii
Christian conscience and Israel, 71-88
Christian mutation, and the Torah, 175
Christian theology, 47-48
Christian view of the Jew, 29-30
Christian views of the state, early, 60-61
Christiani, Pablo, 72
Christianity compared with Judaism, 31-40
Church of Christ, 82
Cohn, Norman, 141, 142, 154
Commission on Social Justice, San Francisco Archdiocese, 85
Commonwealth, Second, 174 destruction, of, 111
Concentration and death camps in Europe, 51, 78-79, 146, 159 *see also* Auschwitz
Conference of Presidents of National Organizations, 171
Congress of Vienna, 2, 18, 91
Conservative Judaism, prayer books of, 41
Conversos, 73
Coptic Orthodox Church, 84
Covenant, Israel's, with God and Abraham, 46, 47, 75, 89, 98, 111, 118, 119, 120, 126, 148, 151, 158, 164, 174
Covenant of Sinai, 54, 158, 168, 174
Covenental character of events, 54
Crescas, Hasdai, 2
Crusades, and Jews under Crusaders, 12, 76, 133
Cullman, Oscar, 60, 61
Cyrus Proclamation, 14
Czechoslovakia, 140, 152

Damascus, 143
Daniel, Book of, 115
Danish democracy, 6
David, 57, 71, 116, 122, 124, 147
David, House of, 124
David, Kingdom of the House of, 1, 147
"David, the dynasty of," 57, 71, 116, 122, 124, 147
Day of Atonement, 34, 35, 173
Day of Judgment War, 169 *See also* Arab-Israeli war
Day schools and university departments, Jewish, 134
Death camps and concentration camps, 51, 78-79, 146, 159 *see also* Auschwitz

Delury, John, 85
Denmark, Lutheran World Federation in, 83
Denmark's democracy, and Christian charity to the Jew, 6, 18
Deputy, The (R. Hochhuth), 112
Der Judenstaat (T. Herzil), 69
Desert tribes, 38, 58, 149
Deutero-Isaiah, 45
Deuteronomy, 44, 45, 46
De Vere, Rev. A. D., 80, 81
Devil and the Jews, The (J. Trachtenberg), 141
"Devil doctrine," and anti-Semitism, 142
Diaspora, 8, 26, 52, 58, 59, 62-72 passim, 75-78 passim, 87, 92, 93, 96, 97, 102, 109, 112, 118, 120, 122, 125, 126, 131, 132, 134, 150, 164, 165
Diaspora-Galut, 134 see also Galut
Dina d'Malkhuta, 62
Doge of Venice, 73
Dohm, Christian Wilhelm, 16
Dreyfus, Alfred, 132
Dubnow, Shimon, 64, 158
Dunn, Bishop, 81
D'VARIM (Warsaw, 1943), 181-183

Easter, 144
Eastern Europe, Jews in, 131, 141, 159
Eban, Abba, 173
Ecclesiastes, 32
Edom and Edomites, 73, 121
Egypt, Israel and Jews in, 38, 73
    departure from, 41, 44
    exile and slavery in, 29, 31, 38, 41, 44, 45, 51, 54, 148
Elazar, Rabbi, 167
Elders of Zion, 133
Elisha, 54
Emancipation, and the Jewish problem, 16, 17, 19, 86, 97, 99, 100, 131
Encyclopaedia Britannica, 66
England, and the Diaspora, 164
England, persecutions in, 72
Enosh, 14
Ephraim, 3
Eretz Yisrael, 26, 65, 71, 89, 90, 91, 94, 103, 135
Europe, liberation of its Jews, 16, 17
Europe, oppression of Israel in, 51, 73
European Jewry, 9, 10, 13, 18-19, 21, 22, 28, 59, 63, 73, 131, 141, 159

European nationalism, 5, 140
Evanston conference, 81, 82, 84, 85, 86
Eved nirtzah, 12
Exile, are we in?, 131-138
Exile, heritage and tyrrany of, 29, 31, 51, 78, 89, 167, 174
Exile, Jewish, 29, 31, 51, 54, 59, 60, 62-63, 65, 70, 72, 75, 77, 86, 89, 112, 125, 139-140, 142, 144, 167, 174
Exodus, 46, 90, 91, 139, 144, 148, 158, 174
Expulsion from Israel, 12-13, 136
Extermination of Jews, 78-79 see also Auschwitz
Ezekiel, 106

Fackenheim, Emil, 156
Fascism in the Arab world, 30
Fichte, Johann Gottlieb, 160
Fiedler, L., 92
First Assembly of the World Council of Churches, 82
First World War. see World War I
Flood, generation of the, 38
For Zion's Sake, 1-14
France, persecutions in, 72
France, slave laborers of, 11
Frank, Jacob, 154
Frank, Waldo, 20
Free World Diaspora, 63
French aristocracy, hatred of democracy by, 10
French Jews, 73, 131
French Revolution, 1, 2
Freud, Sigmund, 28, 51
Friedmann, Peretz, 100
Fromm, Erich, 160
Future as History, The (R. L. Heilbroner), 154

Gabirol, Solomon ibn, 2, 33
Galileo, 33
Galut, 11, 13, 19, 59, 63, 65, 75, 76, 93, 94, 95, 98-104 passim, 107-108, 131-140 passim, 143, 150, 152, 157, 158
Galut and Israel: the unresolved encounter, 157-175
Galut-Israel, 136
Gates of Prayer, 42
Gauls, 119-120
Gemilut hasadim, 40
Genesis, 38
Geneva, 146

German Jewry, 9, 63, 70, 73, 99
Germany, persecutions in, 72
Geulat ha-Shekhinah, 4
Ghetto Warsaw, 53, 99, 106, 133
Gideon, 57
Gilboa, editor of *Maariv*, 132
God and Israel, 41-55
God and Judaism, 31-44 *passim*, 89, 101-102, 105, 111, 118, 119, 120
God's covenant with Israel and Abraham, 46, 47, 75, 89, 102, 105, 111, 118, 119, 120, 126, 148, 151, 158, 164, 174
God's First Love (F. Heer), 155
Goethe, Johann Wolfgang von, 12
Golterman, Dr. 80
Gordon, A. D., 90, 104
Greece, slave laborers of, 11
Gregory the Great, 61

Ha-Am, Ahad, 4, 15, 23, 64, 65, 74, 90, 113, 158, 166
Hadrian 119
Haganah, 120
Haggadah, 44, 148
Halakah, 52
Halakhic illegitimacy, 173
Ha-Levi, Judah, 2, 3, 7, 47, 48, 49, 71, 72, 74, 123, 125, 126
Hanina ben Teradyon, Rabbi, 121
Ha-Parhi, Ashtori, 73
Hartley, David, 3
Hasdai ibn Shaprut, 2
Hasidim, 22, 104, 114, 116, 146, 154
Haskalah, 5
Hasmonean dynasty, 74, 98, 107, 114, 115, 116
Hayim, Levi ben, 74
Hazaz, Hayim, 100
Hazor, 106
He-Atid, 15
Heaven, Kingdom of, 1
Hebrew Bedouins, 148
Hebrew language, rebirth of, 106
Hebrew University, Ben Zvi Library of the, 105
Heer, Friedrich, 155
Hegel, Georg Wilhelm, 4, 6, 62
Heilbroner, Robert L., 154
Hellenism, Jewish, 114
Heraklion, Crete, meeting in, 85
Herder, Johann Gottfried von, 16-17, 159
Herring, Dr., 81

Herzl, Theodor, 4, 15, 28-29, 69, 131, 141, 142, 156, 158, 166
Hess, Moses, 101
Higher Freedom, The (Polish), 113
Hinduism, 69
Hiroshima, 133, 152, 160
History, Jewish, 139, 140, 141, 144, 147, 152, 155, 156, 162, 165
History recent American, 160-161
Hitler, Adolf, 10, 51, 100, 112, 142, 156, 159, 162
Hochhuth, Rolf, 112
Holland, Jews of, 16
Holland's Christian charity to the Jew, 18
Holocaust, the, 76, 86, 104, 106, 112, 145, 146, 155, 157, 158
Hordos ha-Melekh (Schalit), 114
Hosea, 47
How can Jacob Endure?, 151-156

Identity, all Israel's search for, 96-108
Imperium of Rome, 116, 118, 120
India-Pakistan struggle over Kashmir, 119
India, religiosity of, 6
Informed Heart, The (B. Bettelheim), 146
Intermarriage, 134, 159
International Bill of Human Rights, 17
International Committee on the Christian Approach to the Jews, 84
Inyan Elohi, 49
Irgunists, 120
Isaac, 48
Isaiah, 44
Ishmael, Kingdom of, and Ishmaelites, 73, 74
Islam, 32-33, 69, 73
Islamic theology, 48
Israel and Christian conscience, 71-88
Israel and Galut: the unresolved encounter, 157-175 *see also* Galut; Galut-Israel
Israel and God, 41-55, 119, 120 *see also* God and Judaism; God's covenant with Israel and Abraham
Israel-Arab war, 78, 90, 96, 97, 99, 101, 103, 112, 113, 150, 169, 172
Israel as a nation, 4, 19, 26, 29 *see also* under State of Israel entries
Israel, as the Chosen People, 41-55
Israel, expulsion from, 12-13, 136
Israel-Galut relations, viii, 157-175
Israel in Egypt, 29, 31, 38, 41, 44, 45, 51, 54, 73, 148

Israel in Europe, summary of (G. F. Abbott), 25 *see also headings under* Europe; European Jewry
Israel, land of, 52, 74, 94, 112, 126, 138, 139, 148, 149, 163
Israel Menasseh ben, 2
Israel, moral implications of the State of, 24-30
Israel, national character of, 3, 48
Israel, origin of, 148, 149, 163
Israel, people of, 21, 27, 29, 62, 65, 69, 74, 91, 126, 139, 148, 149, 155, 158, 162, 163, 168, 175
Israel religious dimensions of, 89-95
Israel: the meeting of prophecy and power, 56-70
Israel, and the State of Israel, vii, 26, 52, 62, 63, 67, 68, 69, 70, 78, 81, 86, 87, 91-106 *passim*, 112-120 *passim*, 126, 135, 137, 138, 143, 144, 145, 147, 150, 152, 157, 158, 159, 163, 165, 166, 172, 175
Israel, the State of, and the Jewish people, 109-113
Israelis, 63, 162
Israel's covenant with God and Abraham, 46, 47, 75, 89, 98, 111, 118, 119, 120, 126, 148, 151, 158, 164, 174
Israel's search for identity, 96-108
Israel's Supreme Court, 174
Israel's tribes, 38, 58, 149
Italy, Jewry in, 74
Iverson, Earl and Lorraine, viii

Jacob, 44, 45, 48, 151-156
Jeremiah, 1, 6, 7, 14, 32, 36, 47, 57
Jerusalem, 1, 14, 49, 50, 58, 94, 107, 117, 119, 135, 139, 143, 144, 145, 148, 150
    rebuilding of Temple in, 71, 124
    Wall of, 107, 150
Jerusalem Program of the World Zionist Organization, 167
Jesus, Jewish rejection of, 31, 32, 40, 77, 79, 84, 142, 143
Jew in Our Day, The (W. Frank), 20
Jewish assimilation, 5
Jewish Bundists, 154
Jewish Christians, 117
Jewish Commonwealth, 164, 174
Jewish day schools and university departments, 134
Jewish exile, 29, 31, 51, 54, 59, 60, 62-63,

70, 72, 75, 77, 86, 89, 112, 125, 131-138, 139-144 *passim*, 167, 174
Jewish existence, three categories of, 74
Jewish Hellenism, 114
Jewish history, 139, 140, 141, 144, 147, 152, 155, 156, 162, 165
Jewish King, some medieval thinkers on the, 123-130
Jewish literature and history, 139, 140, 141, 144, 147, 155, 156, 162, 165
Jewish mysticisim and spirituality, 110-111
Jewish nationalism, 2-3, 4, 5, 6, 10, 113, 125, 130, 140, 159, 160, 174
Jewish people, the, and the State of Israel, 109-113
Jewish people, the nature of, 110
Jewish prayer book, 111, 135
"Jewish Problem, How to Solve it, The" (L. D. Brandeis), 11
Jewish Radical right and left, 152
Jewish secularism, religious meanings in, 139-150
Jewish State, vii, viii, 2, 3, 4, 12, 27 *see also under all* State of Israel headings
Jewish theology, 35, 63
Jewish universalism, 5, 6 *see also under* "Universalism"
Jewry, African, 21
Jewry, American, 8, 9-10, 22, 67, 92, 93, 99, 110, 134-137 *passim*, 159, 161, 162, 163, 168-174 *passim*
    of foreign extraction, 109-110
Jewry, European, 9, 10, 13, 18-19, 21, 22, 28, 59, 63, 73, 131, 141, 159
Jewry, French, 73, 131
Jewry, German, 9, 63, 70, 73, 99
Jewry, of the Mediterranean area, 21
Jewry, of the Near East, 21
Jewry, Polish, 9, 17, 146, 159
Jewry, Romanian, 9, 159
Jewry, Russian, 140, 141, 175
Jewry, Sephardic, 136
Jewry, Soviet, 98, 99, 104, 135, 148-149, 152
Jewry, Spanish, 87, 131
Jewry, Western, 136, 137, 159
Jews, extermination of, in Europe, 78-79 *see also* Auschwitz; Holocaust
Jews, intermarriage of, with Gentiles, 134, 159
Jews, Reform, and Reform Judaism, 10, 66-67, 112, 151, 173

Jews, Syrian, 73
Job, utterances of, 32
Jose ben Kisma, Rabbi, 121
Joseph, 145
Josephus, 118
Joshua, 158
Josiah, 54
Judah al-Harizi, 72
Judah, cities and tribes of, 14, 38, 58
Judaism, Biblical, 110
Judaism, and Chosen People concept, 41-55
Judaism and God, 31-44 *passim,* 101-102, 105, 111, 118, 119, 120
Judaism compared with Christianity, 31-40, 145
Judaism, cultural contributions of, by Hasidim, 22
Judaism, devotion to, 19, 21
Judaism, essence of, 77, 110, 151
Judaism, historical, 6, 7
Judaism, intermarriage and, 134
Judaism, life (all), as the legitimate concern of, 111
Judaism, pharissaic, 98, 114, 118, 120
Judaism, publications of, viii
Judaism, rabbinic, 2, 149
Judaism, Reform, 10, 66-67, 112, 151, 173 prayer book of, 41
Judaism, teachings of, 77,104,105,135,151
Judaism, uniqueness of, 31-40
Judea, 24, 158
Judenstaat, Der (T. Herzl), 69
Judeo-phobia, 141
Judges, 158

Kabbalistic adage, 63
Kant, Immanuel, 98
Kaplan, Mordecai, 42, 65, 168
Karff, Rabbi Samuel, viii
Karaite mutation, and the Torah, 175
Karaites sect, 2, 63
Karni, Yudah, poem by, 107, 187
Karta, Netorei, 74-75, 101
Kashmir, 119
Kaufmann, Yehezkel, 5, 16, 56
Kautsky, Karl, 25
Kehillah, 172
Kelal Yisrael, 10, 24, 172
Kennedy, John F., 94
Khazar king, 47, 48, 49
Kibbutz galuyyot, 75

Kibbutz movement, 106, 136, 149, 168
Kiddush, 41, 42
Kiddush ha-Shem, 53, 55
Kierkegaard, Sören Aabye, 153
King David, 57, 71, 116, 122, 124, 147
King, Martin Luther, 97
King-Messiah, 116, 118, 122, 124
Kingdom of God, 39
Kingdom of Heaven, 1, 39
Kingdom of the House of David, 1, 71, 147
Kingly government for Israel, arguments pro and con, 126-130
Kings and prophets, 56-57, 58, 61, 62, 128
Kings, sovirgnty of, in the Middle Ages, 61-62
Klatzkin, Yaakov, 66, 167
Klausner, Joseph, 119
Koestler, Arthur, 159
Kohn, Hans, 5
Kol Shiray (Sh. Shalom), 107
Koran, 48
Kristelnacht, 157
Krochmal, Nachman, 4, 25
Kuzari (Ha-Levi), and approaches to philosophy and different theologies, 47-48, 54, 71, 77, 125

Lamdan, 92
Land of Israel, 52, 74, 94, 112, 126, 138, 139, 148, 149, 163
Laski, Harold, 20, 160
Lateran Councils, 12
Law, Rabbinic, 150
Laws (Plato), 60
Lebanon, 136
Lestschinsky, Jacob, 17
Levi, Hayim ben, 74
Levin, Shmarya, 135
Levinson, Isaac Baer, 4
Levi, sons of (priests), 45
Lewin, Kurt, 168
Lewisohn, Ludwig, 92
Lilienblum, Moses, 4, 90
Literature and history, Jewish, 139, 140, 141, 144
Liturgy, Jewish, 43, 50
Livneh, Eliezar, 93
Lo zeh ha-derekh, 151
Loewisohn, Solomon, 3
Luther, Martin, 2

Lutheran World Federation in Denmark, 83

Luzzatto, Samuel David, 3

Maariv (publication), 132
Maccabean dynasty, 118
Maccabean revolution, 74, 116
Maccabees, 114, 116, 118
McCarthyism, 161
Magnes, Judah Leon, 113
Maharal of Prague, 75, 89
Mahgreb, 33
Maimonides, Moses ben, 2, 33, 50, 71, 72, 74, 123-126 *passim,* 147
Makary el Souriany, 84
Making It (N. Podhoretz), 99
Malamud, Bernard, 92
Malkhut bet David, 1
Malkut Shamayim, 1
Manicheism, 64
Mantua, 143
Marranos, 74
Martyrdom reserved for Jews only, 11
Marx, Karl, 98, 105, 132
Masadah, 64
Masaryk, Jan and Thomas, 6
Mashiah ben David, 74, 89
Mashiah ben Yosef, 74, 89
May-June 1967 War, 78, 90, 96, 97, 99, 101, 103, 112, 113, 150, 169, 172
Medieval thinkers, some, on the Jewish King, 123-130
Medinat Yisrael, 65, 104
Mediterranean Jewry, 21
Meir of Rothenburg, 61-62, 73
Menasseh ben Israel, 2
Mendelssohn, Moses, 3, 16
Mesopotamian laws, 56
Messiah, idea of a personal, 43, 60, 71, 74, 89, 91, 107, 116, 118, 119, 122-126 *passim,* 133, 145, 146, 147
Messianic Age, objectives and impulse in, 71, 75, 102
Messianic aspirations, hope, and impulse of Judaism and Israel, 43, 60, 71, 74, 89, 107, 136, 146, 147, 174
Messianism, 122, 146
Metziat Mitzrayim, 48
Mezuzah, 134
Micaiah ben Imlah, 57
Middle East, issues of, and upheaval in, 30, 76, 85, 86, 113, 144, 155, 172

Midrash, 96
Milch, Robert, viii
Miller, Walter, Jr., 133
Mitzvahs, 8, 52, 53, 124, 156
Mitzvah ha-baah ba-averah, 154
Mitzvot, 47, 101, 124, 151
"Mi Yakum Yaakov," viii
*Mi Yakum Yaakov—*How can Jacob Endure?, 151-156
Mohammed, 48
Mohammedan world, 32
Mommsen, Theodor, 5
Monotheism, concept of, 32
Moral implications of the State of Israel, 24-30
Moore, George Foote, 120, 121
More, Thomas, 57
Morgenthau, Hans, 160
Moroccan cave-dwellers, 148
Morse, Arthur, 112
Moscow, 172 *see also* Russian Jewry; Soviet Union
Moses, 3, 38, 48, 129, 139
Moses ben Nahman, 72
Moshave ovdim, 8
Moslem anti-Jewish frenzy, 33
Moslem Spain, 93
Moslem theology, 48
Mount Zion, 58, 73
Muller, Herbert, 61
Mutations, Christian, Karaite, and Shabbatian, 175
My Lai, 161
Mysticism and spirituality, Jewish, 110-111

Nahman of Bratzlav, 2
Nahmanides, 2
Napoleon's Sanhedrin, 1
Nasi, Joseph, 2
Nasis, 72
National Committee of Americans of Polish Descent, 17
Nationalism, European, 5, 140
Nationalism, Jewish, 2-3, 4, 5, 6, 10, 113, 125, 130, 140, 159, 160, 174
Nationalists, anti-, 6, 7, 8
Nation-State, obsolescence of, 160
Nazis, 51, 85, 146 *see also* Hitler, Adolf
Nebuchadnezzar, 122
Negev, cities of the, 14
Negro leaders, and anti-Jewish pro-Arab line, 98

Negroes, and auto-emancipation, 97
Neoemancipation movement and doctrine, of certain Jewish groups, 15-16, 17, 22
New Delhi Assembly of the World Council of Churches, 82, 84, 85
New Testament, 60, 121
New York Times, 17
"New Zionism," 65
Niebuhr, Reinhold, 7
Nietzscheanism, brutality of, 6
Nineveh, 36
Norway, slave laborers of, 11

Obadiah of Bertinoro, 73, 74
Oded, prophet, 56
Oil blackmail, 172
Old Testament, 55, 61
Orbach, Simhah Bunam, 47, 48
Oreah Natah Lalun (S. J. Agnon), 103
Origin of Israel, 148, 149 *see also under all* Israel headings
Orthodox prayer book, 41
Oxnam, Bishop, 81

Palestine, 1, 2, 3, 4, 6, 8, 9, 12, 13, 15, 18, 20-25 *passim,* 52, 58, 59, 63, 72, 73, 74, 76, 81, 111, 112, 113, 119, 122, 125, 126, 140, 143, 146, 149
    Pilgrimages to, 111, 125
Palestine-based Temple, 118, 149
Palliere, Aime, 151
Palmer raids, 161
Paris, Jews of, 16, 87
Parzen, Dr. Herbert, viii
Passover, 44, 144
Paul, 31, 61, 120, 154
Pauline doctrine, 61
Peel Commission, 9
People Israel, 21, 27, 29, 62, 65, 69, 74, 91, 126, 139, 148, 149, 155, 158, 162, 163, 168, 175
Perkins, Dr., 80
Persecution of Jews in England, France, and Germany, 72
Pharaoh, 48, 51
Pharisaic Judaism, 98, 114, 118, 120
Pharisaic party, 115
Pharisaism and political sovereignty, 114-122
Pharisees, 74, 107, 115, 116, 117, 118, 120
Philo, 71, 74

Pilgrimages to Israel, 111, 125, 173
Pinchas, Rabbi, 167
Pinsker, Dr. Leon, 86, 141, 142
Pithom, Egypt, 135
Plague (A. Camus), 133, 161
Plato, 6, 33, 60, 62
Podhoretz, Norman, 99
Pogroms, Armleder, 12
Poland, and American Catholics, 109
Poland, Jews in, 9, 17, 146, 159
Poland, slave laborers of, 11
Polish anti-semitiism, 98, 106
Polish, Rabbi Daniel, viii
Political sovereignty snd Pharisaism, 114-122
Pope Pius X, 142-143, 144
Popes, attitude of, toward Jewry, 73, 131, 142-144 *passim*
Postexilic age, 139
Prague, Maharal of, 75, 89
Prayer books, 41, 42, 111, 135
Presbyterian churches, 136
Presidents of National Organizations, Conference of, 171
Prophecy and messianism, 107, 126
Prophecy and power, the meeting of, 56-70
Prophets, 39, 45, 61, 174
Prophets and kings, 56-57, 58, 61, 62, 128
Prophets of God, 43
Proselytizing the Jews, need for, 78-79
Protestants, American, 110
Psalms of the Bible, 32, 98
"Pursuit of the Millenium" (N. Cohn), 154

Qumran society, 106, 150

Raamses, Egypt, 135
Rabbinic Judaism, 2, 121, 122, 149
Rabbinic law, 150
Rabbinic period, 174
Radical right and left, Jewish, 152
Rapoport, Solomon Judah, 3
Rawidowicz, Shimon, 65
Reconstructionism, 15, 19, 141, 143
Reconstructionist prayer book, 41, 42
Reconstructionist, The (publications of), viii, 78
Redeemer, 73
Redemption, 45, 50, 52, 60, 67, 68, 91, 105, 115, 125, 135, 147
Reform and Zionism, compatibility of, viii
Reform experiment with Torah, 53

Reform Jews and Judaism, 10, 66-67, 112, 151, 173
    prayer book of, 41
Reform movement, 151, 171
Reform prayer book, 41
Reform rabbis of America and Israel, 167-168
Refugees and refugee problem, 77, 78, 86, 112
    Arab-refugee problem, 86
    Refugees in the United States, 75
Religion and religious expression, today's basic untenability of, 20-21
Religious community, world, 7-8
Religious dimensions of Israel, 89-95
Religious meanings in Jewish secularism, 139-150
Remonstrant Brotherhood, 81
Reprise, Warsaw 1943, 176-183
    B'RESHIET, 176-177
    SH'MOT, 177
    VAYIKRA, 177-179
    BEMIDBAR, 179-181
    D'VARIM, 181-183
Restoration, 126
Resurrection, 43
Reuchlin, Johann, 2
Revelation, 43
Rome, Imperium of, 116, 118, 119, 121
Rome, overwhelming of Israel by, 52, 116, 117, 119, 120, 121, 144
Romanian Jewry, 9, 159
Romans (biblical chapter), 61, 83
Roth, Philip, 92
Russian Jewry, 140, 141, 175 see also Sovet Jewry
Russian Revolution, 154

Saadia Gaon (Saadia ben Joseph al-Fayumi), 47, 52
Sabbath, and the festivals, 50
Sabbath Kiddush, 42
Sabbath, laws pertaining to the, 34
Sabbath, prayer of sanctification for, 41, 50
Sabbatian movement, 154
Sacco-Vanzetti case, 161
Sadducees and Sadducee party, 115, 118
Safed, men of, 19
Salvation, in Jewish theology, 35
Samaritans, 149
Samuel, 123

Samuel, Maurice, 92
San Francisco Archdiocese, 85
Sanhedrin, 74
    of Napoleon, 1
Saracens in Palestine, 76
Schalit, Abraham, 114, 115
Schiller, Johann Christoph Friedrich von, 12
Schlesinger, Isaac Baer, 3
Scripture, 43, 44, 46, 67, 71, 127
Sea of Reeds, 175
Second Commonwealth, 174
    destruction of, 111
Second Temple, destruction of, 24, 38, 149
Second World War, 51, 105
Secularism, Jewish, religious meanings in, 139-150
Security Council of the United Nations, 172
Seleucid reign, 116
Sephardic Jewry, 136
Seth, 14
"Seven Days That Shook the World" (L. Steffens), 155
Shabbat, 49, 105
Shabbetai-Tzevi messianic movement and debacle, 92, 135
Shabbatian mutation, and the Covenant and the Messiah, 175
Shadal, 4
Shaftesbury, Lord, 3
Shaldstadt, Rabbi Samuel, 73
Shalom, Sh., 92, 107, 187
Shaprut, Hasdai ibn, 2
Shefelah, cities of the, 14
Shekhinah, 49, 64
Shepherds, wandering bands of, 21
SH'MOT (Warsaw 1943), 177
Shneour, Zalman, 100, 112
Shoah, 105, 163
Shtetl, 59, 135
Shyk, Yeshaya, 174
Simeon bar Yohai, Rabbi, 121
Simon, Ernest, 113
Sinai, 45, 54, 58, 135, 144, 148, 158, 175
    Covenant of, 54, 158, 168, 174
Sinai Peninsula, 54, 149
"Single Ones," 153
Six-Day War, 78, 90, 96, 97, 99, 100, 101, 103, 112, 113, 150, 169, 172
Sixth Zionist Congress, 166
Slave laborers, 11

Slavery in Egypt, 29, 31, 38, 41, 44, 45, 51, 54
Smolenskin, Peretz, 4, 90, 99
Snyder, Louis, 160
Sodom and Gomorrah, 36, 38
Soviet Galut, 93
Soviet Jewry, 98, 99, 104, 135, 148-149, 152
Soviet Union, 119, 148-149, 155, 171
Spain, Almohades in, 33
Spain, Jews in, 87, 131
Spain, Moslem, 93
Spanish Inquisition, 73
Sparta, 136
Spengler, Oswald, 25, 158
Spinoza, Baruch, 66
Spirituality and mysticism, Jewish, 110-111
St. Andrews, meeting in, 84
Stalin, Josef, 142
State and diaspora, issue of, 63-64, 67
State of Israel, The, vii, 26, 52, 62, 63, 66-70 *passim,* 78, 81, 91-99 *passim,* 101-106 *passim,* 112-120 *passim,* 126, 135, 137, 138, 143-147 *passim,* 150, 152, 157, 158, 159, 163, 165, 166, 172, 175
State of Israel, The, and the Jewish People, 109-113
State of Israel, The: Its moral implications, 24-30, 77
Steffens, Lincoln, 155
Strasbourg Cathedral, 145
Study of History (Toynbee), 69
Supreme Court of Israel, 174
Sweden, and American Lutherans, 109
Sweden's Christian charity to the Jew, 18
Synagogue, American, 170
Synagogue, role played by, throughout the war, 170
Synagogue, symbol of, in the Middle Ages, 145
Synagogue Council, The, publications of, viii
Syrian hegemony, 116
Syrian Jews, 73

Talmud, 34, 35, 39, 121
Tanakh, 43, 55, 89, 104, 175
Tefutzot Yisrael, 65
Temple in Jerusalem, rebuilding of, 71, 124
Temple, Palestine-based, 118, 149
Temples, destruction of our, 2, 24, 38, 118, 124, 145, 149

Tenakh, 89
Ten Commandments, 45
Theology, Jewish, 35, 63
Theology, of Christian, Moslem, and Islamic faiths, 37, 47-48
Tikkun Olam, 55, 137
Tillich, Paul, 59, 76, 94, 150
Tmol Shilshom (S. J. Agnon), 103
Torah, 4, 35, 39, 41-53 *passim,* 56, 58, 92, 98, 118, 124, 128, 129, 151, 158, 164, 174, 175
Tortosa, Spain, Jews in, 87
Toynbee, Arnold, 25, 69
Trachtenberg, Joshua, 141
Transjordan, 117
Treitschke, Heinrich von, 6
Tribe of Judah, 38, 58
Tribes of Israel, 38, 58, 149
Trotsky, Leon, 132
Tsarfati, Isaac, 73
Turkey, 73

Uganda, 90, 112, 113, 141
U-Netanneh Tokef, 35
Union of American Hebrew Congregations, The, publications of, viii
   Centennial of, 157
Unitarianism, 154
United Jewish Appeal, 170
United Nations, 10, 91, 157, 172
United States, *see under all* America and American headings
Universal Spirit, 62
"Universalism," 5, 6, 152-153, 168
Universalizing Israel and Judaism out of existence, 151
Ur of the Chaldees, 21
Uzziah, king, 56

Vatican Council, 83, 84, 86
Vatican in 1904, 142
Vatican II, 85, 86
VAYIKRA (Warsaw 1943), 177-179
Venice, 73
   Congress of, 2, 18, 91
   Doge of, 73
Vespasian, 117, 158
Vietnamese war, America's, 96, 97
Volk and *Volkgeist,* idea of, 159-160

Wall, Jerusalem, 107, 150
Wandering shepherds, 21

War, Israel-Arab, 78, 90, 97, 99, 100, 101, 103, 112, 113, 150, 169, 172
Ward, Barbara, 160
Warrant for Genocide (N. Cohn), 141
Warsaw Ghetto, 53, 99, 106, 133
Warsaw Ghetto fighters, 99
Warsaw Reprise, 1943, 176-183
    B'RESHIET, 176-177
    SH'MOT, 177
    VAYIKRA, 177-179
    BEMIDBAR, 179-181
    D'VARIM, 181-183
Watergate crisis, 160, 161
Watts, California, 133
Weimar Republic, 100
Wellhausen, Julius, 66
Wessely, Naftali Herz, 3
Western Arabian desert, wandering shepherds of, 21
Western Europe, attacks upon Jews in, 73
Western Jewry, 136, 137, 159
Western world, dybbuk lurking in people of, 133
While Six Million Died (A. Morse), 112
White Paper, and Britain, 32
World Council, 78-80, 81, 84
World Council of Churches, 81, 82, 85, 106
World Jewish Congress, 146
World religious community, 7-8
World War I, 51, 105
    treaties following, guaranteeing minority rights to Jews, 159
World War II, 51, 105
World Zionist Organization, Jerusalem program of, 167
Writings, 45

Yahrzeit, 35th, of Kristalnacht, 157
Yavneh, 64
Yemei Ziklag, Yizhar's, 64
Yemen, 33
Yemenites, 21
Yetziat Mitzrayim, 48
Yishuv, 8, 9, 21, 23, 26, 120, 164
Yisrael, Kelal, 24
Yizhar's *Yemei Ziklag,* 64
Yohanan ben Zakkai, 120
Yom Kippur, 34, 35, 173
Yom Kippur War, vii, viii, 78, 90, 96, 97, 99, 100, 101, 103, 112, 113, 150, 169, 172
Yoma, 34

Zalmon (Islai), 57, 175
Zangwill, Israel, 90
Zealots, 120
Zion, Elders of, 133
Zion, Mount, 58, 73
Zionism, vii, viii, 5, 6, 1-14, 18, 20, 21, 22, 30, 31, 40, 74, 90, 100, 101, 105, 111, 112, 113, 126, 140, 146, 147, 159, 162, 165
Zionism, modern, 5
"Zionism, new," 65, 90
Zionism, pre-Herzl, 4, 156
Zionism and Reform, compatibility of, viii
Zionism, the twofold task of, 15-23
Zionist Congress, 90
    Sixth, 166
Zionist idea, movement, and issues, vii, viii, 31, 40, 65, 90, 126, 131, 147, 156, 164
Zionists, American, 162
Zionists, anti-, 1-14 *passim,* 16, 18, 23, 143